How Women Saved the City

Daphne Spain

University of Minnesota Press
Minneapolis   London

The University of Minnesota Press gratefully acknowledges financial assistance provided for this book by a grant from the Graham Foundation for Advanced Studies in the Fine Arts.

Published by the University of Minnesota Press
111 Third Avenue South, Suite 290
Minneapolis, MN 55401-2520
http://www.upress.umn.edu

Library of Congress Cataloging-in-Publication Data

Spain, Daphne.
  How women saved the city / Daphne Spain.
      p.   cm.
  Includes bibliographical references and index.
    ISBN 0-8166-3531-5 (HC/J : alk. paper) — ISBN 0-8166-3532-3 (PB : alk. paper)
    1. Women social reformers — United States — History. 2. Women in public life — United States — History. 3. Women — United States — Societies, etc. 4. Social settlements — United States — History. 5. Young Women's Christian Association of the U.S.A. — History. 6. National Association of Colored Women (U.S.) — History. 7. Salvation Army of America — History. I. Title.
  HQ1420 .S64   2000
  305.42'0973 — dc21   00-009648

Printed in the United States of America on acid-free paper

The University of Minnesota is an equal-opportunity educator and employer.

11 10 09 08 07 06 05 04 03 02 01   9 8 7 6 5 4 3 2 1

This book is dedicated to my father,
Frank H. Spain Jr.,
the first and most continuously
supportive feminist in my life.

With a truly remarkable grasp of a widely extended movement,
Mrs. Beard has summarized and emphasized the work that the
women of America have done in behalf of rescuing the city from
the powers of evil and inefficiency, and placing it upon a higher
standard of morality and effectiveness.
— Clinton Rogers Woodruff, introduction to Mary Ritter Beard's
Woman's Work in Municipalities, 1915

Contents

Preface

The time between the Civil War and World War I was an important moment in the evolution of the industrial city — it established the template that guided growth until the 1950s. Architectural, planning, and urban histories recognize the significance of this period and document the accomplishments of the men who built skyscrapers, city halls, and department stores. Few, however, include women as active agents of the city's construction. Like feminist scholars in many fields, I suspected that women had played an obscured role that deserved recognition. This project thus began as a scavenger hunt for women's contributions to the American urban landscape.

One path I could have taken was to search the ranks of architects, urban planners, engineers, and builders for the few women who had made it into these professions. I was more interested, though, in the ways typical women could have engaged in shaping the public sphere. The avenues then open to women for participation in public life were voluntary organizations. Thus voluntary associations with a physical presence in the city became the object of my search.

Four voluntary associations in which women were active that had building programs were founded between 1858 and 1896: the Young Women's Christian Association (YWCA), The Salvation Army, the College Settlements Association (CSA), and the National Association of Colored Women (NACW). The YWCA, NACW, and CSA were operated predominantly by and for women. The Salvation Army, and the larger settlement movement represented by the CSA, included male as well as female members and served the needs of men, women, and children. All four organizations sponsored boarding houses, vocational schools, settlement houses, public baths, and playgrounds in small and large cities throughout the country. Here was evidence of a built environment created by women, not necessarily by professionals for paying clients, but often adapted by volunteers to serve new purposes—what I came to think of as a "voluntary vernacular."

Discovering the places was only the start. The next step was figuring out what they had in common other than their origins in voluntarism. Public baths and vocational schools, after all, seem to share few similarities. One of the clues to the nature of these places emerged when I realized the sponsoring organizations all had religious foundations. The Social Gospel, an activist theology that fueled progressive reform, motivated members of all four organizations. The places they created were "redemptive": they gave newcomers to the city a fresh start, delivered women volunteers from completely domestic lives, and saved the city from being overwhelmed by strangers.

If women volunteers were the sponsors of redemptive places, who were the beneficiaries? Four groups of newcomers presented significant demographic and social challenges to urban order at the end of the nineteenth century: immigrants from Europe, black migrants from the South, independent wage-earning women from small towns, and the women volunteers themselves. All were seeking new identities, but, more important, they were struggling to cope with the opportunities and difficulties of the industrializing city. Lacking the government services and charitable institutions that we now take for granted, these newcomers had to rely on family, friends, or casual acquaintances. Everyone had come to the city from somewhere else, and redemptive places served as safe sites of support and transition. They contributed to the emerging social order by establishing the places in which newcomers could learn to become urban Americans.

The final stage of my search for women's contributions to urban structure suggested that redemptive places were also theaters in which critical issues of the day were negotiated. Could America assimilate all the immigrants arriving daily? Settlement house workers tried to with public baths and playgrounds. What would race relations be like after slavery was abolished? Separate boarding homes for white and African American women suggested intensified segregation. Was it appropriate for women to pursue an education, vote, and hold a job? The YWCA and NACW thought so, and provided women with schools and lodging where they could accomplish those goals. Who was responsible for the poor—individuals, the voluntary sector, or the government? Redemptive places offered one solution and laid the foundations for future government involvement. Contrary to being absent from the construction of the industrializing city, women made a mark at its very core.

It is the physical presence of these voluntary organizations that most interested me. Much like their history, though, a good deal of the material evidence has been erased. Redemptive places are more easily documented in text than in images or remaining sites. I knew places like boarding homes existed because fundraising campaigns were detailed in organizational histories. Sometimes annual reports included sketches of existing or planned facilities. Yet their status as voluntary vernacular means they were seldom considered important enough to record. Locating photographs and prints of redemptive places turned into one of the most challenging parts of the project. The images presented here represent only a small portion of all the places that once existed and have disappeared. Part of the story, therefore, lies in the pictures that are *missing* from this book.

A logical question is whether my search for women's contributions to the urban landscape one hundred years ago has any relevance today. I think it does. Cities confront the same issues now that they did then: poverty, race relations, immigration, and women's status. Welfare reform will make new demands on voluntary organizations, especially those that are faith-based. Immigration is once again at a historic high. The nation continues to grapple with racial equality, and reproductive rights for women is still a subject for national debate. What are the contemporary equivalents of redemptive places? Who will be the army of volunteers now that the majority of women are in the labor force? What roles do women now play in the construction of the city?

These questions give contemporary relevance to this essentially historical work. If readers continue to ponder them after finishing the book, my efforts will have been worthwhile.

Acknowledgments

Years of interdisciplinary teaching and research have nourished this project. I owe special intellectual debts to Eugenie Birch, Dolores Hayden, Lyn Lofland, Beth Moore Milroy, Leonie Sandercock, Suzanne Spencer-Wood, and Catharine Stimpson. I've learned from each of them and would like to thank them publicly for their influence on my work. The ideas in this book and the style in which they are conveyed reflect my efforts to emulate their scholarship.

Among authors whose ideas have contributed to this book from a greater distance are Gerda Lerner, Mary Ryan, Anne Firor Scott, and Kathryn Kish Sklar, all feminist pioneers in women's history. Ephraim Mizruchi's explanation of abeyance structures in *Regulating Society* (1983) gave me a new way to think about the intersection of spatial and sociological phenomena.

The beginning and end of this project were marked, appropriately enough, by consultation with groups of women. The Monday evening student reading group devoted many hours to critiquing my research in the fall of 1995. Jana Lynott, Kristan Mitchell, Debbie Schwartz, Leslie Smith, Megan Teare, and Lynn Ward contributed valuable suggestions while there was still time to incorporate them. Leslie Smith, especially, was a constant source of encouragement. My concluding thoughts were crystallized after I presented this research at a conference on gendered landscapes at Pennsylvania State University in May 1999. I was able to pull together the big picture and benefit from the astute questions raised by other participants. For that capstone experience, I wish to thank conference organizers Josephine Carubia, Lorraine Dowler, and Bonj Szczygiel.

My most constant companion in the development of this book has been my husband, Steven L. Nock, who probably feels that he's read every draft at least a thousand times. I thank him profusely for the contributions he's made during nearly thirty years of walking dogs and talking about ideas.

Many other people who read various drafts improved the final product immensely. Early comments from University of Virginia colleagues Daniel Bluestone, K. Edward Lay, and Camille Wells put me on more solid architectural historical ground. Architectural historian Richard Guy Wilson also contributed substantially to the project. Among friends and family subjected to first (or last) drafts were Susan Bender, Anne Harrington, Kate Johnson, and my dad, Frank Spain, all of whom were extremely encouraging.

Among those who made me rethink the project several times were Bob Beauregard, Genie Birch, Galen Cranz, Mona Domosh, Ann Forsyth, and Beth Moore Milroy. Harry Porter gave me the benefit of his designer's perspective during the semester we taught evening classes at the University of Virginia's Northern Virginia campus. Our midnight drives back to Charlottesville were filled with good conversation punctuated with frequent sightings of the Hale-Bopp comet. My editor at the University of Minnesota Press, Carrie Mullen, helped orchestrate all this input into a coherent whole.

I received the most research help from students Amy Probsdorfer and Leslie Smith. Amy edited numerous drafts of the manuscript, tirelessly pursued Sanborn maps, and helped me organize chapters during the final throes of the project. The most challenging technical job, generating the maps of redemptive places, was aced by Bill Palmer under the direction of Mike Furlough, associate director of the Geospatial and Statistical Data Center at the University of Virginia's Alderman Library. Mike was creative, patient, and helpful *way* beyond the call of duty. The three maps reproduced in this book are mere tips of the iceberg of work it took to create them.

The project could never have happened, of course, without the help of numerous librarians and archivists. The ones with whom I worked most closely were Elizabeth Norris and Dorothy Wick of the YWCA; Scott Bedio and Susan Mitchem of The Salvation Army; Carole Early and Sean Jenkins of the NACW; and Susan Barker and Kathleen Banks Nutter of the Sophia Smith Collection at Smith College. Principal Shirley

G. Hayes of the Nannie Helen Burroughs School in Washington, D.C., was extremely generous with her knowledge of the school's history.

Others who provided invaluable professional archival assistance were Wilbur Meneray, Tulane University Library Special Collections; Thomas Owen, University of Louisville Archives and Records Center; Michael Roudette, Schomberg Center for Research in Black Culture at the New York Public Library; Ann Sindelar, the Western Reserve Historical Society in Cleveland; and Cynthia Van Ness of the Buffalo and Erie County Public Library. I also had the good fortune to correspond with Edward H. McKinley and Norman Murdoch, historians of The Salvation Army.

In Boston Sinclair Hitchings and Aaron Schmidt of the Boston Public Library, Doug Southard of the Boston Historical Society and Museum, and Marie Helene Gold of the Schlesinger Library at Radcliffe College helped me enormously. In Chicago I depended on Cynthia Mathews and Caroline Nutley of the Chicago Historical Society for guidance through the photographs and prints division. Mary Ann Bamberger of the University of Illinois at Chicago was a source of help on matters related to Hull House.

Financial contributions from the Committee on Small Grants, Office of the Vice President for Research and Public Service, and from the Office of the Provost for Sesquicentennial Leave, both at the University of Virginia, are gratefully acknowledged.

This project was supported by a grant from the Graham Foundation for Advanced Studies in the Fine Arts. Their generous award allowed acquisition of most of the images reproduced here.

Finally, as the dedication indicates, I owe the most to my father for making sure I got a college education and a credit card in my own name when the possibility of both seemed remote.

CHAPTER ONE

Voluntary Vernacular

In 1913 the poet Edna St. Vincent Millay joined other adventurous women of her day when she traveled to New York City and stayed at the Young Women's Christian Association. She lived on the eighth floor of the YWCA's recently completed National Training School at East Fifty-second Street and Lexington Avenue. Millay was thrilled with the view. Writing to her family, she observed:

> From my window in the daytime I can see *everything*—just buildings, tho, it is buildings everywhere, seven & eight stories to million and billion stories, washing drying on the roofs and on lines strung between the houses, way up in the air—they flap and *flap!* Children on roller skates playing tag on the sidewalks, smokestacks *and* smokestacks, and windows and windows, and signs way up high on the tops of factories and cars and taxicabs—and *noise,* yes, in New York you can *see* the noise. (Macdougall 1952, 32)

In addition, from the YWCA's twelfth-story rooftop, Millay might have seen the trees of Frederick Law Olmsted's Central Park to the northwest. To the south was the 700-foot-tall Metropolitan Life Insurance Company Tower on Madison Square, completed in 1909 by the architectural firm of Napoleon Le Brun & Sons. On a really clear day, further south, Millay might have been able to discern the newly constructed 800-foot tower of the Woolworth Building designed by Cass Gilbert. It had just surpassed the Metropolitan Life Tower as the city's tallest building. The factories Millay saw were possibly the manufacturing loft buildings of the garment industry creeping up Fifth Avenue from Thirty-second Street, the very ones that prompted New York City to restrict building height in its historic zoning law of 1916 (Fenske and Holdsworth 1992; Weiss 1992).

Had Millay looked to the northeast from her rooftop, it would have been difficult to make out the small public bathhouse at 342 East Fifty-fourth Street that opened in 1911 to serve Irish immigrants. Nor could she have spotted the modest Wesley House Settlement, established in 1908 at 212 East Fifty-eighth Street, much less the more renowned Lenox Hill Settlement on East Seventy-second Street. The settlement houses in Millay's neighborhood that provided kindergartens, libraries, playgrounds, and public baths for poor workers and their families, like their numerous counterparts on the Lower East Side, were less visually prominent than the landmarks typically noted by visitors and historians. Few were designed by an Olmsted, Le Brun, or Gilbert. Easily recognized, skyscrapers and elaborate parks have endured for more than one hundred years. Harder to identify are the buildings and small places that filled the spaces between those towers and parks. In fact, many of these places disappeared as their functions were absorbed by the private or public sector. Yet they were just as important to people living in cities as the more famous structures that survived.

The purpose of this book is to illustrate how women saved the American city between the Civil War and World War I, when women volunteers created hundreds of places like the YWCA boarding house that sheltered Edna St. Vincent Millay. Millay was representative of one type of newcomer to the industrializing city: she was a "woman adrift," seeking her fortune independently of her family. Such women worked and lived in cities on their own and often invited public criticism for rejecting traditional family roles (Meyerowitz 1988). Whether from Europe or from small towns in America, they were strangers to the city who needed to learn how to prosper (or just survive) as soon as they arrived. Some of Millay's neighbors would have been single women living at the YWCA while attending its training school to become "typewriters" for companies like Metropolitan Life.[1]

Two other groups of people, equally unfamiliar with American urban customs, arrived in midwestern and northeastern cities about the same time as single working women: European immigrants and black migrants from the rural South. Few immigrants spoke English, which presented serious difficulties in finding jobs, housing, and schools for their children. Many practiced Catholic or Jewish religious traditions that were out of place in a largely Protestant country. Few had much material wealth when they arrived. Black migrants from the South, although they spoke English and most were Protestant, also were unprepared for urban life. They had low literacy rates and had been agricultural rather than industrial laborers. Like European immigrants, blacks brought few economic resources with them to their new homes. Immigrants and African Americans were the most highly visible poor in the industrializing city.

A fourth category of stranger was the female volunteer. Women had been active in cities for some time, of course. Middle-class women had occupied urban public space for decades, shopping in the streets, demonstrating for temperance, and promenading in parks (Cranz 1982; Ryan 1990). They took part in public life and, in unusual circumstances, they just took, as when Victorian ladies became shoplifters (Abelson 1989; Walkowitz 1992). Women could vote on local issues in some states and they occasionally held public office. Yet the spaces of political activism remained gendered, with men monopolizing the formal discourse carried out in central squares and women relegated to the margins. Before universal suffrage women lacked the range of civic privileges men enjoyed. Voluntary associations, however, gave them new avenues by which to pursue the public good (Ryan 1990, 1997; Sklar 1993).

The end of the nineteenth century marked the first time women played an active role in creating the urban spaces they occupied (Deutsch 1992; Enstam 1998; Spencer-Wood 1996; Turner 1997). Women volunteers were critical to this process. In addition to boarding houses, they produced vocational schools, hotels for transients, playgrounds, and public baths. These were places in which urban newcomers were quickly assimilated, places that simultaneously met women's goals as well as those of the city. The American city was able to accommodate the tremendous onslaught of strangers that threatened social order largely due to the efforts of women volunteers.

Virtually everyone was a newcomer during this period of intense urbanization. Before 1870 three-quarters of the American population were rural and those who lived in cities were predominantly native-born. Most African Americans were slaves, the economy was based on agriculture, only white men could vote, and private charity was the solution to poverty. After 1920 over one-half of the population was urban

1858	*YWCA*	
1861–1865	Civil War	
1870	15th Amendment (Black Suffrage) [U.S. population = 26% urban]	
1879	*The Salvation Army*	
1887	*College Settlements Association*	
1893	World's Columbian Exposition	Peak European Immigration
1896	*NACW*	
1900–1910	City Beautiful Movement	
1914–1918	World War I	
1920	19th Amendment (Woman's Suffrage) [U.S. population = 51% urban]	Major Black Migration

Figure 1.1. Time line of major events associated with the creation of redemptive places.

and more than one-third of those in the largest cities were foreign-born. Slavery had been abolished, industrial production had replaced agriculture, women and blacks could vote, and poverty was defined as a public responsibility. So much change made growing cities a threat to national morals and to Jeffersonian democracy, strengthening Americans' antiurban sentiments of earlier centuries (Beauregard 1993).

Newcomers included a diverse mix of men, women, and children. The men typically were laborers who might or might not speak English. Most young women adrift had chosen to work, but there were also many working mothers who would have stayed home with their children if not for economic necessity. Women volunteers were typically middle or upper class. Some, however, were of the same working-class origins as those they served. Regardless of class affiliation, women in voluntary organizations had many more options than their more traditional sisters who stayed at home.

As Tocqueville observed on his visit to America in the 1830s, voluntary associations make a significant contribution to the cultural health of a nation. They mediate between the individual and the state by educating the electorate and empowering them through political action. Voluntary organizations also define and clarify a nation's values, especially those with a religious affiliation. Faith-based associations, for example, are most likely to promote responsibility for those unable to care for themselves — the poor, the sick, children, and the very old. A strong voluntary sector is thus "a necessary component of a vibrant public sphere in which collective values can be articulated" (Calhoun 1993; Watt 1991; Wuthnow 1991a, 5).

The public sphere can be either a physical place (like the Greek agora) or a process of communication, in which case it may be called "public discourse." Public discourse refers to the kinds of questions we ask ourselves about who we are, how to live morally, or how to create a strong community — what is now called a "national conversation." Public discourse is a continuing process because it represents enduring issues. Tocqueville and others since have argued that the very shape of public discourse depends on the existence of a dynamic voluntary sector (Gamm and Putnam 1998; Habermas 1989; Watt 1991; Wuthnow 1991a, b).

Race relations, immigration, and women's status were controversial at the end of the nineteenth century, just as they are today. That they were subjects for debate meant that they were central to people's daily lives. The sheer numbers of newcomers demanded attention. They changed the demography of the city and placed strains on the newly emerging system. Race relations, of course, were contentious because of the nation's history of slavery. Blacks' Great Migration out of the South was accompanied by violence as African Americans competed for jobs and housing with countless immigrants. Immigrants, in turn, were struggling in factories and tenements just to stay alive. Suffragists were demanding the vote, outraged that black and immigrant men had access to formal political representation before they did. All of these issues found vigorous expression in the city.

Women's voluntary associations created actual spaces in which problems associated with race relations, immigration, and women's status were worked out. A typical day in the life of a settlement house worker illustrates the point. In 1893 the parade of visitors to the Philadelphia College Settlement included children and adults from the neighborhood, "philanthropic ladies," clergymen, and students of social work. In addition, the "general public comes. It insists on discussing Woman Suffrage or the Elizabethan Drama with you while you are trying in vain to put thirty coats on thirty small children simultaneously, without getting mixed" (Scudder 1893). Since the coats belonged to immigrant children attending the settlement-house kindergarten while their mothers worked,

Figure 1.2. Race riots in Chicago in 1919: tenuous calm in front of the Ogden Cafe. (Jun Fujita, photographer. Courtesy Chicago Historical Society, ICHi-21356.)

more was going on than an academic discussion of women's rights. The daycare provided by the settlement house was tangible evidence of its support for employed women.

Race relations were debated in questions about whether to provide separate facilities for whites and blacks. Assimilation of immigrants occurred in settlement houses, on playgrounds, and in public baths. Women boarders who lived and worked away from their families challenged prevailing ideals of "true womanhood" (Welter 1966). These themes were embedded in concerns about poverty, children's welfare, and organized labor. By providing the stages on which these issues played out, women volunteers met a critical need in the industrializing city.

Women's voluntary associations accomplished this feat by occupying territory that sociologist Lyn Lofland (1998) identifies as "parochial" — the world of the neighborhood as opposed to the totally private world of the household and the completely public realm of strangers. Social order in parochial space depends on local institutions and the labor of volunteers (Hunter 1985). This type of labor is not paid, but neither is it voluntary because it is necessary: "Like domestic work, it is cyclical,

Figure 1.3. Couple with cart accompanied by policeman during Chicago race riots, 1919. (Jun Fujita, photographer. Courtesy Chicago Historical Society, ICHi-23869.)

never-ending, and essential. Its spatial location is neither home nor work place, primarily, but community" (Milroy and Wismer 1994, 72).

Community work is a separate area of productive effort that connects the concerns of both private and public spheres. It brings domestic problems like sick children and drunken husbands into the public eye. Community work simultaneously addresses the effects of trends influenced by the market and state, such as unemployment and housing shortages, on private lives. The boundaries between domestic, community, and paid work are porous, just as they are between private, parochial, and public spaces (Lofland 1998; Milroy and Wismer 1994). Women's voluntary associations breached those borders when they translated private troubles into public issues (Mills [1959] 1967).

Initially, many voluntary organizations in which women were active sprang from the Social Gospel theology that took religion out of the church and into the streets. The Social Gospel attributed poverty to social, economic, and political conditions rather than to the personal failings of individuals. Its disciples drew no distinctions between the "deserving" and "undeserving" poor. They believed slums were created by

Figure 1.4. New York City immigrant neighborhood c. 1900. (Courtesy Library of Congress, USZ62-45848.)

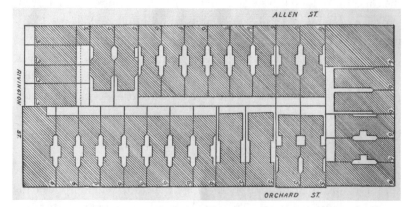

Figure 1.5. Ground plan of the "dumb-bell" tenements in the block surrounding the College Settlement of New York. Nearly 3,000 people lived in the block bounded by Rivington, Allen, Stanton, and Orchard Streets, for a density of over 1,000 people per acre. (From *The College Settlements Association,* 1904. Courtesy Sophia Smith Collection, Smith College, Northampton, Mass.)

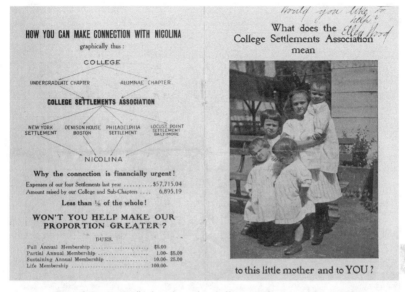

Figure 1.6. Brochure cover, "What does the College Settlements Association mean to this little mother and to you?" c. 1900. (Courtesy Sophia Smith Collection, Smith College, Northampton, Mass.)

society, not by sinners, and that squalid living conditions were a public rather than a private responsibility.

Social Gospel ideas were eventually augmented, and sometimes displaced, by the tenets of "municipal housekeeping," the term used to describe women's responsibility for keeping the city as clean and well functioning as their own homes. Advocates of municipal housekeeping promoted similarities between the home and the city, particularly the need for cleanliness and order, as a way to establish their credentials for civic involvement. The Woman's City Club of Chicago, for example, published a diagram depicting fourteen institutional links that bound the home to city hall. These included food inspection, factory safety, clean air, and marriage and birth licensing bureaus. Municipal housekeeping thus represented a clearly political agenda in an era when women had few direct avenues of influence (Blair 1980; Flanagan 1990).

Women used voluntary associations fueled by religious and domestic doctrine to create a network of places that addressed the needs of new arrivals in large and small cities throughout the country. These places included boarding houses and hotels, vocational schools, settlement houses, public baths, and playgrounds. Settlement houses, for example,

Figure 1.7. Suffrage parade in Washington, D.C., 1913. (Courtesy Library of Congress, USZ6-1266.)

provided essential daycare in immigrant neighborhoods, while settlement workers lived (settled) in the house for months or sometimes years. Middle-class women volunteers who sponsored settlements established their own niche in the city.

The voluntary activities to which Tocqueville referred are now part of a three-sector model of society in which the state represents formal coercive powers, the market involves the exchange of goods and services for profit, and the voluntary sector is composed of activities that are neither coerced nor profit-driven. Participation in the voluntary, or third sector, is free from economic motivation and is chosen willingly (Wuthnow 1991a, b). The concept of voluntarism therefore has dual meanings.

Voluntarism was equally complex at the end of the nineteenth century. Some women donated their labor, while others financed buildings

The Links that Bind the
Home to the City Hall

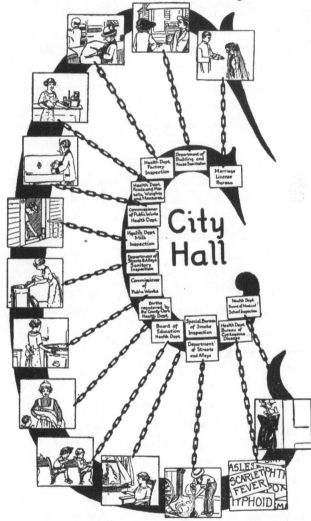

HELP IN THE MUNICIPAL HOUSEKEEPING
The Woman's City Club, Chicago

Figure 1.8. Illustration of links connecting municipal housekeeping and city hall. (*Woman's City Club Yearbook*, 1915. Courtesy Chicago Historical Society, F38JDW8Y.)

or paid the salaries of city employees who supervised public baths and playgrounds. Many of the women whose names appear in this book did both. They were active volunteers *and* philanthropists, like YWCA president Grace Dodge. For each of these women who was recognized in her own time, however, there were hundreds more whose names are lost. It took an army of volunteers to save cities from social disorder.

Of the three sectors, the profit-making sector was the most highly visible in cities one hundred years ago. Urban development in the late nineteenth century was characterized by a commitment to privatism that overshadowed public concerns (Warner 1968). The Gilded Age (roughly 1870 to 1900) championed capitalism and growth. These priorities became manifest in the built environment and were especially obvious in Chicago and New York, where corporatism was the driving force behind the construction of skyscrapers. Those cities dedicated dominant spaces to the enhancement of capitalism. They also tried to counteract its consequences. New York's Central Park, for example, was meant to provide respite from the noisy, polluted city and its relentless rationalization.

Skyscrapers came to represent America's transition from a mercantile to a corporate economy. Compared with the horizontal expanse of department stores like Chicago's Marshall Field and New York's Lord and Taylor, skyscrapers created a vertical skyline that captured the public's imagination. The Woolworth Building in New York was dubbed the "Cathedral of Commerce" when it was built in 1913, and the Metropolitan Life Insurance Company tower became a popular New York City tourist attraction. For America, becoming urban meant becoming corporate, and skyscrapers became the monuments to commercial power that defined the corporate city (Bluestone 1991; Domosh 1996; Landau and Condit 1996; Monkkonen 1988; Trachtenberg 1982; Zunz 1990).

New York City was the quintessential city of contrasts. Architects were designing opulent mansions for millionaires on Fifth Avenue while impoverished workers lived in grim chaos on the Lower East Side. Banks, hotels, and city halls were the domain of the powerful, while back alleys, cheap lodging houses, saloons, and tenements dotted the lower-class landscape. Women's city-building activity was more than just an antidote to men's commercialism, though. Women volunteers often bridged the chasm between social classes (Deutsch 1992).

The turmoil of the late nineteenth century created a strong desire for social order among reformers and businessmen (Boyer 1978; Hays 1995;

Wiebe 1967). Architects and planners had the tools to provide (at least the appearance of) order. Male professionals built grand boulevards and civic monuments in search of the City Beautiful. Female volunteers built the places of everyday life, the neighborhood institutions without which a city is not a city—hallmarks of the City Social movement (Wirka 1996). Gender thus played a significant role in the construction of the emerging urban landscape. Crudely stated, men emphasized economic growth and progress (the City Profitable), while women invoked religiosity and domesticity for the benefit of strangers (the City Livable) (Flanagan 1996). Men and women both built the industrial city.

Municipal housekeeping was more than just the literal effort to sanitize cities. It also created mechanisms by which the city could be cleansed symbolically of strangers. According to anthropologist Mary Douglas, dirt is essentially disorder. Attempts to banish dirt are attempts to reorganize the social system within understandable boundaries. Thinking of dirt as anything out of place implies two conditions: "a set of ordered relations and a contravention of that order. Dirt then, is never a unique, isolated event. Where there is dirt there is a system. Dirt is the by-product of a systematic ordering and classification of matter [that] takes us straight into the field of symbolism." People are considered dirty when they are in a marginal state, placeless, left out of society's patterning by some indefinable status (Douglas 1966, 35, 95).

Douglas's theory presupposes the presence of order, whereas cities at the turn of the century were barely organized. The whole enterprise was new to Americans, who were constructing a novel urban culture out of a world of strangers (Lofland 1973; Schultz 1989, xvi). Thus women volunteers did more to *establish* order than to restore it. This perspective explains the zeal with which nineteenth-century women embraced the Social Gospel and municipal housekeeping. Women volunteers were apostles of sacred and secular campaigns to convert the disorder of so many newcomers into a recognizable pattern by giving them actual places to make the transition into a different life.

The issues most important to the nation one hundred years ago all revolved around who belonged where. Should America open its doors to so many immigrants? Would women abandon their homes completely if they could enter colleges and the workplace? How would society change when blacks left southern farms for northeastern and midwestern cities? If immigrant and black men could vote, why not women? People who were once easy to classify by their proper place—in Europe, at home, on the plantation—were pushing their way into the public realm.

Together the Social Gospel and municipal housekeeping promoted a vision of the good city. Both ideologies legitimized contact with new-comers and justified voluntary activities for middle-class women. By invoking familial metaphors—"Slum Sisters" and boarding-house "ma-trons" taking care of "poor motherless daughters"—women volun-teers positioned themselves to save strangers from being defeated by the city. They also saved cities from being overwhelmed by strangers.

For all these reasons, I have labeled the places created and operated by women volunteers "redemptive places." They were sites of assimila-tion, both socially and politically, and of moral influence. They allowed immigrants to move from Europe to America, black migrants from the rural South to the urban North, and women from dependence on their families to economic independence. Redemptive places were temporary institutions for a society in flux.

The rationale for their existence was the salvation of souls, yet re-demptive places did more than rescue men, women, and children. They also saved the city from the tremendous strains resulting from shifting population dynamics. Through voluntary associations, middle-class women began to shape what municipal governments needed to do to balance the city's exaggerated emphasis on growth and profits. In addi-tion to staffing YWCAs and settlement houses, women volunteers were crucial to the playground movement, the public bath movement, hous-ing reform, and public health. Even if women did not personally design or build redemptive places, such places would not have existed without women's voluntary work. Redemptive places lacked the vertical pres-ence of skyscrapers, the horizontal sweep of City Beautiful public spaces, or the commercial utility of factories and railroad stations, but their im-portance transcends their scale and cost, demonstrating that women, too, shaped the city at the end of the nineteenth century.

Why Cities Needed Saving

Late-nineteenth-century American cities were nasty places. People threw swill out their windows onto muddy, unpaved streets where pigs scav-enged for garbage. Open cesspools fouled the air. Public transit, consist-ing of horse-drawn trolleys, relied on thousands of draft animals that produced tons of manure every day. Horses dropped dead on the streets.

Children played in these same streets unless they were in school or working in factories. Tenement residents had to carry water from the street to their rooms if they wanted to wash, so it was impossible to keep families or homes clean for long. Inadequate municipal water supplies and delivery systems meant that fires regularly killed vast numbers of people and destroyed acres of property.[2] Contaminated drinking water was almost as dangerous as fire, contributing to lethal epidemics and high infant mortality.

The environmental problems of one hundred years ago were accompanied by rampant political corruption. Cartoonist Thomas Nast's images of Boss Tweed personified the worst of big-city machine politics. Ward bosses routinely delivered neighborhood services in exchange for votes before civil service reform was enacted. Journalists Jacob Riis, Lincoln Steffens, and Upton Sinclair made their careers exposing municipal and industrial sins to the public during this era.

Because cities concentrated and highlighted vast inequalities between social classes, they were often the sites of labor riots. Two of the most famous incidents occurred when anarchists bombed Haymarket Square in Chicago in 1886 and when Pinkerton's men fought off rioting workers at Carnegie's Homestead steel plant outside Pittsburgh in 1892. Factories' belching smokestacks made cities literally filthy, while dirty politics and labor unrest made them difficult to clean up. City life seemed messy, dangerous, and out of control.

Cities were symbolically dirty because of the influx of newcomers. Strangers were quite literally "out of place"; they polluted the city by challenging what it meant to be an American. The 27 million European immigrants who arrived between 1870 and 1920 settled mainly in cities, where they spoke strange languages and practiced different religions than native-born Americans. About one million black migrants from the rural South soon added race to the urban ethnic mix. More than distinct cultures and darker skin contributed to the dirty image of poor immigrants and African Americans. They often were physically grimy because they lacked access to water with which to wash their bodies and clothes. The public bath movement was an attempt to provide immigrants with soap and water in the belief that clean citizens were better citizens (Hoy 1995; Williams 1991).

The thousands of women adrift who came to the city were so highly visible that they spawned a new enterprise called "travelers' aid." Volunteers greeted young women at docks and railroad stations before they could be intercepted by "wharf sharks" preying on their innocence. Although women adrift escaped being labeled dirty in the same way immigrants and black migrants were, they were often accused of moral impurity.

Women volunteers also became more noticeable. So many women were involved in so many different voluntary activities that University of Chicago professor Sophonisba Breckinridge refused even to try to count them in her report on women's activities. Her estimate of one million members of the General Federation of Women's Clubs captured only part of the voluntary army of the day (Breckinridge 1933, 11). Women volunteers, while physically clean enough, were almost as suspect as women adrift simply because they chose to spend time away from home. At its best all this diversity created lively democratic practices and rich public events. At its worst it produced urban civic wars (Ryan 1997).

New arrivals often sought relief from the routine grind by visiting "cheap amusements" (Peiss 1986). This was the era of dance halls, ballparks, theaters, World's Fair midways, and moving-picture palaces. The newly developing cinema was governed by the same public desire for spectacle as the department store, the international exposition, and the amusement park (Nasaw 1993; Rabinovitz 1998). Had cities been more pleasant, of course, attempts to escape them might have been less tempting. The greatest collective escape of all took shape in the World's Columbian Exposition of 1893 in Chicago. It was an ideal "White City" that transcended the gritty realities of industrialization.

The World's Columbian Exposition, also known as the World's Fair, was a watershed event that subjected the entire concept of the city to national scrutiny. The fair was nicknamed the White City because it was constructed almost entirely of buildings made of staff (a combination of plaster, hemp, and cement) and painted white. It also demonstrated how clean a city could be when powered by electricity instead of coal, and how brightly it could glow at night. The White City was theoretically free of political corruption, and it was distinctly free of African Americans.

The fair was *the* defining architectural and planning event of the late nineteenth century. It showcased the work of the most prominent architects and landscape architects of the day. Architect Daniel Burnham

of Chicago supervised construction, and Frederick Law Olmsted, the creator of Central Park, designed the grounds around a sweeping Court of Honor. Among the prominent architectural firms participating were McKim, Mead and White of New York City and Peabody and Stearns of Boston. Their emphasis on Roman Revival motifs became the template for the City Beautiful movement that flourished between 1900 and 1910.

One of the ironies of the World's Fair is that it opened its gates at almost the same moment that banks and factories were closing their doors in the worst financial panic of the nation's history. The fair also ended just before the Pullman Strike of 1894 dimmed Americans' hopes of peaceful relations between capital and labor. George Pullman built the town that bore his name outside Chicago in 1880 as an antidote to labor strife. A plaster replica of the model town was displayed at the fair in Louis Sullivan's Transportation Building, and a pamphlet prepared by the Pullman Company for visitors to the fair explained that Pullman was "a town where all that is ugly, and discordant, and demoralizing is eliminated." By May 1894 striking American Railway Union workers led by Eugene V. Debs had shut down the town. Everyone suffered: George Pullman's reputation as a benign paternalist, railroad workers when Clarence Darrow lost his Supreme Court case defending Debs, and the town that eventually was absorbed by Chicago. The Pullman Strike, like the World's Columbian Exposition, symbolized America's transition into the stormy twentieth century (Buder 1967; Smith 1995; Trachtenberg 1982).

Cities from Harrisburg, Pennsylvania, to Kansas City, Missouri, emulated the fair's grand boulevards lined with neoclassical buildings. Imposing libraries, museums, banks, and railroad stations became signatures of the City Beautiful movement, whose disciples believed that elegant design could combat the poverty, squalor, and political corruption of the times. Urban social problems persisted despite the best efforts of male architects and planners, however, leaving plenty of work for women volunteers.

How Cities Were Saved

Redemption connotes salvation, deliverance, conversion, and rescue, all of which were associated with the Social Gospel and municipal housekeeping. These two ideologies justified women's public activities by cloth-

ing them in relatively conservative religious and domestic vocabularies when some of their consequences were quite radical. Municipal housekeeping, for example, was an early form of environmental activism. Many of its advocates lobbied to incinerate garbage rather than bury it, a change that would jeopardize business profits (Flanagan 1996). Municipal housekeepers tried to keep their cities as clean as their homes, a task that included supervision of service delivery and oversight of the politicians who provided those services. They also tried to alleviate the symbolic pollution posed by strangers.

Four voluntary associations influenced by the Social Gospel and municipal housekeeping established a presence in the public sphere. The first was the Young Women's Christian Association (YWCA) founded in 1858. Another was The Salvation Army, established in America in 1879. The College Settlements Association (CSA) was formed in 1887 and is used here to represent the efforts of the settlement movement generally. The fourth organization that made a mark on the urban landscape was the National Association of Colored Women (NACW), created in 1896. These organizations provided actual places in which the processes of assimilation (of blacks, immigrants, and women) occurred.

Together, the YWCA, The Salvation Army, the CSA, and the NACW created a range of redemptive places in hundreds of cities. All four organizations had religious foundations that provided women with the moral and financial strength to shape the built environment on behalf of newcomers. Each organization had a slightly different mission. The YWCA's goal was to help white women become economically self-sufficient. The NACW promoted women's interests, but racial uplift was an equally important part of their agenda. The Salvation Army was clearly committed to saving souls. Only the CSA tried to organize neighborhoods and improve actual living conditions among the poor. All four associations had grand visions that materialized in the urban landscape.

Not surprisingly, these voluntary organizations exhibited some of the same divisions that separated all women activists at the turn of the century (Hewitt 1984). The racial composition of the volunteers and clientele is the most obvious, with the YWCA and NACW providing parallel services for white and black women and their children. Another difference was in the gender composition of the organizations and their clientele. The CSA was founded and governed by women, although men could be members and the larger settlement movement had many male

volunteers. The YWCA and NACW were associations primarily *of* and *for* women; The Salvation Army included male and female volunteers.

The four organizations also differed in the gender and social-class composition of their leadership. YWCA, CSA, and NACW leaders typically were educated, middle-class women, while Salvation Army officers tended to be working-class women and men. Thus the YWCA, CSA, and NACW were class-bridging organizations while The Salvation Army operated within class boundaries (Deutsch 1992).[3] Since most of what we know about the Progressive Era focuses on middle-class white reformers, filling in the history of working-class and black organizations like The Salvation Army and the NACW enhances our understanding of how gender, race, and class intersected in the late nineteenth-century city. Whether white or black, middle-class college graduates or working-class evangelicals, women simultaneously shaped urban spaces on behalf of others while paving avenues out of domesticity for themselves.[4]

Women were active in numerous other voluntary organizations between the Civil War and World War I, of course. The Woman's Christian Temperance Union (WCTU), founded in 1874, developed a huge following under the leadership of Frances Willard.[5] The National American Woman Suffrage Association emerged in 1890 from two competing suffrage organizations first formed in 1869.[6] The General Federation of Women's Clubs (GFWC) became the national umbrella organization for all white women's clubs in 1890, and the National Council of Jewish Women held its first conference in New York City in 1896. The National Congress of Mothers, eventually known as the Parent-Teachers' Association, was established in 1897 in Washington, D.C. The first decade of the twentieth century also saw the birth of associations like the black Woman's Convention of the National Baptist Convention (1900), the Junior League (1901), the National Women's Trade Union League (1903), and the American Home Economics Association (1908) (Breckinridge 1933).

None of these other organizations staked out their presence in the spaces of cities, with the exception of the WCTU. In Chicago the WCTU sponsored day nurseries, an industrial school, temporary lodging for thousands of women and men, and a low-cost restaurant (Bordin 1990, 98). Chicago also was the site of the magnificent WCTU Woman's Temple national headquarters, thirteen stories high, built by Daniel Burnham in 1891 on the corner of LaSalle and Monroe Streets (Weimann 1981,

16).[7] The WCTU in Cleveland created the Friendly Inn Social Settlement, which included a kindergarten, dispensary, classrooms, gym, and public baths, in addition to rooms for the resident workers (Arnold and Martin 1976).

Despite evidence that the WCTU created redemptive places, I omitted it for two reasons. The WCTU's building program was considerably less extensive than those of the YWCA, The Salvation Army, CSA, or NACW, making their impact on urban structure less extensive than of the other organizations. The second reason is that, like social movements for suffrage or the abolition of slavery, the temperance movement had an overtly political agenda. My interest is in organizations that identified themselves in nonpolitical terms, yet accomplished very real political ends by shaping public discourse through the built environment.[8]

Redemptive Places

Few architectural historians would identify redemptive places as "architecture" because they were rarely purpose-built by professionals. However, if one accepts Frank Lloyd Wright's definition that architecture stands for "institutionalized patterns of human relatedness that make possible the endurance of the city, or of society, or of the state" (Smith 1979, 19), redemptive places would surely qualify. They represented organized attempts to construct social order in a time of intense demographic, technological, and cultural change.

Many redemptive places could be described as vernacular. Few were professionally designed or representative of a distinctive formal style. Instead, redemptive places were often ordinary, sometimes adapted from another use (Cromley and Hudgins 1995; Upton and Vlach 1986). Since they were modified by volunteers for the benefit of newcomers and often occupied marginal spaces, I think of them as a voluntary vernacular. The Salvation Army's rescue homes, for example, were once private residences. Some redemptive places, of course, were built specifically for their intended purpose (such as the YWCA boarding home erected in 1892 in Worcester, Massachusetts), but typically they provided background for the more famous foreground of monuments, skyscrapers, and civic buildings described in standard architectural and planning histories.

Landscape historian John Brinckerhoff Jackson might consider redemptive places to be "vernacular space." Vernacular space belongs to

Figure 1.9. Postcard of YWCA boarding home in Worcester, Massachusetts, erected 1892. (Courtesy Archives of the National Board of the YWCA of the USA.)

the community and serves as the site of activities that are too large for dwellings to accommodate, such as weddings or family reunions. Individuals have no legal title to it, but custom allows its use by everyone on a daily basis. "Vernacular space is to be shared, not exploited or monopolized — it is in the literal sense of the term a common ground, a common place, a common denominator which makes each vernacular neighborhood a miniature common-wealth" (Jackson 1994, 67).

The public library is an example of a structure that evolved from the vernacular to the purpose-built. Historian Mary Ritter Beard consid-

Figure 1.10. A rescue home sponsored by The Salvation Army in Philadelphia. (Courtesy The Salvation Army National Archives and Research Center, Alexandria, Va.)

ered libraries to be among the most important educational contributions made by women's clubs at the turn of the century. *Woman's Work in Municipalities* reports that "scarcely a woman's club in the country fails to report [library] activity," whether "in little log cabins on the frontiers" or in "splendid buildings in the cities." Beard observed, however, that "the public that profits by them may not fully realize the number of traveling libraries and stationary and circulating libraries that women have directly established." She concluded that it would be impossible to enumerate them all, because "in settlements, Y.W.C.A.s, homes for working girls, rescue homes, rural centers, villages, churches, institutions, and wherever there is the slightest chance, women have slipped in the books and the magazines" (Beard 1915, 43, 44).

Libraries in small towns were vernacular with a vengeance. Some were in rented commercial rooms, church basements, school classrooms, or drugstores. In Hamburg, Iowa, the library shared space with a ladies' resting room, and in Hamilton, Montana, the library adjoined the room where the horses were kept in the city fire department. When women

Figure 1.11. Fernand Henrotin public bath at 2415 North Marshfield Street in Chicago, 1958. (John McCarthy, photographer. Courtesy Chicago Historical Society, ICHi-21722.)

did manage to build a separate facility, it looked more like conventional domestic architecture than the monumental styles designed by Henry Hobson Richardson for large cities (Van Slyck 1995, 128, 129).

Andrew Carnegie's program of library philanthropy, extending from 1886 to 1917, marked the turning point for library architecture. Carnegie funded 1,679 libraries in 1,412 towns at a total cost of $41 million. Any town with a population of at least one thousand that could provide a site for the building was eligible. The town also had to agree to raise taxes to maintain the building, buy books, and pay staff salaries. Participation in Andrew Carnegie's program was a mixed blessing for women. Although it allowed the construction of a permanent building for book collections, the requirements to cooperate with local officials also meant women often lost control of the facilities. Voluntarism gave way to professionalization, and in the process women's influence waned (Van Slyck 1995, 134).

Redemptive places shared several characteristics. One similarity is that they were *sites of assimilation,* just as factories were the sites of production for manufactured goods and office buildings were the sites of bureaucratic work. Women volunteers devoted endless hours to teaching immigrants from Europe and migrants from the farm how to live, learn, and eat like urban Americans. In the process of helping others, volunteers themselves learned how to administer programs and manage property. Redemptive places were real spaces in which women performed the intangible work of assimilating strangers into a new environment.

In their ability to bring women volunteers into contact with strangers, redemptive places captured the very essence of the city. Cities are more than just large towns; they are different from small towns and rural areas because of the number of strangers encountered in daily life. Parochial space includes people who are known to each other and those who are unknown — "the other" — in close proximity. Cities are so complex because they are the only type of settlement forms that routinely contain private, parochial, and public space (Jacobs 1961; Lofland 1998).

Strangers could compromise a woman's virtue, however. The city was a dangerous place where women risked moral ruin and possibly death, like the prostitutes murdered by Jack the Ripper in the Whitechapel district of London (Walkowitz 1992). Less notorious were the hundreds of "delinquent daughters" whose sexuality was so threatening that localities passed age-of-consent laws making sexual intercourse with teenage girls a criminal offense (Odem 1995). Women volunteers used domestic imagery to create places of refuge from such dangers. The YWCA and NACW, for example, gave young girls alternatives to boarding with families whose husbands or sons might take advantage of them.

Redemptive places also were *abeyance structures* for marginalized populations. Abeyance structures regulate the impact of surplus, potentially disruptive populations by keeping them under surveillance until status vacancies open elsewhere in society (Mizruchi 1983). American cities after the Civil War contained numerous groups that threatened social stability. European immigrants, black migrants from the rural South, unmarried working women, and college-educated women volunteers all strained behavioral norms. The assimilation of immigrants who could neither read nor speak English was only slightly less challenging to Americans than dealing with women who refused to marry, stay home, and have children. Redemptive places thus provided a temporary refuge for urban newcomers making the transition from one place to another, whether from Europe to America, from farm to city, or from domestic to public sphere.

In keeping with their function as abeyance structures, redemptive places were characterized by liminality. *Liminality* refers to the state of transition symbolized by a threshold. Anthropologist Victor Turner (1977) describes liminal phenomena as collective structural adjustments to social crises that appear at natural breaks in the flow of history. Liminal phenomena begin as marginal or unclassifiable concepts and fall between the boundaries of organizing categories, although they eventually are incorporated into the social structure. Liminal phenomena are paradoxical, consisting of *both* this *and* that, or, conversely, consisting of *neither* this *nor* that (Douglas 1966). Two founders of the NACW, Josephine St. Pierre Ruffin and Mary Church Terrell, may have been such successful organizers precisely because of their liminal status. Both women were light-skinned, of racially mixed parentage, and moved easily between white and black worlds (Gatewood 1990).

Redemptive places were liminal because they exhibited characteristics of both private and public space. The Roman architect Vitruvius made the following distinction between the private and public rooms of a house: "the private rooms are those into which nobody has the right to enter without an invitation, such as bedrooms. The common are those which any of the people have a perfect right to enter, even without an invitation" (Morgan 1960, 181). Some redemptive places required an invitation to enter, while others did not. Settlement houses depended on a liberal open-door policy; the ability to invite neighbors inside was the main reason for living in impoverished districts. At South End House in Boston, for example, residents took turns as hostess to greet anyone who stopped by. Even during renovation of new quarters, the "door was never closed, although we lived there under some inconvenience"

(Barrows 1929, 29–41). Settlement houses and Salvation Army hotels seldom turned strangers away, while YWCA and NACW boarding houses limited admission to women who passed a character test.

Redemptive places occupied the parochial space of the neighborhood. Settlement houses simultaneously provided room and board for the settlement workers and classrooms for immigrants. The College Settlements Association described its settlement-house living rooms as family living rooms open to everyone in the neighborhood, encouraging mothers to take their families out of the alley and into their "larger home" (Settlements File, n.d.). The quasi-domestic style of YWCA and NACW boarding houses gave young women a parlor in which to entertain men so they could avoid the temptations of theaters and dance halls.

Redemptive places emerged at a pivotal moment in American history, then virtually disappeared. Voluntary associations offered services that fell between private philanthropy and the public welfare state while America matured into an industrialized nation. Settlement houses provided public baths before the private sector made indoor plumbing readily available, and they sponsored kindergartens and playgrounds before children's welfare became a municipal priority. Hull House founder Jane Addams was well aware of the liminal nature of social settlements. She referred to her work as occupying that "borderland between charitable effort and legislation," a place "where we cooperate in many civic enterprises for I think we may claim that Hull House has always held its activities lightly, ready to hand them over to whosoever would carry them on properly" (Addams [1910] 1960, 221).

Another way in which redemptive places were liminal is that they symbolized a transition in the attribution of responsibility for poverty. Prior to the Civil War the destitute depended on the kindness of family, friends, and neighbors for food and shelter; religious organizations also dispensed benevolence to the deserving poor. As urbanization accelerated and poverty became more concentrated, it evolved from a "private trouble" affecting a few unfortunate individuals into a "public issue" demanding policy solutions (Mills [1959] 1967). Redemptive places created by women volunteers filled the gap between private charity and the welfare state by meeting the needs of the urban poor before municipalities or the federal government accepted that responsibility. In fact, the General Federation of Women's Clubs and the National Congress of Mothers are credited with having sown the seeds of modern maternalist welfare policies (Sklar 1993; Skocpol 1992, 57).

Redemptive places were important to the industrial American city because they assimilated immigrants and migrants, brought women volunteers into legitimate contact with strangers, supervised potentially disruptive groups while they learned to negotiate the city, and redefined the boundaries between charitable and municipal responsibility for poverty. They were liminal places that, for the historical moment, filled certain needs by combining characteristics of private and public space. Redemptive places were a critical part of the urban fabric.

Organization of the Book

Chapter 2 describes why cities needed saving and what types of people needed to be rescued. The years between 1870 and 1920 are known by architectural historians as the "American Renaissance" because of the proliferation of great art and architecture (R. Wilson 1979). Social historians typically divide the period into the Gilded Age (roughly 1870 to 1900) and the Progressive Era (1900 to 1920). This book adds the voluntary vernacular and municipal housekeeping to that era.

The decades between the Civil War and World War I were also the age of America's emerging culture of professionalism that demanded experts to solve social problems (Bledstein 1976). Architects, landscape architects, and urban planners demonstrated how professional designers would address urban problems with the World's Columbian Exposition and the City Beautiful movement. Their efforts proved inadequate to the task, however, as women volunteers soon discovered.

Chapter 3 illustrates how the Social Gospel and municipal housekeeping contributed to progressive reform in the city. Women played particularly important roles in the public bath and playground movements. Black women's efforts to challenge the triple burden of race, gender, and class produced African American associations that gained strength from both sacred and secular sources.

Chapter 4 briefly summarizes the histories of four voluntary associations with a physical presence in the city. The Young Women's Christian Association, The Salvation Army, the College Settlements Association, and the National Association of Colored Women were all established between 1858 and 1896. Each of these organizations created and maintained specific places in which race relations, immigration, and women's status were constantly scrutinized. Although the four organizations shared similar goals, social class and racial distinctions often resulted in parallel services.

Chapters 5 through 7 identify redemptive places sponsored in New York, Boston, and Chicago. These major cities were chosen because each had significant immigrant populations at the turn of the century and because they are well documented in standard architectural and planning histories (Boston Society of Architects 1976; Condit 1964; Reps 1965; Scott 1969; Stern, Gilmartin, and Massengale 1983). Each chapter includes a map of redemptive places, circa 1915, created by the four voluntary associations. The goal is to provide a sense of the importance of redemptive places at the national, local, and neighborhood scales.

The story begins with the connections between New York City and smaller cities throughout the country. Chapter 5 emphasizes the geographic range of the places created by women volunteers by tracing similarities between headquarters in New York City and branches in Cleveland, Washington, D.C., Baltimore, and Philadelphia. All of these cities had a black population large and affluent enough to qualify as "aristocrats of color" (Gatewood 1990). Cleveland and Washington, D.C., important centers of activity for the NACW, were also the sites of City Beautiful plans.

Chapter 6 highlights Boston, Massachusetts. The South End was an especially important district. It was home to Denison House, the second settlement house established by CSA founder Vida Scudder. The first building specifically built for the YWCA was on Warrenton Street in the South End, and The Salvation Army had several hotels located in the vicinity. The Harriet Tubman House was created for black women turned away by the YWCA. This chapter presents a series of city, neighborhood, and block maps to illustrate the depth of coverage in Boston, the origin of so many redemptive places.

Chapter 7 explores the significance of the 1893 World's Fair in Chicago for redemptive places. The fair represented a critical moment in the development of American public discourse about the ideal city, women's proper roles, immigration, and race relations. It was also an event in which three of the four voluntary organizations in this book were intensely involved. This chapter includes a map of recognized landmarks in Chicago to illustrate that redemptive places were as numerous as their famous neighbors.

Chapter 8, the summary, concludes that America could not have made the enormous transition accompanying the beginning of the twentieth century without redemptive places. It speculates on the fate of redemptive places and explores whether the city still needs to be saved as we enter the twenty-first century.

This book builds on scholarship from several fields. Sociologists have written a great deal about assimilation, voluntarism, civil society, and marginality, typically ignoring the places in which they occur. Designers, geographers, and urban planners have devoted a great deal of time to building the public realm, but less attention to the processes by which it is actually created. I am trying to bridge the (narrowing) gap between these spatial and aspatial disciplines. My research, therefore, draws from sociology, geography, and urban planning and is laced with architectural history. The work is also informed by the many excellent histories that have been written about progressive reform, voluntary organizations, women's political activism, and cities (see appendix A). I hope political scientists will find enough food for thought to pursue the implications of redemptive places for citizenship.

How Women Saved the City addresses some of the issues raised by other feminist scholars: the origins of the welfare state, the role settlement houses played in assimilating immigrants, racial and class relations among women in cities, and how women exercised power before they could vote. Each of these topics becomes more meaningful when analyzed in the context of the physical spaces in which they occurred. I am especially concerned with Louise Tilly's (1989) question about what difference it makes to incorporate women into urban history. Recognizing women's roles in creating redemptive places helps us interpret the city differently. It corrects some misperceptions about women's absence from the city-building era, it recovers a history that may inspire other research, and it gives credit to women where it is deserved.

CHAPTER TWO

Why Cities Needed Saving

Mary had a little lamb
Between some bread and butter,
She didn't like its flavor, so
She threw it in the gutter.

Mary had a paper wrapped
About her luncheon neat,
She didn't need it anymore
So threw it in the street.

Mary dropped her orange peel
(She thought it was no harm)
Just where poor I might slip on it
And nearly break my arm.

Mary gaily tripped away
On pleasure she was bound
And, oh, it was so long before
The pick-up man came round.

The American City (November 1909): 134

This ditty was contributed to the *Newport* (Rhode Island) *Civic League Bulletin* by an anonymous author and reprinted in *The American City,* a monthly magazine with a circulation of 8,000 readers. During the years of its publication between 1909 and 1920, *The American City* ran more than one hundred articles about the civic work of women (M. Wilson

1979, 98, 102). The commentary about Mary's slovenly habits illustrates reformers' frustrations with one of the smaller daily irritants of urban life. Noise was another common source of aggravation. A malady known as the "yelling peril" produced nervous tension among people trying to live and work amidst constant uproar (Beard 1915, 93).

Littered streets and noise were minor issues compared with more significant threats to the environment. Air quality and water pollution were major problems in cities one hundred years ago, just as they are today. An editorial in *The American City* titled "The Smoke Evil Must Go" (1909) identified burning soft coal as a major public health threat. Doctors agreed that the "smoke nuisance means uncleanliness, wretchedness, disease and death" because the "breathing of coal smoke predisposes the lungs to tuberculosis and even more violent lung trouble, such as pneumonia." Tuberculosis and pneumonia were, in fact, among the top three leading causes of death in 1900 (U.S. Bureau of the Census 1975, 58).

In addition to contaminated air, late-nineteenth-century city residents also had to worry about filthy water. Cholera was a constant threat, and just breathing could be an unpleasant experience for those who survived epidemics. About one-half of the houses had water closets that drained into sewers, and that water flowed unrestricted into rivers and harbors. Thousands of cattle, sheep, and hogs were shipped out of ports each year. All that manure had to go somewhere, as did the offal (organic refuse known as swill) from dwellings. Not surprisingly, patronage of Boston's public baths in 1880 suffered from the practice of dumping sewage in their immediate vicinity (Waring 1886).

All these causes of death resulted in a life expectancy of forty-seven for white men and forty-nine for white women in 1900. Blacks died even younger. A black man born in 1900 lived an average of only thirty-two years, a black woman just thirty-four years (U.S. Bureau of the Census 1975, 55). This situation demanded reform. Women volunteers took up the crusade by lobbying against litter, noise, smoke, and contaminated water. Voluntary associations sponsored endless public education campaigns about the dangers of dirt. Women refused to accept filth as a necessary byproduct of progress. If the city were to be saved from vile conditions, women would have to do it.

Cities had several ways to deal with dirt, all of which were inadequate to the task. Chicago employed forty-two teams of men to pick up household garbage. Anything that pigs refused to eat was taken outside the

Figure 2.1. Haymarket Square at West Randolph Street, Chicago, c. 1905. (Barnes-Crosby, photographer. Courtesy Chicago Historical Society, ICHi-19202.)

city limits and buried. New York City collected three hundred barrels of offal daily and sent it by steamboat to Barren Island; their night-soil was taken by scow to New Jersey and converted to fertilizer. Boston's Board of Health was responsible for the "scavengering" of offal, ashes, and dry house dirt, and for cleaning privies from hotels, restaurants, markets, tenements, and private dwellings. Boston provided nine carts for refuse collection every other day between May and October, but garbage piled up in yards during the winter. Refuse was thrown down abandoned wells after a municipal water system was installed in 1848, and into abandoned privies once the sewer system was constructed (Spencer-Wood 1987; Waring 1886).[1]

Ashes and house dirt could be used for landfill if they were pure, but people often failed to separate their garbage. The organic matter that crept into benign trash could become a disaster. A federal report acknowledged that it had been a mistake to fill parks near Boston's harbor with contaminated refuse because saltwater liberated foul-smelling gases and "enough sulphureted hydrogen has been generated from half

Figure 2.2. Horse-drawn trolley cars at Howard and Clark Streets, Chicago, 1911. (Courtesy Chicago Historical Society, ICHi-29403.)

an acre of dumping-ground to discolor in a few hours the white paint on all the neighboring houses" (Waring 1886, 128).

Streets were also messy. Unpaved streets were cleaned less often than paved ones, and few streets were paved at all. Chicago had only one mile of stone pavement among its 140 miles of streets in 1880, compared with 114 miles covered with wooden blocks and 25 more covered with cinders, gravel, wood planks, or macadam. Washington, D.C., reported just 55 miles of paving in 1880 compared with 175 miles of gravel, wooden, or unimproved roads. New York City, however, had removed all of its wooden blocks by 1880 and replaced them with 229 miles of stone-paved streets and another 80 miles of cobblestones (Waring 1886).

A popular commercial product of the day was Tarvia, a tar extract produced by the Barrett Manufacturing Company, which sealed macadam and reduced dust more cheaply than stone pavement. Like smoke, dust was considered a menace to public health because it contributed to the spread of tuberculosis. The advertising section of *The American City* boasted that the Tarvia treatment meant "We shall yet hear of the 'dust-

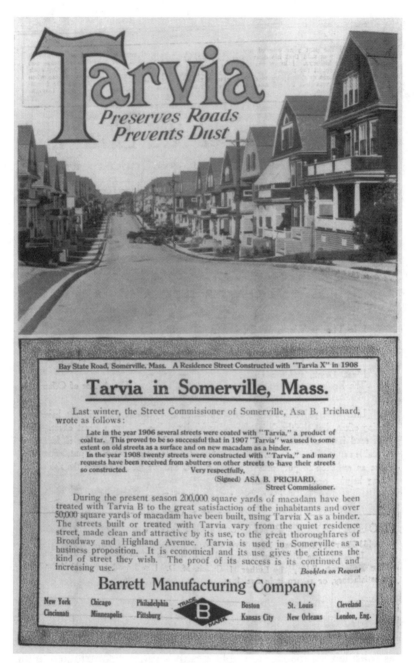

Figure 2.3. Advertisement for Tarvia Road Treatment to reduce dust, including an endorsement of the product by the Street Commissioner of Somerville, Massachusetts. (*The American City*, October 1909.)

Figure 2.4. Children at play in New York City street, c. 1900. The photograph was originally titled, with reference to the horse, "The Close of a Career in New York." (Courtesy Library of Congress, D4-13645.)

less city,' and if such a city is possible, nothing less can claim to be a 'City Beautiful' " (*The American City* 1 [1909]: 95).

Dead animals complicated efforts to keep streets clear. Chicago's extensive system of horse railroads was serviced by more than 4,000 horses and mules in 1880; New York reported nearly 12,000 horses. Sometimes these animals simply dropped in their tracks from exhaustion and had to be removed by the city, along with smaller creatures. In 1879 Chicago public health officials hauled away the carcasses of 1,500 horses, 400 cattle, and about 10,000 cats and dogs to a rendering plant twenty-six miles from the city. The system apparently worked well for people living in Chicago, but residents of the neighborhoods near the rendering establishments were less satisfied. New York removed 15,000 dead horses and about 40,000 dead cats and dogs to Barren Island that year, noting that carcasses seldom remained on the streets for more than three or four hours (Waring 1886).

Washington, D.C., had a particularly difficult time dealing with "the garbage question" even though the city had contracted with private firms for regular removal of trash. The following excerpt from a health officer's report illustrates his degree of frustration with the problem:

> I do not approach the discussion of this subject with any extra degree of pleasant reflection thereon. Indeed, I have become so thoroughly disgusted in ceaseless, untiring, and, withal, unavailing effort to secure some improvement in this service of the collection of garbage, that the very mention of the word is almost sufficient to nauseate.
>
> It seems strange that we of the District of Columbia should have so much trouble with a service which is satisfactorily performed in almost every other city, yet the fact remains; and during the past two years the public has been forced to submit to the greatest discomfort and doubtless, at times, injury to health, resulting from accumulations of decaying animal and vegetable matter allowed to remain for days, and even weeks, upon premises throughout [the city]. (Waring 1886, 46)

One of women's most important crusades concerned municipal responsibility for the incineration of garbage. Adequate garbage and sewage disposal had significant implications for the appearance and health of cities. When Jane Addams organized the Hull House Woman's Club in 1895 to protest the lack of garbage collection in Chicago's Nineteenth Ward, she reported that their greatest achievement was the discovery of a pavement eighteen inches under the surface of rotting fruit and filthy rags. Addams removed the first eight inches of garbage and insisted that the city remove the rest. On their summer-evening walks up and down alleys to inspect garbage boxes, clubwomen discovered more than a thousand health department violations (Addams [1910] 1960, 200–218). Clubwomen also taught neighborhood residents about the importance of clean streets and alleys. Their continued protests to city hall over inadequate services, and the publicity surrounding Jane Addams's bid for the garbage-removal contract in the ward, resulted in eventual reform (Hoy 1980, 190).

Garbage attracted flies, of course, and many cities recognized them as a threat to public health. One alarmist reminded readers of *The American City* that flies had "sticky little feet and innumerable little roughnesses [that] catch and hold and multiply all sorts of germs, finally depositing them with a horrifying liberality in our milk and food" (Fuller 1909, 139). Cleveland embarked on a particularly vigorous crusade against flies. Once again the efforts were organized by women volunteers. Jean Dawson, a local professor of biology, led the charge for a "flyless city of

Cleveland." She issued a "fly catechism" to educate schoolchildren about the dangers of diseases borne by flies. Dawson convinced stable owners to clean out their stalls in the winter to prevent fly eggs from hatching. The mayor was so pleased with the results that he considered "anti-fly campaigning" more important than any other single community public health activity (Beard 1915, 92).

These conditions were an obvious incentive for women's municipal housekeeping activities. Cities became the new battlefields on which to combat the diseases that had killed so many people during the Civil War, since epidemics spread in urban slums as quickly as they had in army camps. The United States Sanitary Commission (of which Frederick Law Olmsted was chief executive officer) had been the training ground for thousands of women who learned from Florence Nightingale's experience in the Crimean War. For municipal housekeepers, a city had to be clean before it could be attractive or beautiful (Hoy 1995, 75).

Americans at the end of the nineteenth century believed disease was caused by dirt and bad smells, so they assumed that cleaning the city would also make it healthier. Women volunteers' efforts were encouraged by sanitary engineer George Waring, "the greatest apostle of cleanliness" working in the field of municipal sanitation. Waring, whose career began as Frederick Law Olmsted's agricultural and drainage engineer for Central Park, published numerous articles in the *Atlantic Monthly* and *Scribner's Monthly* about the need for urban sewage systems. Waring and other experts promoted the notion that filth bred chaos, and that the country's progress depended on clean, orderly cities. Public and private cleanliness soon became the American Way (Hoy 1995).

Garbage disposal, dust, and water supplies were clearly a problem in American cities, but there was another cleanliness issue. If dirt is anything that appears to be out of place, the influx of newcomers who were strangers to America's urban culture constituted a major symbolic source of contamination.

The Threat of New Arrivals

American cities were still struggling to define themselves when an onslaught of immigrants arrived from three origins. Approximately six million European immigrants entered the United States during each decade between the Civil War and World War I, when the Immigration Act of 1917 codified all previous restrictions by country of origin. The year 1917 also heralded the "Great Migration" of blacks from the South to north-eastern and midwestern cities. These immigrants and migrants included thousands of independent women seeking jobs in the city. All of these groups demanded a niche, as did the women volunteers who provided them with redemptive places.

This demographic context is relevant to the history of redemptive places because redemptive places often were racially segregated. Many redemptive places were established in northern and midwestern cities when European immigration was at its peak and before black migration from the South reached significant numbers. Thus the most visible urban poor—the users of redemptive places—at the end of the nineteenth century were white ethnics. By the beginning of the twentieth century, however, the most visible urban poor were African Americans, with residential segregation and racial discrimination exacerbating their need for services.

Immigration

Images of immigrants arriving at Ellis Island are almost as symbolic as the Statue of Liberty in evoking the foundations on which America is based. Between 1870 and 1920 approximately 27 million immigrants arrived from Europe (nearly nine million between 1900 and 1910). Most of them settled in cities, giving many cities higher proportions of first- and second-generation immigrants than of the native-born. In 1910 the cities with the highest proportions of foreign-born were Boston, Chicago, Cleveland, and New York. Since internal migration from farms and small towns accelerated during the same period, the majority of Americans lived in cities by 1920 (Dorsett 1968, v; Hofstadter 1955; Still 1974; Ward 1971).

In 1890, when social reformer and photojournalist Jacob Riis asked an agent of New York City's Fourth Ward how many people lived there, he was told "one hundred Irish, thirty-eight Italian, and two that spoke the German tongue"; there were no native-born Americans (Riis [1890] 1957, 15). Another notorious immigrant section was the Sixth Ward, known as Five Points, where the revivalist Phoebe Palmer first ministered to the poor. Its architectural center was the Old Brewery, squalid quarters for hundreds of Italians and blacks. During an 1842 visit Charles Dickens described Five Points as an urban hell rivaling London's Whitechapel district (Bergmann 1995).

Immigrants, the "strangers within our gates" (Wilson [1916] 1987), were perceived by native-born Americans as a threat to social order. Public sentiment against immigrants was intense. In 1889 Wisconsin and Illinois passed legislation forbidding instruction in foreign languages. The American Protective Association, a virulent anti-Catholic group, attracted half a million members after the Depression of 1893 with claims that the pope could seize power in the United States. In 1894 Sen. Henry Cabot Lodge of Massachusetts founded the Immigration Restriction League. The league lobbied for the literacy test, which Congress approved in 1897, but Pres. Grover Cleveland later vetoed. The president of the Daughters

Figure 2.5. Photograph of immigrant family included in *News of the College Settlement of Philadelphia* 3, no. 8 (September 1912). (Courtesy Sophia Smith Collection, Smith College, Northampton, Mass.)

of the American Revolution cautioned members in 1910 that Americans should be more selective about who was let into the country "to trample the mud of millions of alien feet into our spring" (Hays 1995, 140).

Between 1870 and 1921 Congress passed twenty pieces of legislation restricting immigration. When measures aimed at controlling the origins of immigrants failed to work, Congress imposed a numerical limit with the Quota Law of 1921 (U.S. Department of Justice 1997). Thus ended the massive European infusion. The proportion of Americans who were foreign-born peaked at about 15 percent in 1910 and declined steadily thereafter until beginning to rise again in the 1980s (U.S. Bureau of the Census 1997).

Industrialization proceeded relentlessly despite the ban on immigration, and black men and women soon joined Europeans as a cheap source of urban labor.

Race Relations after the Civil War

Slavery ended symbolically with President Lincoln's Emancipation Proclamation in 1863 and legally in 1865 with ratification of the Thirteenth Amendment to the Constitution. Federal Reconstruction efforts enacted in 1867 granted some civil rights to blacks (through the Fourteenth and Fifteenth Amendments), but those evaporated when Pres. Rutherford B. Hayes withdrew Union troops in the Compromise of 1877. Within the next decade Jim Crow laws mandating racially segregated public facilities were passed throughout the South. In 1896 the Supreme Court upheld states' rights to impose racial separation when it declared in *Plessy v. Ferguson* that Louisiana could legally require whites and blacks to ride in different train cars. Blacks effectively lost their voting rights when states introduced poll taxes, literacy tests, white primaries, and grandfather clauses to subvert the Fifteenth Amendment (Brands 1995, 215–28, 251).

Declining legal rights were accompanied by increasing violence. The number of lynchings tripled between 1882 and 1892 as the Ku Klux Klan terrorized blacks and any whites who defended them. Former slaves could rarely read or write and the new system of sharecropping produced almost as much poverty as slavery had. Although blacks were free to move north after the Civil War, few did. Social Darwinism had created racial prejudices among northern employers; illiteracy and rural isolation made contact with the larger world difficult; and many southern states passed laws to capture blacks as a cheap labor pool. In Georgia, for example, northern recruiters were charged a $25,000 license fee and required to supply forty-five character references; blacks were sometimes arrested for vagrancy as they waited to board northbound trains; and the Freedmen's Bureau encouraged blacks to work for plantations rather than move north. It is not surprising, therefore, that 90 percent of blacks still lived in the South at the turn of the century (Farley and Allen 1987, 109–12; A. Jones 1990, 20).[2]

It was this milieu in which both Booker T. Washington and W. E. B. Du Bois gained national recognition. Washington and Du Bois were the principal African American participants in the debate about race relations. One spoke with the authority of humble beginnings shared by most blacks. The other spoke for the "colored aristocracy" (Gatewood 1990).

Washington was born a slave in Virginia in 1856, attended Virginia's Hampton Normal and Agricultural Institute, and founded Tuskegee Institute in Alabama in 1881. Washington believed that industrial education would be most effective in preparing the majority of blacks for useful jobs, and that blacks needed to prove themselves economically before entering white society. He articulated his philosophy in an address delivered to an audience of blacks and whites at the 1895 Cotton States and International Exposition in Atlanta:

> No race that has anything to contribute to the markets of the world is
> long in any degree ostracized. It is important and right that all privileges
> of law be ours, but it is vastly more important that we be prepared for
> the exercise of these privileges. The opportunity to earn a dollar in a
> factory just now is worth infinitely more than the opportunity to spend
> a dollar in an opera house. (Brands 1995, 246)

W. E. B. Du Bois advocated a completely different approach. Like Washington, Du Bois attended school in the same state in which he was born, but Du Bois was born free in Massachusetts and graduated with a Ph.D. from Harvard. Du Bois placed his hopes in the "talented tenth" — the black ministers, teachers, doctors, lawyers, and writers who would demonstrate that blacks could match the achievements of whites. Du Bois fought for the elite, while Washington fought for the masses. The breach between their two camps was illustrated in Du Bois's *The Souls of Black Folk* (1903), in which he accused Washington of asking blacks to give

up political power, civil rights, and higher education in favor of industrial training, material goods, and compromise with the South. According to Du Bois, Washington's "propaganda" had accomplished: "1. The
disfranchisement of the Negro. 2. The legal creation of a distinct status
of civil inferiority for the Negro. [and] 3. The steady withdrawal of aid
from institutions for the higher training of the Negro" (DuBois [1903]
1961, 48). At the turn of the century, therefore, blacks were faced not
only with white hostility, but with disagreement among their leaders
about the best avenue out of oppression.

The nation's largest-selling black newspaper, the *Chicago Defender*,
actively encouraged blacks to come north. The *Chicago Defender* advertised throughout the South that May 15, 1917, would be the date of "the
Great Northern Drive," causing Carl Sandburg to comment in the *Chicago
Daily News* that "[t]he Defender more than any other one agency was
the big cause of the 'Northern fever' and the big exodus from the South,"
and prompting a Georgia newspaper to call it "the greatest disturbing
element that has yet entered Georgia" (Henri 1975, 63). More than one

Figure 2.6. Lantern slide of nurse from the Chicago Visiting Nurse Association in
home of African American family, c. 1910. (Photographer unknown. Courtesy
Chicago Historical Society, ICHi-21072.)

million blacks left, and the South lost approximately 8 percent of its black population between 1870 and 1920 (Farley and Allen 1987).

As a result of the *Defender*'s campaign, Chicago was one of the northern cities that attracted thousands of southern black migrants. Chicago's black population tripled between the 1870s and early 1890s (from 5,000 to 15,000) and more than tripled again (from about 30,000 to 109,000) between 1900 and 1920. The "Black Belt" of Chicago, already established by the time of the World's Columbian Exposition, became increasingly more pronounced. Conflicts produced by demographic pressures intensified competition for jobs and scarce housing, sparking race riots in Chicago in 1919 (Drake and Cayton 1962, 47–65; Farley and Allen 1987, 109–15; Hirsch 1983, 17; Osofsky 1966, 46–52).

Women Adrift

The Civil War and subsequent economic depressions forced many young women to seek their fortunes outside the family. Fathers, brothers, and potential husbands were either dead or bankrupt. Between 1870 and 1920 the number of wage-earning women in the United States rose from less than two million to almost nine million, while the proportion of all women in the labor force rose from 13 to 21 percent (U.S. Bureau of the Census 1975, 128). A large number of these women who lived with neither their own families nor as a domestic servant in an employer's family were labeled "adrift" by a 1910 federal report. The majority were young and single, but some were separated, divorced, or widowed. White and black migrants from America's farms and towns joined European immigrants, and by 1900 one in five urban wage-earning women lived "adrift," most of them in boarding or lodging houses. The census of 1900 reported that between one-tenth and one-third of all adult working women lived as boarders or lodgers in the twenty-eight largest cities (Meyerowitz 1988; Mjagkij and Spratt 1997).

The boarding home of the early nineteenth century, in which communal meals were served, was gradually replaced by the more impersonal rooming house lacking dining room or parlor. Rapid growth in rooming houses began in the 1880s. By 1893, the year of the Columbian Exposition, the number of furnished rooms in Chicago surpassed the number of boarding houses, and by 1917 the number of furnished rooms had risen to almost three thousand. As married and widowed women found more profitable ways to earn an income and as standards of privacy rose among both lodgers and families, fewer private homes took in strangers (Meyerowitz 1988, 73–77).

"Women bachelors" in New York City solved their lodging problems by living cheaply in halls converted into bedrooms. Hall-rooms were furnished with family castoffs: broken chairs, cracked mirrors, and faded carpets. These "Pariahs of the community of rooms, the Cinderellas of the domestic roof" seldom had heat, plumbing, or lighting comparable to other rooms in the house, leaving their occupants stifling in the summer and freezing in the winter. Their small size also induced the "hall-room habit" — the psychological necessity of having everything within reach. The number of hall-rooms was enormous despite their numerous drawbacks. One estimate is that fifteen thousand hall-rooms existed near Washington Square between Fifth and Sixth Avenues at the end of the century (Humphreys 1896).

Women Volunteers

Women volunteers were scandalized that working women had so few rooming options. In trying to provide alternatives, volunteers gained as much from redemptive places as the clientele they served. The YWCA, for example, gave young women room, board, and recreational space at the same time it educated volunteers about the real estate market and institutional management. Settlement houses established social work and city planning as respectable professions for women at the same time they provided kindergartens, playgrounds, and public baths for immigrants.

Urban conditions and gender relations at the turn of the century were ripe for women's voluntarism. Historian Barbara Berg argues that middle-class men's pursuit of an affluent lifestyle coupled with industrialization removed their wives from economically productive roles. Women responded to this change in status with an explosion of voluntary association networks through which they established acceptable public identities (Berg 1978). The steady stream of newcomers demanded the services women volunteers began to offer.

One type of voluntarism, the women's club, was almost exclusively an urban phenomenon. Many began as reading clubs to educate middle-class women, few of whom had attended college. They soon adopted a more active agenda. Two of the first clubs to take civic issues seriously

A Typical Hall Bedroom.

Figure 2.7. Typical New York City hall bedroom for single working women. (*Scribner's Magazine* 20 [1896]: 630.)

were New York's Sorosis, founded in 1869 by newspaper columnist Jane Cunningham Croly for white women, and Boston's Woman's Era club, founded in 1893 by Josephine St. Pierre Ruffin for black women. By the beginning of the twentieth century, a clubwoman considered it "folly" to waste her time on esoteric subjects like "the Moorish invasion of Spain" when the health of her home and family was menaced by "impure water supply, poor lighting, smoky, rubbish-laden streets, or lack of play space for her children" (*The American City* 1909, 1:90; M. Wilson 1979).

Members of women's organizations participated enthusiastically in shaping the Progressive social reform agenda by disseminating Social Gospel and municipal housekeeping ideas nationally through the General Federation of Women's Clubs (GFWC) and the National Association of Colored Women (NACW). The GFWC was a national network founded in 1892 to coordinate the activities of thousands of white

Figure 2.8. Grace Dodge at groundbreaking ceremony for St. Paul YWCA with Mrs. C. P. Noyes and other women volunteers. (Courtesy Archives of the National Board of the YWCA of the USA.)

women's voluntary associations. The GFWC had nearly one million members by 1910, the majority of whom were "home-staying, church-going women with no career and no [desire] for one" (M. Wilson 1979, 98–102). Many of the women involved with the YWCA and CSA were also members of a local GFWC affiliate.

In 1909 GFWC president Eva Perry Moore wrote an essay titled "Woman's Interest in Civic Welfare" for the first volume of *The American City*. Moore identified the city as "a home, clean and beautiful" where every citizen should find the opportunity for physical, mental, and moral development (Moore 1909). On behalf of the GFWC, Moore promoted municipal housekeeping as an ideology that urged women to keep the city as clean as their homes. The GFWC sponsored sanitary campaigns for streets and sidewalks, cleared alleys of debris, and lobbied for clean air during the peak of industrialization. The GFWC was successful because it clothed its activities in the guise of domestic duties. More secular than the Social Gospel and less radical than the suffrage movement, municipal housekeeping was the vehicle by which women became involved in city government before they could vote. Municipal housekeeping allowed women to define the public city as a private space they could understand and influence: as a home, clean and beautiful.

Clean Cities, Clean Americans

When immigrants began arriving from Europe, blacks from the rural South, and women adrift "from the West in regiments, and from the South in brigades," the city was overrun by people who were out of place. These strangers became a symbolic source of pollution (Douglas 1966; Humphreys 1896, 627). British journalist William Stead's Social Gospel manifesto, *If Christ Came to Chicago!*, documented hundreds of tramps in the streets, "[l]ike the frogs in the Egyptian plague." These jobless and homeless men slept in police stations, City Hall, even outhouses. Stead chastised city officials for diverting resources to host the World's Fair when so many of the poor needed help. He warned them that "[f]rom poverty and homelessness comes despondency, loss of self-respect follows on enforced dirtiness, and the undescribable squalor of filthy clothes" (Stead [1894] 1978, 17–31).[3]

Women volunteers turned their attention to cleansing newcomers in the belief that clean bodies were closely linked with public sanitation. As historian Suellen Hoy (1995, 87) put it, "cleanliness became some-

thing more than a way to prevent epidemics and make cities livable—
it became a route to citizenship, to becoming American." That message
was conveyed incessantly to immigrants. It began with Ellis Island, which
had enough showers for eight thousand immigrants a day, continued
through English lessons that taught adults and children how to read,
and extended to settlement-house classes about the hazards of slaugh-
tering sheep in the basement or drinking water from horse troughs.
Settlement workers often set up model centers so immigrant women
could copy white, middle-class American styles of housekeeping by learning how to clean each room. Classes in hygiene stressed the importance
of soap and water, and immigrant women soon learned that being American meant scrubbing floors, doing laundry, and washing windows as
well as bathing (Hoy 1995, chapter 4).

Every settlement house promoted a cleanliness agenda. They provided
nurseries to feed and bathe infants whose mothers worked at neighborhood factories. Settlement kindergartens offered early instruction
in American values. For example, an adaptation of the kindergarten
known as the "kitchen garden" was developed by settlement worker Emily
Huntington to teach homemaking skills to immigrant children by let-
ting them play with miniature pots, pans, and brooms. Huntington's *Little Lessons for Little Housekeepers,* published in 1875, gained quite a following among settlement workers (Weimann 1981, 339).[4] A former resident
of Boston's South End House recalled being shown the home furnishings by a proud new bride, who never made up the bed "without singing
the verses she had learned in the Little Housekeepers' Class, where she
had been introduced to some of the first principles of housekeeping at
seven or eight years of age" (Barrows 1929, 41).

Settlement houses also functioned as kindergartens for adults, since
few European immigrants spoke English or knew American customs
when they arrived. Through public kitchens, cooking classes, cookbooks,
and model tenements, settlement workers taught immigrant women
how to keep house like Americans. Most important, settlement houses
sponsored public baths to transform "dirty immigrants" into clean citizens (Davis 1967, 44; Hoy 1995).

Black migrants from the South were also subject to a catechism of
cleanliness, both from whites and from middle-class blacks. Booker T.
Washington actively preached the "gospel of the toothbrush," a doctrine of personal hygiene promoted by Virginia's Hampton Institute. The

Chicago Defender urged newcomers to "use water freely" to prevent both illness and "hostile comments against the race" (Hoy 1995, chapter 4).

Of the three types of migrants, only working women escaped a concerted cleanliness campaign, presumably because they were already white Americans. Europeans and blacks were more visibly the "other" and out of place than women adrift, and therefore bore the brunt of efforts to equate Americanization with cleanliness. Just as municipal housekeepers considered the only worthy citizen a clean citizen, they defined the only attractive city as a clean city.

The cleanest city of them all was the World's Columbian Exposition held in Chicago in 1893. The World's Fair was a fantasy of what a city could and *should* look like. It was a stage on which all the newest technology was displayed, an illusion of efficiency, order, and cleanliness. It was nicknamed "The White City" in honor of this image. White is the cleanest of colors, one that reveals dirt most clearly.

The White City, the City Beautiful Movement, and Village Improvement Societies

An international exposition was held almost every year between 1851 and 1925, each one bigger and better than the last. The exposition, as an urban event, was an important educational and entertainment venue during the last part of the nineteenth century. It began as a showcase for new technological discoveries and evolved into a way for countries to advertise their cultural accomplishments. The first one, the Great Exhibition in London, boasted a major large-scale, prefabricated iron and glass building—the Crystal Palace. The exposition in Paris in 1889 was celebrated for its Eiffel Tower. The United States was intent on outdoing both for the four-hundredth anniversary of the discovery of America. While Paris, London, and other host cities had temporarily transformed the appearance of a few districts for fair exhibits, Chicago created an entirely new place. The World's Columbian Exposition of 1893 proved that elegant cities could be designed from the ground up (Badger 1979; Burg 1976).[5]

The White City

The man who executed this impressive feat was Daniel Burnham, a local architect hired by the Commercial Club of Chicago when the city won the national competition to host the fair. In addition to Burnham, the exposition was designed by Burnham's partner, John Wellborn Root (who died before the fair opened), Frederick Law Olmsted, and Olmsted's partner, Henry Sargent Codman. The team chose Jackson Park, now the site of the University of Chicago, for its creation. They juxtaposed a large naturalistic lagoon with neoclassical buildings to create a Court of Honor that grouped the major buildings together. They also agreed to total unanimity of style, color, and cornice height, features that contributed to the fair's distinctive design (Bolotin and Laing 1992; R. Wilson 1979).

The sheer enormity of the fair and its impact on the public imagination are hard to overestimate. Described as the "greatest theatrical production of the century," the fairgrounds were three times larger than any previous fair and had twice as much space under roof (five million square feet); total costs exceeded $30 million. The main attractions were buildings exhibiting the nation's technological and cultural wealth. The Midway Plaisance was part carnival and part circus, with rides and games and "villages" displaying exotic people from around the world. Every important author, journalist, and photographer of the day chronicled the fair's events for newspapers and souvenir albums. The fair supposedly inspired composer Katherine Lee Bates to finish the lyrics for "Amer-

Figure 2.9. View of the Court of Honor, World's Columbian Exposition, Chicago, 1893. (C. D. Arnold, photographer. Courtesy Chicago Historical Society, ICHi-13883.)

ica the Beautiful." Frederick Jackson Turner delivered his treatise on the closing of the American frontier at a historian's conference in Chicago convened to add intellectual respectability to the fair. Between the time it opened on May 1 and closed in October 1893, nearly 28 million people had visited the fair (Bolotin and Laing 1992; Brands 1995, 20; Burg 1976; Rabinovitz 1998).

The legacy of the World's Columbian Exposition extended far beyond its short six-month installation, although professionals disagreed about its worth. Daniel Burnham thought the fair had made a profound and positive impression on the public. Architect Louis Sullivan, on the other hand, suspected that the damage to architectural standards wrought by the neoclassical theme of the fair would last for "half a century" (Reps 1965, 501). For better or worse, "the whole regal scene was a prophecy, a forecast of monumental city halls, public libraries, museums, union stations, banks, and academic halls to be built in the next twenty or thirty years" under the banner of the City Beautiful movement (Scott 1969, 36).

The City Beautiful Movement

The City Beautiful movement that flourished between 1900 and 1910 was an architectural and planning campaign to make cities more aesthetically pleasing, to enhance civic pride, and to improve public morals. Its advocates were among the first to practice comprehensive city planning. Like the White City, the ideal City Beautiful would unify all the forms of physical design into one coordinated plan applicable to the entire city. In its emphasis on the healing power of well-balanced buildings and landscapes, the City Beautiful movement tried to clean up the visual and moral disorder of the industrial city (Foglesong 1986; Peterson 1985; Wilson 1989; R. Wilson 1979).

The City Beautiful movement celebrated the virtues of urban beauty and utility, or "beautility" in the words of advocate Arnold Brunner (Wilson 1989, 83). The movement had both ideological and aesthetic components. It was part of the general reform zeal to instill civic responsibility by enhancing the urban environment. A well-ordered, harmonious system of neoclassical public buildings amidst natural landscapes would help. Design professionals would work with citizens to develop a visionary plan and secure funding. The construction of neoclassical post offices, for example, required the cooperation of elected officials and voter approval of bond issues. Although the City Beautiful movement concentrated on public spaces and left residential planning to the private sector, it addressed such functional concerns as sewerage and water supply, landscaping, recreation, and transportation. The goal was to create a coherent grouping of grand architecture — spread horizontally rather than vertically like skyscrapers — to promote civic values, improve worker productivity, and boost a city's image as a good place to live and conduct business (Foglesong 1986; Wilson 1989).

One of the reasons the Columbian Exposition is often identified as the foundation of the City Beautiful movement is that Daniel Burnham designed two of the most famous City Beautiful plans, one for Washington, D.C., and one for Chicago. A more realistic interpretation is that both the exposition and the City Beautiful movement were responses to contemporary reformist concerns for park planning, municipal art, and civic improvement. City Beautiful ideals spread beyond Chicago to smaller cities like Denver, Kansas City, Dallas, Seattle, and Roanoke, Virginia. Grand civic centers and railroad stations were signatures of the movement. The municipal art movement developed simultaneously to provide public monuments, while volunteers with civic improvement leagues worked on sanitary reforms (Bluestone 1991; Gilmartin 1995; Peterson 1976; Wilson 1964).

City Beautiful efforts typically involved major redevelopment schemes. Primary among these was the 1901 plan for Washington, D.C. (sometimes called the McMillan Plan because it was sponsored by Sen. James McMillan and his Senate Park Commission). Daniel Burnham and Frederick Law Olmsted Jr. were hired to update L'Enfant's 1791 design for the city. The intervening century had produced a hodge podge of architectural styles among the federal buildings, a cast-iron market shed on Pennsylvania Avenue, and a Mall marred by a railroad depot. A series of political, financial, and artistic compromises ensued. Eventually Burnham, Olmsted Jr., and Charles McKim (another World's Fair architect) designed a "Renaissance complex" of imposing buildings. They moved the railroad station off the Mall and restored some of L'Enfant's original dignity to the city (Gutheim 1977; Peterson 1985).

Burnham's design for Chicago was less successful. Sponsored by the Chicago Commercial Club in 1909, the *Plan of Chicago* represented materially the culmination of the search for moral order in American cities (Boyer 1978, 272–75). It reoriented the city toward the lakefront and ignored the skyscrapers that already existed by proposing a uniform cor-

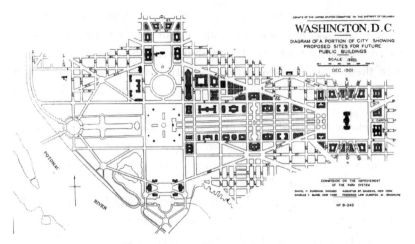

Figure 2.10. City Beautiful Plan proposed by Daniel Burnham, Charles McKim, Augustus St. Gaudens, and Frederick Law Olmsted Jr., 1901. (Courtesy Library of Congress, USZ62-60164.)

nice line for low commercial buildings reminiscent of the Columbian Exposition. The civic center would be connected to the museum on the lake by a landscaped boulevard and the visual balance would be shifted from the business domain to the civic realm (Bluestone 1991, 194–96). Coming to fruition as the City Beautiful movement was waning, the Chicago Plan met opposition; some of its suggestions were implemented but many more remained unrealized. Burnham's plans for Cleveland (1903), San Francisco (1905, just before the earthquake), and Manilla (1905) were even less well developed (Barth 1980, 31; Hines 1974).

Urban planners credit Charles Mulford Robinson's *Modern Civic Art, or, The City Made Beautiful*, first published in 1903, as the "bible" of the City Beautiful movement.[6] The publication of this book, followed by Robinson's death in 1917, marked the symbolic beginning and end of the movement. Unlike most City Beautiful professionals, Robinson had *not* been trained as a designer. He had a liberal arts college degree and wrote for a newspaper, experience that helped him become a major popularizer of the movement. His education also helps explain why Robinson believed that "[s]tatues, monuments, and skylines can wait but bodies and minds must be fed; aesthetic improvement comes last" (Peterson 1976, 428; R. Wilson 1979).

Robinson believed that modern civic art could provide visually pleasing harmonious surroundings, even in humble slums. In opposition to the urban eyesores of the early twentieth century, Robinson anticipated "a new day for cities," in which "water is had in abundance to clean the pavements and lay the dust. The mesh of wires that inventions brought with them as a temporary urban evil are now assembling in orderly strands beneath the ground; and there is promise that the smoke, which has hung in a dark cloud about the modern industrial community, is shortly to be dissipated" (Robinson [1918] 1970, 6). *Modern Civic Art* was so popular it was reprinted three times between 1903 and 1918.

Compare Robinson's words with those of Mary Ritter Beard in *Woman's Work in Municipalities* published (only once) in 1915. Beard introduced the section on "Clean Streets" with a vignette in which a woman looks out the windows of her home and notices "that portion of municipal dusting and sweeping assigned to men: namely, street cleaning." Whereas Robinson's prose implied that clean cities would just happen, Beard knew better. She recited story after story of volunteers who cleaned streets themselves, then turned over maintenance to Boards of Public Works. The work women considered "just housekeeping as usual" soon became paid labor for the public sector (Beard 1915, 84–92).

Village Improvement Societies

The work of women's organizations extended beyond municipal boundaries and into the countryside. While Daniel Burnham and Charles Mulford Robinson are the names typically associated with the City Beautiful movement, historians acknowledge that the movement emerged from a national network of antebellum village improvement societies typically organized by women volunteers (Peterson 1976; Wilson 1989). The first Village Improvement Society is generally acknowledged as the Laurel Hill Association of Stockbridge, Massachusetts, founded by Mary Hopkins in 1853. Hopkins supposedly formed her association after overhearing a tourist deriding the intelligence of people willing to live in a community "devoid of any attempt at sanitation or adornment." Summer visitors wanted to see porches and bay windows, not "old-time country makeshifts." Within a few years the Laurel Hill Association had transformed Stockbridge from a "rough, shabby village" to a handsome, orderly town (Hoy 1995, 74). A journalist for the *Atlantic Monthly* proposed that tourists came in search of the same conveniences they had in the city, so "[v]illage improvement is the offspring of the cities, and in most cases it is paid for and engineered by those who have enjoyed city advantages" (Robbins 1897, 214).

Perhaps Mary Hopkins had just read Andrew Jackson Downing's newly released *Rural Essays*. Downing was a highly influential writer on gardening and rural architecture who died in an 1852 Hudson River steamboat fire. A volume of his editorials for *The Horticulturist* was published in 1853 in his honor. In an essay titled "On the Improvement of Country Villages" that appeared originally in 1849, Downing exhorted village residents to plant trees, for "once planted, there is some assurance that, with the aid of time and nature, we can at least cast a graceful veil over the deformity of a country home." Downing thought a village without trees was like a community without a schoolmaster. He counted on two principles of American character traits to disseminate the gospel of tree-planting: "the principle of imitation, which will never allow a Yankee to be outdone by his neighbors; and the principle of progress, which will not allow him to stand still when he discovers his neighbor has really made an improvement" (Downing [1853] 1974, 230).

Downing's message lived on through the work of his disciple, Rev. Nathaniel Hillyer Egleston. Egleston published a collection of essays in 1878 dedicated to Downing's memory titled *Villages and Village Life: Hints for Their Improvement*. Egleston was impatient with Downing's reliance on individual imitation, though, and proposed that collective action was the key to success. He urged readers to talk with neighbors, hold meetings, and "organize themselves into a visible and formal society or association." Egleston cared less about the name of the group or its first project than that the group should make a start and establish an identity; he thought Stockbridge's Laurel Hill Association had originated in the effort to preserve a wooded hill in the middle of town that was heavily covered with wild mountain laurel (Egleston 1878, 52–61).

Regardless of its origins, the Laurel Hill Association's reputation spread quickly through New England and the Middle Atlantic states. Egleston was so impressed with the Laurel Hill Association that he reprinted its bylaws for the benefit of other organizations. He considered Laurel Hill a model for women's participation in public affairs because "the sexes should combine in the work of improving their common home" (Egleston 1878, 59). The idea that women were particularly well suited to keeping cities clean gained momentum during the 1870s. In an 1877 article

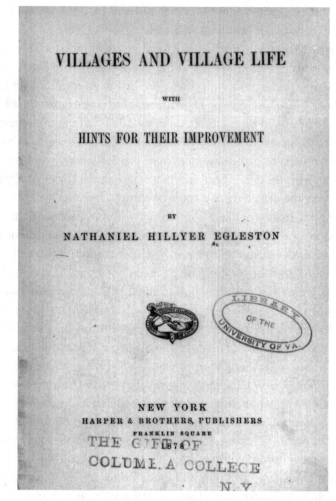

Figure 2.11. Title page of *Villages and Village Life, with Hints for Their Improvement,* by Nathaniel Hillyer Egleston (New York: Harper and Brothers, 1878).

in *Scribner's Monthly,* noted sanitary engineer George Waring expressed the opinion that "the organization and control of the village society is especially woman's work. It requires the sort of systematized attention to detail, especially in the constantly recurring duty of 'cleaning up,' that grows more naturally out of the habit of good housekeeping than out of any occupation to which men are accustomed" (Waring 1877, 16).

Professional and popular periodicals took up the village improvement cause. An 1889 article in the journal *Garden and Forest* noted that the main goal of village improvement societies was to "improve the sanitary condition of towns and their general appearance, and in this way to improve the well-being of the inhabitants, and then to elevate their intelligence, stimulate their love of Nature and develop their artistic feelings." Securing an abundant supply of pure water and a good sewage-removal system were the first steps in this campaign. Officers of the society should accomplish these goals by first raising a "good round sum of money, for education and reform cost money," then follow up with "an educational crusade against popular ignorance and indifference to everything connected with public health, convenience, and taste" ("The Improvement of Villages" 1889, 145).

Nearly a decade later Mary Caroline Robbins wrote an article for the *Atlantic Monthly* in which she applauded that "admirable body of executive women" conducting village improvement work in their communities. Robbins believed there was something about village improvement that made it compatible with the feminine temperament, "even as the intimate connection between a woman and a broom-handle is an obvious and natural fact" (Robbins 1897).

In 1900 the publisher of *Home and Flowers* magazine sponsored a conference of village improvement societies, out of which grew the National League of Improvement Associations. Miss Jesse M. Good, "an energetic spinster" who wrote for *Home and Flowers*, served as the league's national organizer. In 1901 the second president, Charles Zueblin, a University of Chicago sociologist who frequently visited Hull House, allied the organization with the national Progressive movement and renamed it the American League for Civic Improvement. By 1902 the league had created fourteen advisory councils of nationally known experts to direct its campaign in municipal arts, social settlements, sanitation, and recreation (Peterson 1976, 421–23).

Village improvement campaigns proliferated after 1902. Local groups typically "pursued piecemeal programs . . . often stressing small, feasible goals" (Peterson 1976, 416). For example, the Village Improvement Society of Idaho Falls, Idaho, eventually transformed the city from a "treeless, grassless desert village . . . to an oasis." The women of the society, known as City Mothers, encouraged lawns and flowers: they granted annual prizes for the best landscaping, bought land for a park, founded a library, supplied alleys with garbage boxes, and bought "the site of a nest of vile resorts and caused the removal of tenants." The Woman's Town Improvement Association of Westport, Connecticut, laid an impressive two thousand feet of sidewalk; a women's club in Arkansas "filled mud holes in three streets and planted trees along the sides"; and the Woman's Improvement Club of Roseville, California, planted date palms and thousands of lilies, roses, and magnolia trees to beautify the entrance to the train station (Beard 1915, 313–14).

The American City ran a monthly column titled "Town and Village" that listed the accomplishments of various civic improvement societies around the country. The 1909 volume recognized the women of Bamberg, South Carolina, for placing a magazine rack in the railway station, beautifying the courthouse square, and cleaning up the cemetery. The Woman's Club of Tallahassee, Florida, was commended for work on their cemetery, while ladies of Kingwood, West Virginia, were congratulated for cleaning up cesspools. Women in Enosburg Falls, Vermont, started a village improvement association that raised $12,000 by serving meals at the county fair, hosting bazaars, and sponsoring ladies' minstrel shows (Hartman 1909).

Despite their numerous successes, women's improvement societies were sometimes viewed with skepticism. Mrs. Harmon, vice president of the Civic League of Yankton, South Dakota, reported the following difficulties:

> At first our existence was looked upon with much disfavor by the city officials, being regarded as a standing criticism of their administration. Our speedy demise was predicted. Now, after a year of existence and a campaign of education, the Civic League is referred to as an arbiter of difficulties and a court of complaint.
> We have largely succeeded in shutting up chickens. Alleys may no longer be used as dumping grounds. We have become the sponsors for the development of a new park to be donated to the city. We have interested the Commissioners in employing a landscape architect to make a permanent city plan. Further, we are in the field to stay. (Beard 1915, 315)

Charles Mulford Robinson learned a great deal from village improvement societies. He undoubtedly gained an appreciation for smaller-scale projects through his visits to women's clubs around the nation. He knew, for example, that the Woman's Clubs of Brooklyn and Chicago were working to beautify parks, that women in Boston were behind the Charlesbank playground, and that the United Women of Maryland had created a Children's Playground Association in Baltimore. He also cited the Laurel Hill Association for its successful tree-planting campaign, in which they planted more than four hundred trees in their first year "by offering prizes for their planting by others and rewards for evidence leading to the conviction of those who injured the trees" (Robinson [1901] 1913, chapter 10, 124). Robinson also was commissioned by two women's clubs in Colorado Springs to submit a comprehensive plan for city improvement. After his presentation, his plan was approved by the women, "but the City Fathers did not manifest the same concern," forcing the women to lobby (successfully) for a city planning commission (Beard 1915, 314).

Much of Robinson's success as the prophet of the City Beautiful movement was due to his grasp of its small side compared with Daniel Burnham's emphasis on grand plans (Peterson 1976, 421). Robinson somewhat grudgingly acknowledged his debt to women's clubs in regard to modest projects for playgrounds and parks. The following excerpt from the 1913 edition of *The Improvement of Towns and Cities* is one of the few places in which he talks about the role of women:

> It is well that [the women's clubs'] appreciation of the desirability of beauty as an element in civic development should reach small matters as well as large. Grand schemes for vast public improvements with parks, drives, and boulevards naturally stir enthusiasm and allure to effort; but these smaller plans for making a city attractive are also discussed and promoted. With the beginning of 1900, for instance, the Woman's Club of Brooklyn, the largest organization of its kind in the boroughs, resolved to begin its effort to beautify the city by trying to secure a lovelier treatment of the small parks and squares which had hitherto been sadly neglected. And almost simultaneously the Woman's Club of Chicago, which occupies a like distinguished local position, voted to spend from its own funds $1000 for the improvement of one such little area. The two examples are no more than types of a deal of feminine endeavor to be found in many cities. (Robinson [1901] 1913, 176)

Robinson was engaged in professionalizing the design and planning activities performed by volunteer societies with his publication in 1901 of *The Improvement of Towns and Cities; or, the Practical Basis of Civic Aesthetics*. With the publication of *Modern Civic Art* in 1903, the trend toward reliance on experts was well under way (Wilson 1989, 42–45). As the City Beautiful movement, and then urban planning, became the domain of authorities, women's influence on the shape of cities took backstage to the great names of the architectural and planning professions. Because women had no formal higher education and only volunteer experience, they lacked the qualifications for membership when the American Civic Association was formed in 1904, the National Conference on City Planning was organized in 1909, and when the American City Planning Institute was founded in 1917 (Birch 1994, 479).[7]

Charles Mulford Robinson believed that "[w]e shall not be able to attain to cities and villages that are beautiful until we learn artistically to plan them. . . . [A] mended article is never as good as one well made at first. The problem in our cities is mainly, to be sure, one of mending, but even yet it is not wholly so" (Robinson [1901] 1913, 18). While Daniel Burnham was busy trying to create cities from whole new cloth, women volunteers were strengthening the existing urban fabric by focusing not on commerce and large public spaces, but on daily life and the neighborhood. The salvation of cities, they believed, depended on more than the restructuring of space and the construction of monumental buildings. Women volunteers understood that people were as important as the places they occupied. In order to save the industrial city and its vast array of newcomers, women depended on both sacred and secular paths.

I
Paths to Salvation

CHAPTER THREE

Sacred and Secular Organizational Ideologies

> One of the first lessons we learned at Hull House was that private beneficence is totally inadequate to deal with the vast number of the city's disinherited.
>
> — Jane Addams ([1910] 1960, 219)

Settlement workers like Jane Addams of Chicago's Hull House were not the first women to discover urban poverty, but they were among the first to identify it as a systemic problem rather than a personal failing. Benevolent societies of the eighteenth century and charity organizations of the nineteenth century assumed poverty was a *private trouble* that individuals could control, but the Social Gospel defined poverty as a *public issue* warranting institutional reform (see Mills [1959] 1967). Thus the Social Gospel strongly justified women's work outside the home.

The Social Gospel movement applied Christian principles to the problems of daily life. It linked individual salvation to the salvation of society by focusing on such issues as workers' rights, race relations, immigration, and housing conditions. Advocates of the Social Gospel believed poverty had structural roots. Not surprisingly, many leaders of the Social Gospel shared a critique of capitalist society with those on the political left. This association, and the intense civic boosterism among city leaders, explained why Hull House and other settlements were often at odds with municipal officials. Religion and reform went hand in hand to shape many cities at the turn of the century (Hopkins 1967; Luker 1991; Turner 1997).

In addition to religion, women invoked domestic ideology to justify their participation in city affairs. The idea that women's service to the state was best rendered through obligations associated with motherhood dates back to the early Republic (Kerber 1980). The late-nineteenth-century version of this message was called "municipal housekeeping," a rhetorical strategy used to justify women's entry into a range of public activities. By encouraging women to take responsibility for air quality, purity of food, and clean streets and sidewalks, municipal housekeeping allowed women to define the city as an expansion of private space they could understand and influence: as a home, clean and beautiful (Moore 1909). Municipal housekeepers also tried to clean up corrupt local governments through moral persuasion while fighting for the right to vote. Women argued that their experience as household managers qualified them to reform city government. A final advantage of domestic imagery was that it allowed women legitimate contact with strangers, whom they could socialize in the same ways they would influence their own children.

Neither the Social Gospel nor municipal housekeeping threatened women's traditional sphere. Rather, they expanded the definition of that sphere. Both ideologies were reflected in feminist journalist Rheta Childe Dorr's hope that "[t]he city will be like a great, well-ordered, comfortable, sanitary household. Everything will be as clean as in a good home. Every one, as in a family, will have enough to eat, clothes to wear, and a good bed to sleep on. There will be no slums, no sweat shops, no sad women and children toiling in tenement rooms" (Dorr [1910] 1971, 328). According to historian Marlene Stein Wortman, "In an intensely political society, the home and church stood out as apolitical forces. And as these two institutions were isolated from worldly affairs, each came to rely on the other to promote its causes" (1977, 541). Municipal housekeeping and the Social Gospel were cornerstones of the City Social movement that joined the City Beautiful and the City Practical among movements predating the origins of contemporary urban planning (Wirka 1996).

The Social Gospel and municipal housekeeping together fueled the voluntary associations that created redemptive places in cities at the turn of the last century. Two social movements loosely associated with municipal housekeeping are of particular importance. The public bath movement, from approximately 1840 to 1920, was part of a larger demand for public health reform. Jacob Riis noted that the cities' "great un-washed" were not so by choice, challenging municipal housekeepers to keep new immigrants as neat and orderly as cities (Williams 1991). Reformers also recognized the need for recreation. Between 1885 and 1917 the "play movement" contributed more than five hundred sand gardens, model playgrounds, and small parks to urban landscapes (Cranz 1982; Rainwater 1922). Public baths and playgrounds were intended to create better citizens of immigrants and their children, giving redemptive places a central position in the industrial city.

Women's contributions to the construction of urban culture are more apparent when the Social Gospel and municipal housekeeping are situated within the same time frame as the City Beautiful movement. It puts women on the scene, so to speak, as American cities took shape. Women volunteers became a symbol by which public health and morals were connected. They believed that better public health led to higher moral standards, which in turn facilitated efficient governance and a respectable community. Assimilating newcomers to the city was less an attempt to restore urban order, since cities were ill-defined right after the Civil War, than to help create a new urban culture (Schultz 1989).

The Social Gospel

The Social Gospel practiced in America at the end of the nineteenth century had origins in the Second Great Awakening. During the 1820s and 1830s Protestants of all denominations were swept up in evangelical campaigns to eliminate intemperance, slavery, prostitution, profanity, and Sabbath-breaking. Passions in upstate New York were so heated that the region became known as the "Burned-Over District." The zealous revivalists Charles Finney, James Caughey, and Phoebe Palmer earned reputations in the Burned-Over District that took them on lecture tours to England, where their sermons subsequently convinced William and Catherine Booth to form The Salvation Army. Finney also influenced the young Dwight Moody, who grew up to become a great urban evangelist. Moody lived in Chicago at the end of the century and used the World's Columbian Exposition as his own personal theater to merge popular culture and revival Protestantism (Degler 1980; Gilbert 1991; Murdoch 1994, 22–23; Ryan 1981).[1]

The Social Gospel also had roots in mid-nineteenth-century charitable and benevolent societies. The "business of benevolence," as historian Lori Ginzberg (1990) called it, became bureaucratized after the Civil War with the formation of the Charity Organization movement. The movement's association, the Charity Organization Society (COS), operated with three assumptions: first, that urban poverty was caused by moral deficiencies and character flaws among the poor; second, that eliminating slums depended on the poor recognizing and correcting these deficiencies; and third, that preventing slums would require coordination among urban charity associations (Boyer 1978, 144).

One of the movement's best-known national leaders was Josephine Shaw Lowell. Lowell gained prominence for her lifelong work in the New York City Charity Organization and for her book, *Public Relief and Private Charity* (1884). Lowell believed that moral oversight of the poor was more important than alleviating physical hardship and that society should "refuse to support any except those whom it can control" (Boyer 1978, 147, 148). One form of control was exerted by "friendly visitors" — usually middle-class female volunteers — who collected information about slum families at the same time they preached Christianity. By the early 1890s more than four thousand friendly visitors operated in cities across the country. Mary Richmond's *Friendly Visiting among the Poor* (1899) distilled their experiences and became the manual for the next generation of women volunteers (Boyer 1978, 149–59; Gittell and Shtob 1980).

Not all charitable associations adopted this approach. The Salvation Army preferred to work independently because its refusal to distinguish between deserving and undeserving poor set it apart from contemporary attitudes toward poverty. Indeed, it was their reputation for "promiscuous alms-giving" that excluded The Salvation Army from the COS during the 1890s (McKinley 1995, 73). Although The Salvation Army operated a vast network of shelters at the turn of the century, their volunteers had little contact with the YWCA, the NACW, or settlement houses. Their aloofness was deliberate, for they believed that other organizations would accomplish nothing for individuals or society unless they emphasized Christian evangelism (McKinley 1996). General Booth was openly skeptical of social reform, telling his son Bramwell that reformers "have no sympathy with The Salvation Army, nor with salvation from worldliness and sin" (Murdoch 1994, 167).

Jane Addams also disagreed with the COS philosophy. Where friendly visitors saw personal moral deficiency, settlement workers saw institutional failure as the causes of poverty. Consequently, a low-level feud characterized relations between charity and settlement workers. Charity workers accused settlement workers of being naive and unduly influenced by radical politics; settlement workers thought charity workers were self-righteous in expecting the poor to change slum conditions they could not control. While charity workers studied families to change their behavior, settlement workers gathered data about neighborhoods so families could change society (see Residents of Hull House [1895] 1970).[2]

Despite ideological disagreements between charity and settlement workers, the settlement house emerged as a site of intersection between them (and later between the Social Gospel and municipal housekeeping). Settlement workers were sympathetic to union organizers like Eugene Debs and often sponsored branches of the Women's Trade Union League. Labor reformer Florence Kelley, who corresponded with Frederick Engels for many years, promoted her political agenda through Hull House (Sklar 1995b). This shift in emphasis from private troubles to public issues was characteristic of the shift from charity to the Social Gospel as the compelling model for urban change.

Cities became the focus of moral criticism in America as the nineteenth century progressed. Social and economic disruptions following the Civil War convinced the clergy to shift emphasis from saving individuals to addressing social problems caused by rapid urbanization (Boyer 1978, 222; Hays 1995, 103; Wiebe 1967, 137). The Reverend Richard Storrs of Brooklyn exhorted his congregation to "preach Him in the cities; for nowhere else is the need of this greater" (Bender 1975, 11). Evangelical Protestant minister Josiah Strong's *The Twentieth Century City* (1898) warned that cities were the source of "crime . . . vice and wretchedness" that would spell the downfall of the nation (Hofstadter 1955, 175). Walter Rauschenbusch became the most prominent representative of the Social Gospel. Influenced by Henry George's *Progress and Poverty* (1879), Rauschenbusch wrote *The Social Principles of Jesus* in 1916 for the YWCA and *A Theology for the Social Gospel* in 1917. Rauschenbusch believed that advocates of the Social Gospel should form a working partnership with "real social and psychological science" (Hopkins 1967, 232).

The Protestant clergy had pragmatic as well as spiritual reasons to promote the Social Gospel. Ministers began to lose their congregations as cities filled with Jewish and Catholic immigrants who displaced previous residents. In Manhattan between 1868 and 1888, for example, the area below Fourteenth Street gained 250,000 people but lost seventeen Protestant churches. Episcopalians, Methodists, Unitarians, Presbyterians, and Congregationalists banded together to conduct studies of the slums on which later reform efforts were based. At least part of their missionary zeal was prompted by the possibility of converting immigrants to Protestantism (Glaab and Brown 1976, 214).

Josiah Strong organized three major conferences to address the church's nonsectarian responsibility for urban problems. Meetings of the Evangelical Alliance of the United States were held in 1887, 1889, and 1893 (the latter in conjunction with the World's Columbian Exposition in Chicago). A spate of now-classic Social Gospel books followed: William Stead's *If Christ Came to Chicago!* (1894); Strong's *The Next Great Awakening* (1902); Shailer Mathews's *The Church and the Changing Order* (1907) and *The Social Gospel* (1910); and Washington Gladden's *Social Salvation* (1902) and *The Church and Modern Life* (1908) (Hopkins 1967, 215).

Ministers disseminated the Social Gospel through churches, schools, and volunteer organizations. In 1908 the American Institute of Social Service published the first issue of *The Gospel of the Kingdom,* edited by Josiah Strong, which was a "course of study on living social problems in the light of the gospel of Jesus Christ." These lessons reached more than forty thousand readers in churches, YMCAs, YWCAs, and colleges and universities (Hopkins 1967, 262). That same year disciples of social Christianity were organized into the Federal Council of the Churches of Christ in America. This formalized the cooperation among religious groups such as the YMCAs and YWCAs, the United Society of Christian Endeavor, the American Bible Society, and the American Tract Society, which had existed since the Evangelical Alliance conferences (Hopkins 1967, 302).

While men preached the Social Gospel from the pulpit, women translated their faith into activities sponsored by volunteer groups outside the church. Women adrift were their particular concern. Girls coming to cities were joining the National Women's Trade Union League, many of them going out on the garment workers' "Strike of the Forty Thousand," and some dying in New York City's notorious Triangle Shirtwaist factory fire. Against this backdrop, the YWCA commissioned Dr. Annie Marion MacLean's investigation into the conditions of women's work (published in 1910 as *Wage-Earning Women*). Their own work, combined with convention speeches by Dr. Walter Rauschenbusch (such as "Jesus, and the Social Problem of Our Age," delivered in 1909), solidified the YWCA's advocacy of the Social Gospel (Wilson 1933, 26–28). YWCA members considered it their Christian duty to protect young working girls as they arrived in the city, and proselytizing was part of that process. The first constitution of the New York Ladies' Christian Association stipulated that "the spread of Evangelical Religion can be best accomplished by associated effort" and that members should help "young women of the operative class" obtain employment and "suitable boarding places" (Wilson [1916] 1987, 23).

Some university students, especially women, became interested in settlement work as a way to apply the Social Gospel. At the turn of the century it was often difficult to distinguish a settlement house from an urban mission sponsored by a church. The settlement house tried to save each city neighborhood and to create, in Rauschenbusch's words, "a Christian social order which will serve as the spiritual environment of the individual." When a visitor to Vida Scudder's College Settlement in New York asked about religious work, the settlement worker replied, "We think all our work is religious" (Crocker 1992, 114).

Members of religious missions were more discerning. They believed settlements were not religious enough. In 1903 the *Nashville Christian Advocate* of the Methodist Episcopal Church, South, criticized college students who thought secular work was more important than church work:

> It is an excellent thing to have free baths and reading rooms and gymnasiums. Agencies for the placing of the unemployed often serve a most useful purpose. But it is a truth which this generation is coming to see more clearly every day, that the only way to save a man's body is to save his soul. Let us, therefore, openly accept also the corollary that the best way to save his soul is by the time-honored and spirit-honored agency of the Church of God. (Lasch-Quinn 1993, 54)

The *Handbook of Settlements* elaborated the distinction between settlements and institutional churches or missions when it was published in 1911. Its guidelines, endorsed by the National Federation of Settlements, advised that "[t]he typical settlement, under American conditions, is one which provides neutral territory traversing all the lines of racial and re-

ligious cleavage." Settlements preferred to be identified with social action associated with the state and municipality rather than with a religious affiliation. Many overtly religious black settlements were omitted
from the *Handbook* because of this decision (Crocker 1992; Lasch-Quinn
1993; Woods and Kennedy [1911] 1970, v, vi).[3]

Eventually settlement houses tried to distance themselves from religious affiliation, just as they had tried to differentiate themselves initially from the Charity Organization movement. Jane Addams founded
Hull House on the principles of the Social Gospel because she thought
"a simple acceptance of Christ's message and methods is what a settlement should stand for" (Davis 1973, 73, 74). By the 1920s, however, she
had discontinued even its interdenominational services because she believed that residents of Hull House came together "on the basis of the
deed and our common aim" rather than on the basis of a shared faith
(Crocker 1992, 114). Strict adherence to Protestant theology also would
have jeopardized Hull House efforts to reach immigrant Jews and
Catholics.

World War I signaled the end of the major settlement era. Public interest was diverted to international politics, funding once provided by
personal benefactors was replaced by the Community Chest, and young
workers who would live in poor neighborhoods became harder to recruit. Not coincidentally, women won the vote and became less involved
in volunteer activities. Settlements thus provided a historical bridge between two generations of women: those with evangelical voluntary outlets and those with public political options. Settlement workers were
"in, but not of, the Social Gospel movement, . . . a political boat on a
religious stream, advancing political solutions to social problems that
were fundamentally ethical or moral" (Sklar 1985, 663).

Several women symbolized the transitional nature of settlement houses
in their personal careers. Mary Kingsbury Simkhovitch, for example,
worked at the CSA's Rivington Street Settlement in New York City before she founded Greenwich House with Jacob Riis in 1902. Her experiences in poor neighborhoods made her a lifelong advocate of housing
reform. Before joining the settlement movement, Simkhovitch earned
degrees from Boston University and Radcliffe and studied history and
sociology in Berlin on a scholarship from the Women's Educational and
Industrial Union. She eventually became chair of the Committee on Con-

gestion of Population in New York City. Under the committee's auspices she and Florence Kelley organized the first national planning conference in the United States, the National Conference on City Planning held in Washington, D.C., in 1909. The theme of the conference was "using planning to deal with social problems," and Simkhovitch was the only woman to deliver a presentation (Birch 1994; Wirka 1996).

Florence Kelley, a graduate of Cornell University, was a Hull House resident from 1891 to 1899. She then moved to New York City's Henry Street Settlement, was appointed general secretary of the National Consumers' League, and remained active in settlement work for the next twenty-seven years. Kelley is best known for influencing legislation that instituted the eight-hour workday and prohibited child labor in factories (Sklar 1995b; Wirka 1996).

Other women with settlement ties established professional careers in nontraditional occupations. Sophonisba Breckinridge, who was forbidden by her father to become a settlement worker, received a scholarship from the CSA that she put to good use. Breckinridge founded the School of Social Service Administration at the University of Chicago. As a professor of public welfare administration, she published *Women in the Twentieth Century: A Study of Their Political, Social, and Economic Activities* (1933). Bookbinder Mary Kenney O'Sullivan, an organizer for the American Federation of Labor and founder of the National Women's Trade Union League, worked closely with members of Hull House and Boston's Denison House throughout her life. A University of Chicago graduate student, Frances Kellor, received a CSA fellowship in 1902, and in 1904 she published her report on "Employment Bureaus for Women." As a result of that study Kellor organized New York's Inter-Municipal Committee on Household Research. By 1912 Kellor was directing Teddy Roosevelt's Bull Moose campaign for the Progressive Party (Fitzpatrick 1990, 80; Woods and Kennedy [1911] 1970, 3).

Simkhovitch, Kellor, Kelley, Breckinridge, and O'Sullivan all worked at the borders of theory and practice as the disciplines of sociology and urban planning began to take shape. Their dedication to action, however, penalized them in the academic world. Partly by choice and partly due to discrimination, few of the settlement workers' accomplishments were incorporated into the classroom. Nevertheless, they represented the first generation of women to move through the quasi-private settlement movement and emerge fully into the public sphere (Bender 1996; Deegan 1988; Nutter 1997; Sibley 1995).

Municipal Housekeeping

The major vehicle by which the principles of municipal housekeeping were transmitted from one town to another was the General Federation of Women's Clubs (GFWC). In 1906 Mary I. Wood, public information director for the GFWC, observed that GFWC members "began to realize that the one calling in which they were, as a body, proficient, that of housekeeping and homemaking, had its outdoor as well as its indoor application.... It was the extension of the homemaking instinct . . . that led them into the paths of civic usefulness" (Scott 1991, 146).

Mrs. Frank Pattison, president of the New Jersey Federation of Women's Clubs, used her position to promote municipal housekeeping. In "The Relation of the Woman's Club to the American City" (1909), she stated:

> [W]e find the Woman's Club is in many cities providing its place as an aid in municipal housekeeping, standing for the City Cleanly, as is shown in its demand for clean streets, rubbish cans, and orderly backyards; the City Sanitary, through its work for the cure of tuberculosis, pure milk, district nurses, baths, and public health generally; the City Beautiful, in numberless efforts, from the growing of vines and flowers to the work of having established municipal art committees whose duty it may be to plan a city, and the standard of art therein. In fact there is not a town of any size to which the Woman's Club is not in some of these ways related. (130)

Rheta Childe Dorr dedicated her book, *What Eight Million Women Want* (1910), to the "American representatives of the eight million — the eight hundred thousand members of the General Federation of Women's Clubs." Dorr believed women wanted more involvement in civic affairs, stating, "Woman's place is Home. Her task is homemaking. But Home is not contained within the four walls of an individual home. Home is the community. The city full of people is the Family" (Dorr [1910] 1971, 327).

Mrs. T. J. Bowlker, president of the Women's Municipal League of Boston, expressed similar sentiments in 1912 when she reported that "our work is founded on the belief that woman has a special function in developing the welfare of humanity which man cannot perform. This function consists in her power to make, of any place in which she may happen to live, a *home* for all those who come there. Women must now learn to make of their cities great community homes for all the people." Educating women to these goals began early. The Ice Cream and Butter Committee of Boston's Women's Municipal League owned a play shop that it loaned to kindergartens and settlement houses to teach children "the necessity of cleanly conditions in the buying and selling of food" (Bowlker 1912, 863, 864).

Boston was the home of another women's voluntary association that espoused a municipal housekeeping agenda. The Women's Educational and Industrial Union (WEIU) was founded in 1877 by Dr. Harriet Clisby with forty-one other women. The union had four hundred members within one year and forty-five hundred members by 1915. Among its contributions to the urban landscape were a health clinic, lunchrooms for women, and salesrooms where the "genteel poor" among housewives could sell handicrafts and baked goods on commission (Deutsch 1992; Sander 1998; Spencer-Wood 1987). The WEIU developed branches in twenty American cities and in two European cities (Geneva and Paris). The second WEIU opened in Buffalo, N.Y., where a downtown "Noon Rest" provided safe and inexpensive lunches for women, an Exchange and Bake Shop sold women's homemade goods, and the Mary C. Ripley Memorial Library circulated more than five hundred books and periodicals. Harriet Austin Townsend was president of the Buffalo WEIU from its founding in 1884 to its demise in 1916. The union donated its home at North 86 Delaware Avenue to the University of Buffalo in 1915 with the stipulation that the university establish a department of liberal arts and sciences named "Harriet A. Townsend Hall" (Blair 1980, 91, 140; "Women Approve Plan" 1915).[4]

The YWCA was similar to the WEIU in its secular mission. The YWCA promoted a municipal housekeeping agenda in addition to its evangelical efforts in nearly every large city in the country. The Dayton, Ohio, YWCA issued a statement in 1876 claiming that "[o]ur field is our entire city and the public institutions in its vicinity," and proceeded to offer members help with lodging, employment, libraries, recreation, and various free classes. The Pittsburgh YWCA had similarly wide-ranging influence throughout the city. By 1880 they had opened a Temporary Home for Destitute Women, a Home for Aged Women, Sheltering Arms (for unmarried mothers), the Hospital for Incurables, an industrial school, and the Ladies' Depository and Exchange for Women's Work (Sims 1936, 12, 13).[5]

In 1884 the Ladies' Health Protective Association of New York City complained to the mayor about dirty streets, recommending that annual appropriations for street cleaning be increased, street sweeping be done at night, that householders be required to own trashcans, that the city burn the garbage, and that garbage collectors be paid by the piece rather than by the day. They also suggested that women be appointed as sanitary inspectors, since "keeping things clean, like the training of children and the care of the sick, has ever been one of the instinctive and recognized functions of women" (Hoy 1980, 176).

The Chicago Woman's Club helped create Chicago's reputation as a leader in municipal housekeeping. The Woman's Club supported the founding of Hull House in 1889, through which it was connected to the local WCTU, YWCA, the Women's Trade Union League, the Association of Collegiate Alumnae, the elite Fortnightly club, and the radical Illinois Women's Alliance. More than four hundred clubmembers were involved with the Columbian Exposition of 1893, coordinating and staffing exhibits at the Woman's Building. The club created kindergartens, low-cost housing projects, and public baths as part of its municipal housekeeping mission (Scott 1991, 142, 143).

One of the most famous professional municipal housekeepers at this time was Caroline Bartlett Crane of Kalamazoo, Michigan, hired as a consultant by over sixty cities to survey their sanitary conditions. Crane was influenced by the Social Gospel and settlement movements of her youth and by summer courses in sociology at the University of Chicago. She began her career as the pastor of Kalamazoo's First Unitarian Church, which she convinced the congregation to rename "The People's Church." During the 1890s the church opened a kindergarten, manual training and mechanical drawing classes for boys, a Frederick Douglass Club for African Americans, and a lunchroom for working women. Crane encouraged the city to absorb the budget for the church's services and by 1899 the kindergarten had been incorporated into the public school system (Hoy 1980, 182).

Crane pursued studies in household science in 1902 while conducting a survey of sanitary practices in Kalamazoo's slaughterhouses. She formed the Women's Civic Improvement League of Kalamazoo in 1904

with the purpose of promoting "higher ideals of civic life and beauty...
out-door art, public sanitation, and the general welfare of the city." Their
first street-cleaning project was so successful that it garnered national
attention (Hoy 1980). In response to this demand, Crane published an
article titled "Some Factors of the Street Cleaning Problem" in a 1912
edition of *The American City*. Among her observations were that cities
typically paved streets too widely, often with materials insufficient for
the traffic load, and graded them incorrectly for proper drainage. She
ended the article with the admonition that "a clean city is not something which is to be accomplished by the sole and unsupported effort
of the street cleaning department," but by collaboration between the city
and its residents (Crane 1912).

Crane thought women bore a special responsibility for clean cities. She
advised women to "keep our city — that is to say, our common house —
clean. The floor should be clean. The air should be clean. The individual houses and premises, the schools, the places of public assembly, the
places of trade, the factories, the places where foods are prepared, sold,
served, should be clean" (Hoy 1980, 183).

Successful municipal housekeeping required constant vigilance, and
advocates had to choose their battles carefully. Imogen Oakley reported
that the Woman's Club of Green Cove Springs, Florida, had placed nicely
decorated refuse cans on street corners and they were used so consistently that the town became known as the "Parlor City of the South"

> until one sad day, when the town fathers decided that it was only right
> and proper that the owners of cows should be allowed the privilege of
> pasturing them in the streets. The protests of the Woman's Club were of
> no avail against the influence of the cow owners, so its members gave up
> the street question and devoted themselves to founding and equipping a
> town library. (Oakley 1912, 808)

In the opinion of many advocates of municipal housekeeping, men had
"done nobly in some particular lines," but were "not natural-born housekeepers. It is in the field of municipal housekeeping that they are looking to the new citizen, woman, for assistance" (Van Buren 1915, 105).

The fact that the new citizen could not yet vote rankled many municipal housekeepers. Oakley, chair of the Civil Service Reform Committee of the GFWC, thought women should take charge of municipal
housekeeping because "owing to partisan politics, the authorities are
prone to spend so much time wrangling over the spoils of office that

they have little left over for civic improvement" (Oakley 1912). Zona Gale, chair of the Civic Department of the GFWC, agreed with Oakley. Gale recounted the cases of the Juvenile Court, ambulance service, and playgrounds created by the Chicago Woman's Club which were then turned over to the city to own and operate. She lamented that "as soon as the women gave over control and maintenance [of the Juvenile Court] to the City Council, it became immediately one more prize in the spoils politics of its city.... [T]he women who inaugurated it and sacrificed themselves for the work were helpless to touch it, for it had become a part of the city machinery in which they had no part." Gale's conclusion was that there was "only one direct means of cooperation between women's clubs and city officials — the franchise for women" (Gale 1914).

In addition to the vote, advocates of municipal housekeeping endorsed public baths. Baths, after all, were the most effective direct attacks against dirt. "We shall never have a beautiful city till we have a clean city, and the city will never be clean when masses of its inhabitants are dirty" were the words of a 1902 *Brooklyn Daily Eagle* editorial following a public meeting on municipal baths sponsored by the Women's Municipal League (Williams 1991, 58).

The Public Bath Movement

In the current era of almost universal indoor plumbing, it is hard to imagine the filthy condition of nineteenth-century tenements. Survey after survey found grossly inadequate plumbing and bathing facilities in cities, most estimating that fewer than one-fifth of tenement families had access to a private bath (Gerhard 1908; Williams 1991, 28; Zueblin 1902, 288–96). Organizations like the Baltimore Bath Commission considered public baths neither "a luxury nor charity, but a public necessity and obligation" (Williams 1991, 28).

Bath reformers were driven by several concerns: public health, assimilation of immigrants, and civic boosterism. To Progressives public baths could provide immigrants with the moral uplift they needed to become better citizens; at the same time, they could demonstrate the city's good-faith efforts to curb disease and provide a healthy environment for people and commerce (Williams 1991, chapter 2).

Millions patronized public baths. Between 1910 and 1915, the cities of Baltimore, Boston, Chicago, and New York reported a combined average of over 10 million bathers per year (Williams 1991, 66, 81, 94, 123). Standard works like William Gerhard's *Modern Baths and Bath Houses* (1908) were written to guide municipalities in the construction of "cheap spray or rain baths for the masses of working people, who lack bathing facilities in the tenement" in order to reduce the morbidity and mortality rates in cities and to "improve the air of classrooms" in public schools. It instructed reformers about how to place baths and facilities in hospitals, factories, and schools, and included data on water supplies and construction costs (ix, 6, 7). The *Journal of the American Association for Promoting Hygiene and Public Baths* was still publishing similar instructional articles well into the 1920s (Phillips 1926).

Large cities were leaders in the public bath movement, but smaller cities also gained recognition for their efforts. One of the most complete bathing and gymnasium facilities, for example, was in Milwaukee. The first year-round free public bath to provide a swimming pool and showers was the West Side Natatorium erected in Milwaukee in 1889. In 1900 the natatorium furnished 215,000 baths at a cost to the city of $4,755. The city of Brookline, Massachusetts, provided baths for 50,000 people for a small fee (Mero 1909; Zueblin 1902, 292).

Sarah Dickson Lowrie, an upper-class white woman who conducted sewing courses in a mission building, was the organizing force behind providing facilities in Philadelphia. The Public Baths Association of Philadelphia was formed in 1895, and in 1898 the Gaskill Street Bath was opened. It was a two-and-one-half-story structure with twenty-six showers and one tub for men and fourteen showers and three tubs for women. A laundry was located in the basement and the superintendent's living quarters were on the second floor. The bath was built on a 40- by 60-foot lot in a colonial-style building of red brick. A five-cent fee was charged for a shower, ten cents for a tub bath (both included towel and soap), but children under ten with their parents were admitted free; the laundry cost five cents per hour (Williams 1991, 98–108). The fact that Philadelphia provided more facilities for men than women and children suggests that a clean labor force was more important than clean families.

Public baths constructed by women's efforts in Boston, Chicago, and Philadelphia were small and economical. They were established to promote habits of personal cleanliness by providing facilities so people could "observe the fundamental rules of health and sanitation" (Williams 1991, 83). In New York City, however, where women were less involved, baths were built on a much grander scale. In 1889 *Cosmopolitan* sponsored a competition for the design of public baths that retained Cornelius Vanderbilt, among others, as a judge. First prize went to John Galen Howard's "extraordinarily elaborate" plan invoking a Roman bath. Critics observed that it was too monumental, and that instead "what poor people need...is a little place, well-lighted and warm...they do not need tepidariums...or porticos; and the less magnificence is put into the new buildings, the more comfortable they will be for the people who use them, and the more profitable for those who own them" (Stern, Gilmartin, and Massengale 1983, 138).

The Salvation Army depended on just such modest public baths. The Workingmen's Metropole in Philadelphia, for example, had no bathing facilities. The hotel's 110 residents used the public bathhouse, whose owner gave the Metropole free tickets to distribute to "worthy bathers" (McKinley 1986, 57). The closest public bath was probably the second one built in Philadelphia by the Public Baths Association at 718 Wood Street. It was near the Metropole's Eighth and Vine location in the Northern Liberties neighborhood (now Olde City) of Russian Jews and Irish immigrants. The Wood Street Bath had twenty-four showers for men and six for women, in addition to a public laundry (Williams 1991, 106).

Municipal governments eventually took over the provision of baths from charitable associations. By 1904 eight of the ten largest cities in the country had public baths; by 1922 more than forty cities operated year-round municipal baths. Bath reformers believed, however, that an unpaid commission appointed by the municipal government was the best system by which to administer public baths. This decision perpetuated the structure of volunteer labor under which the movement began. Women volunteers in Newark, N.J., for example, continued to monitor the municipal bath system to insure its cleanliness even after the city had taken over fiscal responsibility (Beard 1915, 82; Williams 1991, 39).

Open space was as important to everyday life as public baths, since both served as "an insurance policy of good citizenship" (Mero 1909, 73). While public baths instilled principles of cleanliness, playgrounds taught children rules that would form their adult character. The slogan of the Massachusetts playground movement was "the boy without a playground is the father of the man without a job" (Dorr [1910] 1971,

36). Like public baths, playgrounds were operated initially by women volunteers.

The Playground Movement

Precursors to playgrounds were first established in Boston in the 1880s by Dr. Marie Zakrsewska, who lobbied the Massachusetts Emergency and Hygiene Association (MEHA) to create "sand gardens" for slum children to protect them from unsupervised play. Playgrounds followed sand gardens as places that removed immigrant children from dangerous public streets. The MEHA reported that supervision of its three mission-yard playgrounds in 1886 was voluntarily performed by mothers in the neighborhood. Public subsidies began soon thereafter. The city of Boston employed matrons for ten sand gardens in the city's poorest districts by 1887, and by 1889 the city had twenty-one sand piles (Cavallo 1981; Cranz 1982; Rainwater 1922; Spencer-Wood 1994).

The Civic Club of Philadelphia started the first public playground in that city and maintained it until municipal authorities recognized its importance. By 1912 the city maintained eighty school playgrounds and ten large public playgrounds. The Civic Club also started the first school gardens project. By 1911 the city had taken over eight large school gardens, nineteen "gardens for kindergarten scholars," and numerous window-box home gardens, for a total of five thousand separate gardens (Oakley 1912, 811).

When Lillian Wald and Mary Brewster founded New York City's Henry Street Settlement in 1895, they converted the backyard, an adjacent schoolyard, and the yard of a third house into a "miniature but very complete playground." They were such pioneers in the effort that their facility was called the "Bunker Hill" of playgrounds by the National Playground Association. The playground contained a big sandpile, swings, gymnastic equipment, and "baby hammocks"; the only greenery consisted of a border of flowers, a wisteria-covered trellis, and two ailanthus trees (Wald 1915, 82). Lillian Wald was one of several women who eventually formed the Playground Association of America in 1906 with Luther Gulick and settlement workers Jane Addams, Mary McDowell, and Graham Taylor (Cavallo 1981, 23, 36).

The playground movement coexisted somewhat uneasily with the City Beautiful movement (Cranz 1982). Recreational enthusiasts thought passive park space designed by Olmsted and his disciples was wasted, while

City Beautiful advocates feared that the money spent on playgrounds would be diverted from parks and monuments (Boyer 1978, 244). Chicago tried to reconcile the aesthetic tensions between City Beautiful and playground proponents by having the Chicago Architectural League design playground shelters and fences in a "simple and graceful outline painted in appropriate shades of green and red" (Zueblin 1902, 287).

Charles Mulford Robinson was especially conflicted about the tension between function and appearance. In the original 1901 edition of *The Improvement of Towns and Cities,* he described the dilemma somewhat sympathetically:

> The playground is a bit of land seized from the builder's clutch and set apart for the children, consecrated to their use to help them keep their souls pure though they soil their hands. It may or may not be beautiful.... While they contain possibilities for the adornment of the city, that part of their advantage is secondary.... As a result, some of the most famous playgrounds in the world are bare even of grass, gaining such beauty as they have from the grace of the trees and the happiness of the children. (Robinson [1901] 1913, 179)

By 1909 Robinson seemed to prefer Olmsted's vision of vast open spaces. He wrote:

> the whole playground conception has heretofore been wrong. We have taken as our ideal a bare city lot equipped with paraphernalia for children's exercise. The truer ideal would be an acre or so of natural looking country, which we should create if necessary and where a chance for the city child to know the delights of a real outdoors, of a place where in the night there might be fairies, as there never would be in the ordinary playground. (Cavallo 1981, 26)

"An acre or so of natural looking country" was rarely feasible in cities at the end of the nineteenth century. Whether financed by private philanthropy or public coffers, there was seldom enough money for grandiose plans. The point was also to bring play opportunities to children where they lived, rather than making them travel to some distant place, even in pursuit of fairies (Cranz 1982).

As difficult as it was to convince municipalities to provide playgrounds for immigrant children, it was even harder to get localities to provide for the children of black migrants. Residential segregation was already well entrenched by the turn of the century, so playgrounds that were accessible to immigrant children were often unavailable to black children. Women in voluntary associations provided what the city did not.

The African American Experience

Although most historians have focused on the activities of white ministries in the Northeast and Midwest, the Social Gospel also flourished in black churches in the South. The credo of interdenominationalism was difficult to implement, however, since southern blacks had strong denominational ties and little time or money to contribute to causes outside their own churches. The Social Gospel also may have suffered in the African American community from the reputation of its white leaders. Josiah Strong was suspected of racism, Lyman Abbott of "faithlessness," and Washington Gladden and Walter Rauschenbusch of a "complicity in silence" on racial issues (Lasch-Quinn 1993, 55; Luker 1991, 2).

The two most important voluntary organizations for black women at the time were the National Association of Colored Women (NACW), founded in 1896, and the Woman's Convention (WC) Auxiliary to the National Baptist Convention, formed in 1900. These associations drew inspiration from both the Social Gospel and from municipal housekeeping. The NACW is described in greater detail in the next chapter, but is outlined here because of its important relationship with the WC.

The National Association of Colored Women

The work of the NACW was a "special kind of municipal housekeeping, carried out with limited resources, which meant that the women themselves did a great deal of hands-on labor in their projects" (Scott 1991, 148). The club's motto, "Lifting as we climb," reflected its mission to improve the status of the entire race as its members rose on the socioeconomic ladder. Their goal was "raising to the highest plane the home life, moral standards, and civic life of the race" (Davis [1935] 1981, 5, 14, 86). By 1914 the NACW had fifty thousand members in more than one thousand clubs (Shaw 1991). These women were an educated elite, typically married to professional men, who defined their duties as acknowledging their "weak sisters," having compassion for their "inferiors," and helping "waifs and strays of the alley come in contact with intelligence and virtue" (Hine 1990b, 31). Their outreach efforts often took form in the built environment. The NACW sponsored homes for the aged, for working women, and for unwed mothers. They also built hospitals and clinics, kindergartens, libraries, and settlement houses.

Nannie Helen Burroughs formed a critical link between the NACW and the WC. Although Burroughs was not among the founders of the NACW in 1896, her name began to appear in records of NACW conference proceedings in 1906. She gave antilynching speeches, raised money to save the Frederick Douglass home in the Anacostia neighborhood of Washington, D.C., served as a regional president, and directed pageants at important NACW events (Wesley 1984). Before Burroughs became active in the NACW, however, she formed an organization that vigorously promoted the Social Gospel: the Woman's Convention Auxiliary to the National Baptist Convention.

The Woman's Convention

The Woman's Convention (WC) Auxiliary to the National Baptist Convention emerged in 1900 when Nannie Helen Burroughs delivered a speech titled "How the Sisters Are Hindered from Helping" at the Baptists' annual conference in Richmond, Virginia. Burroughs, only twenty-one at the time, proclaimed that black women had been unequal members in the church for too long and this discrimination had fueled a "righteous discontent" with their status. Burroughs's speech galvanized more than one million black women who were already active in church work at the local and state levels (Higginbotham 1993, 8, 150, 171).

As a leader of the WC, Burroughs also endorsed municipal house-keeping. She reminded women that "[a]s a practical part of our Home Mission work, we urge the women here to give more attention to civic improvement.... Clean out the rubbish; whitewash and put things in order.... This is the only practical way to show that education and Christianity are counting in the development of the race" (Higginbotham 1993, 134, 202).

Burroughs was a strong advocate of community reform, endorsing the creation of a social service committee in her 1912 annual report to the Woman's Convention. The 1913 manifesto of the WC listed the following at the top of "What We Want and What We Must Have": "Well-built, sanitary dwellings ... and streets that are paved and kept just as clean as others in the town are kept" (Higginbotham 1993, 203, 222, 276).

The WC agenda clearly had been influenced by the NACW. Delegates to the 1904 NACW conference resolved that "the women of our association prepare themselves by the study of civil government and kindred subjects for the problems of city, state and national life, that they may be able to perform intelligently the duties that have come to some and will come to others in the natural progress of the woman's suffrage question" (Wesley 1984, 63).

Strong ties bound the National Association of Colored Women and the Woman's Convention. The NACW held its first convention at the Nineteenth Street Baptist Church in Washington, D.C., and several leaders of the WC also held offices in the NACW. Members of the NACW and the WC attended each other's annual meetings to report on their respective activities, while delegates to the WC often invoked the NACW's "Lifting as we climb" motto. The NACW, despite its secular constitution, included departments on church clubs, evangelical work, and religious work along with those on domestic science and temperance. One of the clearest examples of collaborative effort between the two organizations was the National Training School for Women and Girls. The school was technically controlled by the WC, but local branches of the NACW contributed money for its maintenance (Higginbotham 1993, 182, 183).

Burroughs became increasingly active in the NACW as its platform became further oriented toward municipal housekeeping. Part of this shift was reflected in the choice of biennial meeting places. Whereas the first NACW conferences occurred in churches, the third biennial convention met in 1901 at the Buffalo Women's Educational and Industrial Union Building and the eighth biennial convention was held at Ohio's Wilberforce University in 1914—both secular spaces (Wesley 1984, 59, 70).

Blurring the Boundaries

Black women's church and club work were so intertwined during the late nineteenth century that it is difficult to separate their activities into religious and secular categories. This complexity "precludes attempts to bifurcate black women's activities neatly into dichotomous categories such as religious versus secular, private versus public, or accommodation versus resistance" (Higginbotham 1993, 17). This lack of bound-

aries made the NACW and WC more effective than if they had operated completely independently.

Women's church societies had long been a training ground for leadership and organizational skills; they also had been agents of self-help
in the black community, providing schools and social services when cities
did not. Leaders of the NACW acknowledged their debt to the church.
In 1900 Chicago author and founding member of the NACW, Fannie
Barrier Williams, stated that "[t]he training which first enabled colored
women to organize and successfully carry on club work was originally
obtained in church work. These churches have been and still are the great
preparatory schools in which the primary lessons of social order, mutual trustfulness and united effort have been taught." In his commence-
ment address to the Fisk University class of 1898, W. E. B. Du Bois stated
that black churches were "for the most part, curiously composite institutions, which combine the work of churches, theaters, newspapers, homes,
schools, and lodges" (Higginbotham 1993, 17, 173).

The Baptist Woman's Convention and the NACW formed links between local problems and the national Progressive reform movement.
Although the WC continued charity work in rural areas, it turned its
attention more to urban conditions as the distribution of the black population shifted from farms to cities. By 1912 the WC had adopted the
Social Gospel agenda of secular progressivism in regard to labor problems, housing, race, and immigration issues. As the Social Gospel linked
individual salvation with the salvation of society, black women's groups
began to establish settlement houses and training schools (Higginbotham
1993, 172). Baptist and African Methodist Episcopal (A.M.E.) churches
promoted programs similar to institutional white churches and settlement houses to address the needs of the urban poor. Black churches
sponsored schools, health clinics, libraries, and recreation centers for
their urban congregations. In 1901 a Baptist minister established Bethel
Institutional Church in Jacksonville, Florida, which operated a kindergarten, cooking school, and night school; it also created the Afro-
American Life Insurance Company. At about the same time in Washington, D.C., the Shiloh Church and the Nineteenth Street Baptist Church
opened daycare centers and clinics for the poor (Higginbotham 1993, 174).

One of the most famous black Social Gospel efforts was launched in
1900 by an A.M.E. minister in Chicago. Reverend Reverdy Ransom opened
the Institutional Church and Social Settlement at 3825 Dearborn Street,

with an auditorium that could seat twelve hundred people, a dining room, kitchen, and a gymnasium. The settlement sponsored a daycare center, kindergarten, mothers' and children's clubs, print shop, sewing and cooking classes, an employment bureau, and a penny savings bank. Some of the white progressive reformers with whom Reverend Ransom worked included Jane Addams, Mary McDowell of the University of Chicago Settlement, Social Gospel minister Shailer Mathews, and renowned lawyer Clarence Darrow (Luker 1991, 174; Woods and Kennedy [1911] 1970).

Black women relied on the socially acceptable NACW and WC rather than the more radical suffrage movement to press their claims for citizenship. Most black clubwomen, like most white women of the day, supported women's traditional sphere and feared that voting might "unsex" a woman. Black women, though, were in an even more delicate position than white women regarding suffrage. Some black women believed that if they lobbied for suffrage for themselves, they risked diminishing one of the few sources of power black men enjoyed (White 1993). Others were less optimistic. Among NACW members supporting woman's suffrage were Josephine St. Pierre Ruffin, Mary Church Terrell, Hallie Q. Brown, and Nannie Helen Burroughs. Most outspoken of all was Burroughs, who challenged WC members in a 1912 speech to mobilize because "[i]f women cannot vote, they should make it very uncomfortable for the men who have the ballot but do not know its value" (Higginbotham 1993, 203; Hine 1990, 38).

Members of the National Association of Colored Women and the Woman's Convention had a vision of a better urban life for African Americans, one they implemented by minimizing borders between the two organizations. Black women's voluntary work at the liminal edge between the public and private sectors helped shape a more humanitarian city for newcomers. Their story is a reminder that middle-class black women, lifting as they rose, built bridges to the city for succeeding generations of their sisters.

The four prominent voluntary organizations of this era, the YWCA, NACW, Salvation Army, and CSA, firmly staked out their positions within the Social Gospel and municipal housekeeping ideologies. The YWCA evolved from an evangelical to a Social Gospel organization, while The Salvation Army remained firmly rooted in the Social Gospel and became the prototype for the urban institutional church. The College

Settlements Association and the National Association of Colored Women straddled philosophical lines between the Social Gospel and municipal housekeeping. The fact that both movements existed simultaneously is a reflection of the intellectual vitality of the era. It also suggests the confusion surrounding race relations, immigration, and the role of women in public life.

CHAPTER FOUR

Voluntary Associations with an Urban Presence

An abundance of voluntary associations during the nineteenth century led Tocqueville to recognize them as the foundation of American democracy. By constructing the private problems of numerous individuals as public issues, women's voluntary organizations played a pivotal role in determining the shape of public discourse (Bender 1975; Clarke, Staeheli, and Brunell 1995; Ryan 1997). The president of the General Federation of Women's Clubs, for example, boasted that her organization was "in no sense political, yet its influence and power are to be seen in every State legislature" (Decker 1906, 204).

Women were actively engaged in four voluntary associations that transformed the physical fabric of cities between the Civil War and World War I. The first two were founded *by* women primarily *for* women (and sometimes children): The Young Women's Christian Association (YWCA) and the National Association of Colored Women (NACW). Many American and European women started their journeys into the city under the auspices of the YWCA and NACW. Both organizations provided safe places to live while women tested their new independence.

Two other organizations, The Salvation Army and the College Settlements Association (CSA), included both women and men. Men were more visible in The Salvation Army than in the CSA. The CSA's original constitution, stipulating that only women could be members, was amended at their first annual meeting in 1890 to allow membership to "persons," but college-educated women were the majority of members and they remained firmly in control of the organization (Settlements

Figure 4.1. "Comfortable Accommodations." An early YWCA poster depicting an African American woman. (Courtesy Archives of the National Board of the YWCA of the USA.)

File, n.d.). Just as with the larger American settlement movement it represented, the CSA was a predominantly female endeavor.

Members of the CSA tried to produce better neighborhoods for women, men, and children. They saw themselves as leaders in the effort to "awaken the social conscience [that] has lagged behind the fierce development of industrialism" threatening city life (Scudder 1915, 32).

The Salvation Army, on the other hand, focused less on neighborhood reform and more on rescuing individuals. Their members dealt with conditions as they were in an attempt to save souls. All four of these organizations shared a Social Gospel ideology that united them in their attempts to create redemptive places.

In the midst of these similarities, of course, sits the most glaring difference. The YWCA, The Salvation Army, and the CSA were predominantly white associations, while the NACW was predominantly black. In fact, the YWCA actively encouraged the NACW's parallel efforts to provide inexpensive lodging and vocational training for black women. Thus these voluntary groups both reflected and perpetuated the racial and class divisions prevalent in American society.

The Young Women's Christian Association (YWCA)

Seeds for the Young Women's Christian Association (YWCA) were sown during the Second Great Awakening and were nurtured by the Social Gospel. The YWCA was formed in "the period of the great social awakening when the responsibility of Christians for a more Christian social order was proclaimed as an evangel." (*The Evangel* would become the name of the *Young Women's Christian Association Quarterly* in 1889.) The revivalist Reverend Charles Finney christened the first American YWCA. YWCA leaders were enthusiastic supporters of Walter Rauschenbusch's *Social Principles of Jesus* (1916) and for many years the mandatory Sunday afternoon gospel meeting was the heart of the YWCA (Bittar 1979, 15; Sims 1936, 105, 106).

The YWCA in the United States dates from 1858, when a Ladies' Christian Association was formed in New York City under the leadership of Mrs. Marshall O. Roberts.[1] The most important duty of YWCA members was to help young working girls find suitable housing. One of the first requests received by the original New York City YWCA was for lodging. The Reverend Heman Dyer was asked to find safe accommodations for a colleague's daughter, who could not afford the prices charged by families or boarding houses. Reverend Dyer challenged Mrs. Roberts to "open such a Home for such young girls," and by 1860 she had done just that (Wilson [1916] 1987, 25). Although historians recognize the New York group as the first American YWCA, that name was not used formally in the United States until 1866, when thirty women met as the Boston Young Women's Christian Association. New York and Boston were just the beginning. YWCAs sprang up in Providence, Hartford, and Pittsburgh in 1867; in Cincinnati, Cleveland, and St. Louis in 1868; and in Dayton, Utica, Washington, D.C., Buffalo, and Philadelphia in 1870. There were at least twenty-eight associations by 1875, nearly one-half of which maintained boarding homes for fifty or more women (Sims 1936, 5–7; Wilson [1916] 1987, 22–32).

As the urban organizations were growing to meet the needs of working women, college groups were also forming. The first association started at Normal University in Illinois in 1873 and was soon followed by a national alliance calling itself the American Committee of YWCAs. In 1891 attempts to combine the students' American Committee and the existing International Board (so called due to the international conferences sponsored annually by the original urban YWCAs) were rejected. Finally, in 1906, both associations met in New York City and agreed to merge. The conference was attended by representatives of 147 city and 469 student groups. The new organization was called the Young Women's Christian Association of the United States of America and established its national headquarters in New York City with Grace Dodge as its first president (Sims 1936, 21–24, 48, 49).

The YWCA's priority of safe housing was emphasized in an 1878 editorial in *Faith and Works,* the local magazine of the Philadelphia YWCA that served for many years as a resource for all associations:

> The chief cornerstone on which rests the foundation of Women's Christian Association work is the purpose to "help those who help themselves." One of the chief out-growths of this purpose thus far is the *establishment of safe, suitable, and economical homes for girls who earn their own support.* In making this statement we have by no means overlooked the great variety of good work done in various ways by our Associations at large, employment bureaus, libraries, industrial classes, etc. We speak merely of the feature of work in which a large proportion are alike engaged. (Sims 1936, 27; emphasis added)

The expectation of self-support applied to boarding homes as well as to those living in them. The 1879 annual conference addressed the question, "Should Boarding Homes Be Self-sustaining?" and the answer was a resounding yes. The members based their decision on a survey of residents who expressed a preference for higher rates to cover all operating expenses to insure their independence. They feared that "the independent principle God has implanted in the human heart is no light thing to be tampered with.... Once degrade a young girl to a spirit of dependence, and you take her to the brink of a precipice" (Sims 1936, 29).

The decision to be self-supporting meant that it cost more to live at the YWCA than in facilities that operated at a loss, but they were more affordable than living alone. The U.S. Commissioner of Labor recognized the YWCA boarding house as an important way for working women to stretch their housing budgets. His 1894 annual report stated:

> [YWCA] homes should not be regarded as "charities," for they are not such. They should be looked upon rather as cooperative enterprises, where the funds which the women would individually expend for a poor and insufficient living are, by combination and judicious management, rendered sufficient to give all those advantages which without such combination would be beyond the reach of any. (Sims 1936, 31)

After housing, the next most pressing need shared by young girls was employment. Providing both lodging and jobs maximized the opportunities for YWCA members to proselytize. The first constitution of the New York Ladies' Christian Association identified the duties of members to:

> seek out especially young women of the operative class, aid them in procuring employment and in obtaining suitable boarding places, furnish them with proper reading matter, establish Bible classes and meetings for religious exercises at such times and places as shall be most convenient for them during the week, secure their attendance at places of public worship on the Sabbath, surround them with Christian influences and use all practicable means for the increase of true piety in themselves and others. (Wilson [1916] 1987, 23)

"All practicable means for the increase of true piety" sometimes, out of necessity, took the form of entertainment. Members of the YWCA feared that working-class women, left to their own recreational devices, would choose dance halls, nickel movies, or the street, where they were "so apt to grow noisy and bold." They suspected that young women preferred exciting amusements to a homey evening around the hearth, so they tried to "provide attractions which should give the pleasure-loving girl all the brightness and entertainment possible" — even to the extent of occasionally allowing men into the home for events. Understanding that "the enemies of girls' souls are working when the lights are brightest," new YWCA boarding houses included gyms, swimming pools in the basement, and movies and soda fountains on the roof, in addition to the traditional concerts, libraries, and educational classes (Peiss 1986, 164–67; Wilson [1916] 1987, 100, 281–85).

YWCA volunteers served as personal mediators between potential employers and employees, and opened their own boarding houses when suitable accommodations could not be found. They also took prayer meetings to women where they worked. The 1860 annual report of the New York City Ladies' Christian Association recorded noon-hour religious services for five hundred women at a hoop-skirt factory, and a rent of $850 paid for a boarding house at 21 Amity Place. The association's effort to reduce the time women spent eating and increase their time for self-improvement led to the invention of the cafeteria in Kansas City in 1891. In a small made-over school building the YWCA bought for $10,000, members passed between a brass rail and the counter, selected their hot or cold food, and carried their trays to a table that they later cleared themselves. By 1913 the Kansas City YWCA cafeteria was feeding one hundred women a day. This novelty spread quickly because the reductions in time and labor made it profitable for both customers and sponsors (Geary 1913; Wilson [1916] 1987, 24, 25, 84).

Eligibility requirements reflected the YWCA's philosophy that their boarding houses should inoculate young girls from trouble, not cure them once problems developed. Women applying to live at Boston's YWCA were reminded that "[a]s the Institution is not designed to be a reformatory, no one will be admitted whose references in regard to character are not perfectly satisfactory" (Wilson [1916] 1987, 34). YWCA homes gave preference to women who lodged all year, although many residents stayed only a few weeks or months. Thus two to three times as many residents lived in the home over the course of a year as could be accommodated at any one time. Thousands of women lived in the homes for two weeks or less on a space-available basis (Meyerowitz 1988, 83).

The YWCA tried to provide a "home in every sense of the word," a place where (white) women "might come and feel at home in a city of strangers." Residents and managers alike were called "family" and they were mutually responsible for each other. The familial imagery may have helped middle-class sponsors bridge the class barrier between themselves and the working girls. It also may have driven away women seeking privacy and left a clientele of those predisposed to virtue. Matrons of the early boarding homes were expected to provide beds and food, but, more important, they were to "guide the young women under their care along the swiftly widening paths of opportunity" (YWCA of the USA 1954). Some independent Chicago YWCA residents resented the condescending supervision of the matrons, complaining of "funereal" rooms and poor food, and referring to themselves as "victims of the home"; the malcontents were subsequently asked to leave (Meyerowitz 1988, 50, 53, 85; Rothman 1978, 90).

The YWCA changed the names of its "homes" to "residences" at the turn of the century because "homes" had the connotation of a poorly run boarding house with too many rules (Sims 1936, 61). By then the YWCA had firmly established itself as a provider of safe housing for working girls. The capacity of all homes nationally in 1916 was 7,000, but the transient nature of the clientele meant that over 157,000 women found rooms in YWCA lodgings in any given year. The YWCA emphasized that its mission was accomplished through "members, not building," although it recognized that the building "is the embodiment of the loyalty and enthusiasm of the members, that glorifies it as nothing else can adorn it" (Wilson [1916] 1987, 281–83).

Training schools, employment bureaus, gymnasia, and administrative centers soon joined residence homes in the repertoire of YWCA buildings. Some were free-standing buildings and others combined functions. "Combination buildings" were controversial because some members believed dorm rooms should be kept separate from administrative functions. The flagship combination building for the YWCA was its headquarters at 600 Lexington Avenue in New York City, built in 1912. (This was the building from which Edna St. Vincent Millay wrote of "seeing the noise" of the city, and is described more fully in chapter 5.) Young women lived there for a year while they trained to be "typewriters" by attending classes for eight hours a day. Teaching typewriting was a radical endeavor because the work of a typist was considered a physical and mental strain for women (Sims 1936, 31).[2]

Prospective employers were typically looking for household help, sewing skills, or clerical talents. Since many girls coming to their doors were ill equipped for any kind of work, the YWCA opened training schools as feeder systems to their employment bureaus. These schools taught classes in the new technologies of the sewing machine and the typewriter. Perhaps because household chores took less skill, employment bureaus typically were more successful in placing domestics than white-collar workers (Rothman 1978, 76, 90).

Training schools were the YWCA's answer to upward mobility and economic independence for women. The YWCA's goal was to make educational opportunities available for women who might otherwise miss them due to lack of time or money. Organized schools existed in forty of the largest cities by the 1920s. The Ballard School in New York enrolled thirty-five hundred students in forty-six different classes, two-thirds of which were offered at night. The most popular subjects were secretarial and business courses, taken by employed women ambitious to gain better positions and salaries. Other courses in high demand were English, elocution, and public speaking. Girls would take these classes to win an employer's trust, acquire greater responsibility, and become more acceptably American. Courses in tea-room management and nursing also were offered at the Ballard School (U.S. Department of the Interior 1923, 3).

The curriculum at YWCA training schools varied depending on the location of the school. The YWCA School of Opportunity in Harlem had a curriculum devised for girls with less than a high school education. It offered courses for girls and women who wanted "preparation for making a living or a better living." In Cincinnati the YWCA offered citizenship classes sponsored by the League of Women Voters that included lectures on city government and political parties (U.S. Department of the Interior 1923, 5).

Grace H. Dodge was appointed the first president of the YWCA of the United States when the college and city branches merged in 1906 (Sims 1936, 21–24, 48, 49). Grace was heiress to the Dodge copper fortune and daughter of William Dodge, a founder of New York City's YMCA. Dodge had been involved with working women since the 1880s, when she organized the Association of Working Girls Societies. Although the Working Girls Societies seldom provided boarding houses, they duplicated the YWCA's services and philosophy in almost every other respect. They had clubhouses with libraries, pianos, sewing classes, and weekly meetings to instill "The Three Ps — Purity, Perseverance and Pleasantness" (Murolo 1997).

Dodge took a personal interest in "her friends" at the Thirty-eighth Street Working Girls Society. Her series of talks from Tuesday evening meetings was published in 1887 as *A Bundle of Letters to Busy Girls on Practical Matters*. The booklet's message transferred easily to the YWCA. Topics included tips on personal health and hygiene, working, saving money, prospective husbands, housekeeping, and moral advice. Dodge thought young women should work hard and establish economic independence. She also thought they should guard their virtue. Dodge advised women that there was nothing wrong with having men friends, only with "trying to attract the attention of strangers." She was adamant, advising girls that "[i]t is dangerous as well as wrong to allow a man to give you money or presents of value, to accept invitations from one you do not know all about, to put yourselves in any way in a man's power" (Dodge 1887, 103). Dodge herself, of course, had little need for others' money, nor did she marry.

In addition to the Working Girls clubs, Dodge founded the Industrial Education Association and the New York College for the Training of Teachers (now the Teachers College of Columbia University) (Kaminer 1984, 37; Rothman 1978, 77, 91; Wilson 1933, 9–11). She also established a Travelers' Aid Society that grew out of Victoria Earle Matthews's model for black girls seeking the White Rose Mission in New York (Best n.d.). Dodge was an impressive leader with all the right credentials. She possessed wealth, social connections, and a commanding presence — she was nearly six feet tall. Dodge was extremely self-conscious about her height, however. She avoided being photographed at all and, if it was necessary, usually insisted on a seated pose. One of the few pictures of Grace Dodge that exists is at a ground-breaking ceremony for a YWCA in St. Paul, where she is stooped slightly over her shovel (see figure 2.8).

A concern about the homogeneity of its membership emerged during the 1880s, and the YWCA began to address the needs of immigrants, industrial workers, and blacks. Although the YWCA prided itself on crossing class lines, there was a vast gulf between the Protestant middle-class members and most of the women they served. YWCA historian Mary Sims acknowledged, "Left to itself any local Association tends to become homogeneous and slough off the most different parts." Yet the national leadership "recognized that if the really different groups of the community, such as women and girls in industry, the foreign-born who do not speak English and the Negro girls, were to be a part of any Young Women's Christian Association it was necessary to make special provision for them." Sims warned that constant vigilance was needed to reach and maintain the organization's "principle of diversity" (Sims, 1936, 71).

In 1910 YWCA member Edith Terry Bremer opened an International Institute in New York City for the "protection and welfare of immigrant girls." Bremer, who was also a settlement worker, pushed the YWCA to establish an educational center in Greenwich Village. It served newcomers by providing English classes, recreation, and help with housing, employment, and naturalization. Its goal was to develop leadership and self-governing clubs among immigrants by using organizers who knew their language and could "help to adjust to American life girls and women strange not only to the language but to the customs and conventions of the new land" (Sims 1936, 60). Bremer's idea spread to fifty-five other cities by the 1920s. The YWCA thus complemented the work of settlement houses in assimilating immigrants as it evolved from a strict proselytizing agenda (Mohl 1997, 113).

The YWCA had more trouble assimilating blacks than immigrants because it subscribed to the racially segregated conventions of the late nineteenth century. Elizabeth Wilson's noteworthy history of the YWCA, *Fifty Years of Association Work among Young Women*, 1866–1916 ([1916] 1987), makes few references to "Colored Associations," although "The Girls in Industry" and "The Strangers within Our Gates" each warrant a separate chapter. The Chicago YWCA voted to deny black women admission to its boarding home in 1877, and a "colored branch" was eventually opened (Meyerowitz 1988, 47). Jane Edna Hunter could not find lodging at the YWCA when she arrived in Cleveland twenty-eight years later (in 1905), prompting her to found the Phillis Wheatley Association (described further in chapter 5).

The newly organized YWCA national board began to discuss the issue of racially segregated facilities in 1907. That year the YWCA hired Addie Waite Hunton to investigate work in black women's associations across the country; Elizabeth Ross Haynes joined her in 1908. Together they visited campuses and cities throughout the southern and eastern states. Hunton and Haynes found that most of the leaders of local black associations were also active members of the NACW and that the YWCA and NACW shared similar goals. At the 1914 general national conference, the record reports a "general awakening in the country over for our colored girls. . . . Just as the immigrant and industrial girls are special girls, so the colored girl is fast coming in for her share of development. We must be prepared to meet her needs" (Higginbotham 1993, 35–48; Jones 1997; Scott 1991, 109; Sims 1936, 60–173).

During the years the YWCA excluded black women it tried to maintain some control by establishing *branches* of the local association rather than separate organizations. Leaders debated whether this practice contributed to segregation, and apparently bowed to financial and political realities of the time. Whites' tolerance for integrated activities varied by region. In Atlanta in the early 1900s, Mrs. Lugenia Burns Hope, wife of the president of Atlanta University, was successful in convincing the YWCA to accept black members. In Cleveland, however, the YWCA and Phillis Wheatley Association existed side by side. Issues of interracial relations appear to have been worked out locally by trial and error, with little official policy or action (Matthews 1992, 193; Sims 1936, 174, 175).

Evidence exists that the YWCA actively encouraged the NACW's parallel efforts to provide inexpensive lodging for black women. In St. Louis the Wheatley Branch of the YWCA inherited the building abandoned when the white YWCA moved to new quarters, and when the City Federation of Washington, D.C., decided to join the NACW in 1920, it met at the YWCA building (Davis [1935] 1981, 54, 60, 235, 409). The first YWCA building specifically for colored women and girls in the North was opened in New York City in 1919, marking the beginning of an effort to provide equal facilities and leadership training (Sims 1936, 66). Similar parallel homes for black women opened in Philadelphia, Dayton, Baltimore, New York, and Washington, D.C. (Geary 1913; Jones 1997).

Black women's organizations sometimes depended on the YWCA. Jane Edna Hunter's Phillis Wheatley Association in Cleveland had a governing board dominated by whites, many of whom were on the YWCA board, as a condition of funding from a white benefactor. Relations between the two organizations were not altogether smooth. After 1914, when the national YWCA began to address seriously the issue of segregated facilities, Cleveland was considered a model to emulate. Eva Bowles, YWCA national secretary for colored work, traveled to Cleveland several times between 1915 and 1917 to mediate a merger of the YWCA and the Phillis Wheatley Association. But Hunter resisted the idea and negotiations were dropped. Hunter eventually joined forces with the NACW instead (A. Jones 1990, 59–68).

Historians disagree about whether the YWCA was regressive or progressive on the issue of race relations (Jones 1997; Meyerowitz 1988; Scott 1991). The probable reality is that they were liberal on some issues and conservative on others, given the size of the organization and its decentralized administration. It seems clear that Grace Dodge was committed to racial cooperation. She supported the White Rose Mission for black women throughout her life, and insisted that the rights of black associations in the Jim Crow South be "guarded just as carefully and unflinchingly as those of the whites." When Dodge died in 1914, the National Association for the Advancement of Colored People called her a "friend to the American Negro" in its periodical, *The Crisis*. The article compared the records of the YWCA with those of the YMCA and concluded that "it was due to her [Dodge] more than any other person that the YWCA, while gravely deficient in some respects, still is so much more Christian and decent than the YMCA." The article ended with the hope that Dodge's death would not herald "the gradual encroachment of Negro-hating tendencies" in the YWCA (Lasch-Quinn 1993, 133).

The National Association of Colored Women was established thirty years after the YWCA. Like the YWCA, the NACW began with strong religious affiliations and its goals became more secular as the association matured. Like The Salvation Army, black women adopted a rallying cry of "The World for Christ" (Higginbotham 1993, 157, 225). Like the CSA, the NACW tried to improve poor neighborhoods. Under the motto "Lifting as we climb," members of the NACW inspired racial uplift by sponsoring ordinary kindergartens, boarding homes, and vocational schools for newcomers.

The National Association of Colored Women (NACW)

The NACW had roots in antebellum organizations, just like white women's voluntary organizations. Black women formed numerous antislavery and literary societies during the 1830s. The United Daughters of Allen, for example (affiliated with the A.M.E. church), stressed temperance and educational and welfare reform in large eastern and midwestern cities. Many free black women assisted runaway slaves through the Underground Railroad. Eventually, church groups like Christian Endeavor Societies, Daughters of Zion, and Epworth Leagues provided black women with "spaces of resistance" in which to articulate their goals for racial and community uplift. Howard, Fisk, and Spelman Universities began offering college degrees to black women in the 1860s (Higginbotham 1993; Lerner 1972; Shaw 1991; Solomon 1985; Wesley 1984, 1–12). The combination of traditional activism, new educational opportunities, and rural-to-urban migration laid the foundation for secular black women's clubs by the end of the nineteenth century. It developed an urban emphasis, but members of the NACW still tried to take "the light of knowledge and the gospel of cleanliness to their benighted sisters on the plantations" of the South (Terrell 1898).

One of the factors contributing to the birth of the NACW was black women's exclusion from the 1893 World's Columbian Exposition in Chicago. White women had difficulty joining men in preparations for the fair and had to settle for representation through a Board of Lady Managers composed of women's clubs members. Black women had worse luck. They found it impossible to participate because eligibility for the Board of Lady Managers was determined by organizational affiliation and they had no nationally recognized association (Weimann 1981).

Hallie Q. Brown, a graduate of Wilberforce University, lobbied most actively for black women's inclusion in the fair. Brown protested the absence of black women from exhibits in the Woman's Building in a letter to one of the Lady Managers, observing that "if the object of the women's department of the Columbian Exposition is to present to the world the industrial and educational progress of the bread-winners, the wage-winners, how immeasurably incomplete will that work be without the exhibit of the thousands of colored women of this country" (Wesley 1984, 27). Brown's lobbying failed, but it strengthened her resolve to form a national organization for black women. She eventually collaborated with Josephine St. Pierre Ruffin to found the National Association of Colored Women in 1896.

Josephine St. Pierre Ruffin was the daughter of an English mother and a father of African, French, and Indian heritage. Ruffin and her husband, a judge, were members of Boston's "colored aristocracy" (Gatewood 1990). As a result of her light-skinned features and high social status, she was active in both black and white women's clubs. Ruffin's most significant contribution was the Woman's Era Club she founded in 1893 (discussed further in chapter 6). She also belonged to the Domestic Reform League Committee of Boston's Women's Educational and Industrial Union; the Massachusetts School Suffrage Association (with Lucy Stone and Julia Ward Howe); the New England Women's Club; the Boston Movement for the Kansas Exodus; and the League of Women for Community Service. Like many white women, Ruffin gained organizational experience during the Civil War with the U.S. Sanitary Commission (Wesley 1984; Women's Educational and Industrial Union 1907).

Historian Gerda Lerner credits Ida B. Wells for inspiring Ruffin's activism and for transforming black women's local charitable concerns into a national political agenda. In 1892 Wells, an outspoken journalist in Memphis, wrote a series of editorials that exposed economic motives for the lynching of three local black businessmen. Her newspaper office was subsequently destroyed and her life threatened. Wells moved to New York City to work for the *New York Age* and continued to write and speak out publicly against lynching. "Thus [Wells] expressed what was to become the ideological direction of the organized movement of black women — a defense of black womanhood as part of a defense of the race from terror and abuse" (Lerner 1974, 160).

As she was preparing to depart on a lecture tour to England in 1892, Wells spoke at a fundraising rally in New York City organized by another woman who would become instrumental in the formation of the NACW: Victoria Earle Matthews. Matthews established the Women's Loyal Union of New York that same year and later opened the White Rose Mission in New York. The Women's Loyal Union and Ruffin's Woman's Era Club were two of the first black women's clubs in the country.[3] Wells established the Ida B. Wells Club in Chicago in 1893 (Lerner 1974).

For ten years Ruffin and her daughter published a monthly magazine for club members, *Woman's Era,* which gained her membership in the Women's Press Club of Boston. (That membership, ironically, eventually allowed her to join the all-white General Federation of Women's Clubs [Wesley 1984, 13, 14].) Ruffin used the *Woman's Era* to widely publicize the First National Conference of Colored Women in Boston in 1895. The specific incident that spurred Ruffin's invitation was her receipt of a letter from the president of the Missouri Press Association claiming that black women were "wholly devoid of morality and that they were prostitutes, thieves, and liars." Outraged and worried about the effects of giving such comments a public forum, Ruffin did not publish the letter in *Woman's Era,* but issued a call for black women to confer about the assault on the moral character of colored women. The conference was timed to coincide with a Boston meeting of the Christian Endeavor Society; its fifty thousand delegates insured low railroad rates around the country and an overlapping constituency. The circular announcing the conference reminded black women that one of the reasons they had been excluded from white women's clubs was their individual reputations for being immoral (Wesley 1984, 31).

The four-day conference at Berkeley Hall in Boston included a speech by Margaret Murray (Mrs. Booker T.) Washington titled "Individual

Work for Mental Elevation," one by abolitionist William Lloyd Garrison on "Political Equality," and one by Victoria Earle Matthews on the "Value of Race Literature." Other sessions dealt with "social purity," temperance, industrial training, and women in higher education. A resolution was adopted endorsing the Republican Party for condemning lynching in its platform and expressing regret that the Democratic Party had failed to include a comparable statement. Margaret Murray Washington was elected president of what became known as the National Federation of Afro-American Women. The announcement of the federation's meeting for the following year included among the general topics "The need of rescue work among our people, by our women" and "The establishment of Christian homes and asylums for our fallen and wayward" (Davis [1935] 1981, 21, 22).

As Ruffin was organizing the National Federation of Afro-American Women in Boston, Mrs. Helen Cook was forming the Colored Women's League in Washington, D.C. The league was formally incorporated in 1894. In addition to Hallie Q. Brown, one of its original members was Mary Church Terrell, a college graduate who would soon be elected first president of the NACW. In 1896 Cook's Colored Women's League and Ruffin's National Federation of Afro-American Women met in Washington, D.C. The Colored Women's League Convention was held at the Fifteenth Street Presbyterian Church on July 14–16, and the National Federation's Conference was held at the Nineteenth Street Baptist Church the following week. Rivalry for leadership was resolved when the groups combined as the National Association of Colored Women under the presidency of Mary Church Terrell (who had a B.A. and an M.A. from Oberlin in contrast to Ruffin's lack of formal higher education) (Lerner 1974; Salem 1990, chapter 2; Wesley 1984, 33–42). The NACW became the umbrella group for black women's organizations at the state and local levels. It operated through departments and an executive cabinet and kept its members informed of events through *National Notes*, its official publication. The first two conventions included reports on kindergartens, temperance, suffrage, lynching, domestic service, and education (Williams 1995).

Ruffin's *Woman's Era* became the official publication of the NACW. The August 1896 edition carried new president Mary Church Terrell's announcement of the formation of the NACW, in which she pledged that the association would promote the welfare of the race through every means possible, leaving each organization to fulfill that mission in its own way (B. Jones 1990, 131, 132). Terrell also justified including the word "colored" in the name of the organization because "our peculiar status in this country at the present time seems to demand that we stand by ourselves in the special work" (Salem 1990, 30).

Terrell was concerned about the attack on black women's moral character, but her own words reflected similar middle-class concerns:

> It has been suggested... that this Association should take as its motto—
> *Lifting as we climb*. In no way could we live up to such a sentiment better
> than by coming in closer touch with the masses of our women, by
> whom, whether we will nor not, the world will always judge the
> womanhood of the race. Even though we wish to shun them, and hold
> ourselves entirely aloof from them, we cannot escape the consequences
> of their acts. So, that, if the call of duty were disregarded altogether,
> policy and self-preservation would demand that we go down among the
> lowly, the illiterate, and even the vicious to whom we are bound by the
> ties of race and sex, and put forth every possible effort to uplift and
> reclaim them. (Terrell, as quoted in B. Jones 1990, 144)

Terrell's 1897 presidential address noted that mothers, wives, daughters, and sisters could accomplish the NACW's goals more effectively than fathers, husbands, sons, and brothers. Better homes and free kindergartens were central to the NACW's mission. Terrell believed that black women had a special responsibility to save children from the "miles of inhumanity that infest... the most noisome sections" of the city (B. Jones 1990, 136). Intervention was most effective before the age of six, when "evil habits [were] formed that no amount of civilizing and Christianizing can ever completely break" (Terrell 1898). The necessity for action was immediate:

> Let the women of the National Association see to it that the little strays
> of the alleys come in contact with intelligence and virtue, at least a few
> times a week, that the noble aspirations with which they are born may
> not be entirely throttled by the evil influences which these poor little
> ones are powerless to escape.... Let the women of the race once be
> thoroughly aroused to their duty to the children, let them be consumed
> with desire to save them from lives of degradation and shame, and the
> establishment of free kindergartens for the poor will become a living,
> breathing, saving reality at no distant day. (B. Jones 1990, 136)

When various regional associations of black women's clubs united under the umbrella of the NACW, black women created an organizational structure similar to that of the racially exclusive General Federation of Women's Clubs (GFWC) founded in 1892 to coordinate the activities of thousands of white women's clubs. Relations between the NACW and GFWC were strained from the start. At its 1898 conference the GFWC declined "fraternal greetings" from the NACW, and at its conference in 1900 it refused to accept Josephine St. Pierre Ruffin as a representative of her Woman's Era Club. Although Ruffin eventually was admitted as a representative from the white New England Federation of Women's Clubs, of which she was also a member, the damage from "the Ruffin Incident" was done (Cash 1992a; Hine 1990a; Wesley 1984, 39–44).

As with white women's volunteer work, much of what black women did went unrecognized outside their own organizations (Ruffins 1994). If it was unusual for white women to receive credit for saving cities, it was almost impossible for black women. As historian Anne Firor Scott remarked, "The problems with which [black women] grappled were so huge and were growing so fast that their accomplishments tended to be swallowed up in a sea of poverty and prejudice. Yet without their work things would have been much worse" (Scott 1990b, 18).[4]

The Salvation Army

Under the motto "Soup, Soap, and Salvation," Salvation Army volunteers worked to assimilate the poorest of the poor into urban America. Historian Paul Boyer acknowledged that "the Salvation Army did more than any other religious group to adapt the moral outlook and social values of Protestant America to the immigrant cities of the late nineteenth century" (Boyer 1978, 141).

William and Catherine Booth laid the groundwork for The Salvation Army in 1865 with their London urban home mission. They had been strongly influenced during the 1840s and 1850s by visiting American revivalists James Caughey (who baptized their second son), Charles G. Finney, and Phoebe Palmer. Finney's *Lectures on Revivals by Religion* (1837) was especially valuable because it revealed how to entice new converts to testify, how to hold meetings in unconsecrated halls, and how to encourage women to pray in public. The Bible and Finney's *Lectures* became the Booths' primary texts. By the time the Booths' emissaries arrived in the United States in 1879, however, those American roots had been obscured (Murdoch 1994, 12–17; Winston 1999, 53).

The Booths were innovative and none too picky about their facilities: one was in a stable, one in a "covered skittle alley," one in a carpenter's shop, and another in a pigsty. As the number of stations, leaders, and members increased, William and Catherine added paid employees and sought a building suitable for headquarters. He found it in 1867 on Whitechapel Road (where the settlement house Toynbee Hall would be established in 1884 and the same area Jack the Ripper would terrorize in 1888) at "The Eastern Star," formerly a "low beerhouse, notorious for immorality." William cultivated a music-hall atmosphere to attract converts. He also provided outdoor relief of food and clothing, soup kitchens and free teas during the economic panic and cholera epidemic of the winters of 1866 and 1867. Free breakfasts were followed by religious services for hundreds of "Negroes, mulattos, and denizens of distant countries clad in rags and tatters." William used a variety of means to draw his listeners toward conversion: retail shops, poor relief, classes, home visits, and prayer meetings. He believed that men must be fed and clothed before they could experience redemption (Murdoch 1994, 41–87).[5]

William first referred to his mission as "a salvation army" in the *Christian Mission Magazine* of 1878 (changed to *The War Cry* in 1879). "Evangelists" became "field officers" and "stations" of the mission became "corps"; William used the title "General" for the first time in 1879. Catherine designed a flag of red, blue, and yellow, its crimson symbolic of the "redeeming blood of Christ; its blue for purity" and its yellow for the fire of the Holy Spirit. Field officers were assigned ranks; uniforms for volunteers followed soon thereafter. By 1890 William had published *In Darkest England and the Way Out*, his answer to the needs of the "submerged tenth" laboring in England's cities. This book, based on ideas in Henry George's *Progress and Poverty* (1879) and Andrew Mearns's *Bitter Cry of Outcast London* (1883), was released in the United States at the same time as Jacob Riis's *How the Other Half Lives*. Booth's volume sold 200,000 copies in its first two years and enhanced The Salvation Army's reputation in America (Green 1989; McKinley 1995, 48; Murdoch 1994, 104–11, 146; Winston 1999, 61).[6]

The Salvation Army began in America in 1879 when sixteen-year-old convert Eliza Shirley immigrated to Philadelphia with her parents. General Booth was suspicious about achieving success overseas, but he grudgingly gave his consent for use of The Salvation Army name. While Mr. Shirley worked at a local silk factory, Eliza and her mother scoured the poor neighborhoods of Philadelphia for a suitable meeting hall. They settled on an abandoned chair factory between Fifth and Sixth on Oxford Street. They could afford the rent because it was dirty, unfurnished, and had holes in the roof (McKinley 1995, 7).

Mr. Shirley advertised the first meeting with flyers announcing that "Two Hallelujah Females" would "speak and sing on behalf of God and Precious Souls" at the "Salvation Factory." On the way to the meeting the Shirleys held a street-corner service to attract followers. That event had few spectators, but within a few weeks a propitious fire that drew large crowds and resulted in the dramatic conversion of a notorious drunkard improved the Shirleys' luck. Soon they were reaching so many people that Eliza opened a second corps in January 1880 at Forty-Second and Market Streets (McKinley 1995, 10).

The Shirleys' success prompted General Booth to send a formal emissary to America. In 1880 he appointed George Scott Railton to lead an expedition to New York City. Railton selected seven "Hallelujah Lasses" to accompany him, and they departed for Castle Garden in New York City on the oceanliner *Australia*. The Shirleys were at the dock to greet them, as were several reporters who routinely met steamships. Commissioner Railton and the seven sisters gave them a show. They marched down the gangplank waving a Salvation Army flag and singing, "With a sorrow for sin, let repentance begin" (McKinley 1995, 15). The next day (March 11, 1880) the *New York Times* reported that

> they [the Salvationists] created quite a sensation in the Garden and subsequently in the streets. . . . They were all attired in a uniform of dark blue cloth, edged with bright yellow binding and around their hats were broad bands of scarlet ribbon inscribed with the words: "The Salvation Army" in gilt letters. . . . They intend to spread themselves throughout the principal cities of the Union. (Chesham 1965, 59)

They spread themselves rapidly. Salvationists paraded through cities and preached in the "Cathedral of the Open Air," claiming forty thousand converts by 1895. General Booth's motto was *Attract attention.* This philosophy incited ridicule from traditional religious leaders and provoked violence among some spectators. Salvationists, even women, were beat up and harassed repeatedly. Yet the Army's sensationalism resonated with the emerging consumer culture. The Salvation Army cultivated media coverage to advertise its presence to its audience by "saving souls and savoring headlines" (Winston 1999, 19).

The Salvation Army did both in Chicago in 1893. It conducted extensive relief efforts for families left destitute by the loss of jobs following
the closing of the Columbian Exposition and the financial panic of that
year. In the Pullman Strike of 1894, Gov. John P. Altgeld accepted the
Army's offer to collect and distribute food for starving strikers. The
Army's official position on the labor movement was neutral because it
believed in conversion of individuals, not social class reform. The Army
was once endorsed by the United Mine Workers, however, and Eugene
V. Debs, leader of the Pullman strike, called the Army "Christianity in
action" (McKinley 1995, 78, 132). By the turn of the century The Salvation
Army was so well established that Presidents Cleveland, Harrison, and
McKinley all endorsed its programs (McKinley 1995, 23–25, 81; Murdoch 1994, 127).

Catherine Booth's Legacy

Catherine Booth established a professional identity long before women
could vote, own property, or develop careers in England. She told William
after their engagement that only when women were "educated as man's
equal will unions be perfect." Catherine apparently was responsible for
a great deal of William's education on the topic of women's rights. In
1855 she challenged him with the issue of equality in the pulpit. His response was, "I would not stop a woman preaching on any account. I
would not encourage one to begin . . . [but] I am for the world's salvation. I will quarrel with no means that promises help" (Chesham 1965,
33). Catherine needed no encouragement. She began to teach Sunday
school at Brighouse Chapel and wrote to her parents, "If I get on well
and find I really possess any ability for public speaking, I don't intend
to finish with juveniles" (Murdoch 1994, 32, 33).

After William and Catherine's marriage in 1855 Catherine interspersed
childbearing with preaching; by 1864 she had established a successful
ministry in London's West End. She formed contacts with London's Midnight Movement for Fallen Women and her interest in prostitutes and
unmarried mothers would translate eventually into a network of "rescue homes" sponsored by The Salvation Army.

Her eight children were one of Catherine's most enduring contributions to The Salvation Army. All but one, the mentally handicapped
Marian, assumed positions of leadership in the organization. Long be-

fore hyphenated names were in vogue William insisted that his married daughters retain the Booth identity to accompany their positions of power. Thus four couples extended William and Catherine's legacy: first daughter Catherine (Kate) and her husband Arthur Sydney Booth-Clibborn worked on behalf of the Army in France and Switzerland during the early 1880s; son Ballington and his wife Maud commanded the American Army between 1887 and 1896; Emma and Frederick St. George de Lautour Booth-Tucker were joint commanders of the American Salvation Army during the late 1890s; and Lucy and Emmanuel Daniel Booth-Hellberg led the Scandinavian Army at the turn of the century (McKinley 1995, 102–5; Murdoch 1994, 124–26).

Ballington and Maud Booth did the most to Americanize The Salvation Army, a decision that cost them General Booth's support. They chose to leave the organization rather than be transferred out of America, and formed the Volunteers of America to continue their mission work. The Booth-Tuckers replaced Ballington and Maud in 1896, and the next heir to the American post was the daughter who remained single, Evangeline Cory Booth. Christened Eveline and called Eva by her father, she changed her name to Evangeline and began using her middle name at the suggestion of Woman's Christian Temperence Union president Frances Willard. Willard convinced Eva that a dignified name helped bestow authority to a woman. William made Evangeline the National Commander of the American Salvation Army in 1904, a post she held until 1934. Her flair for dramatic leadership was signaled by her first official meeting at Carnegie Hall, where she made a grand entrance on horseback surrounded by flags, flowers, and a brass band. Evangeline was a charismatic speaker whose motto was "The World for God!" She was the only woman to hold the post of Commander during the history of The Salvation Army, and when she left that position in 1934 the Booth family dynasty ended as well (Chesham 1965, 119; McKinley 1995, 122).

The Salvation Army gave women opportunities they could not find elsewhere. Most of the female officers came from small towns with few options, so women who wanted to practice religion on an equal footing with men turned to The Salvation Army. Their rather unorthodox career choice (and uniforms) often made female officers the target of public harassment. Maud Booth tried to counteract any resulting discouragement by devoting a special column of the weekly *War Cry* to bolster the spirits of her "Woman Warriors." The Woman Warrior combined "tender, gentle, loving attributes" with "courage, strength, action, sacrifice, and loyalty" in service to the Army (Winston 1999, 78).

Many Woman Warriors craved legitimacy. A *War Cry* correspondent wanted to set the record straight:

> To those of our readers or critics who have "with the larger majority" always held that the ranks of the Salvation Army are altogether made up and recruited from the riff-raff and bob-taildom of society, we say "Hold it a bit!" Perhaps they will be surprised to find that a great many have been gathered in, not from the slums or the haunts of shame but from the ranks of upper tendom and aristocracy. (Winston 1999, 79)

Although occasionally the daughter of a wealthy family (the "upper tendom") would join the Army, the typical recruit was from a farm or family business of modest means.

Frances Willard was as supportive of women's roles in The Salvation Army as she was of Evangeline Booth. She wrote that the Army represented "the nearest approach to primitive Christianity" at the turn of the century because it "placed woman side by side with man as a teacher, worker, and administrator." British journalist William T. Stead declared in London's *Pall Mall Gazette* that one key to The Salvation Army's success was its "perfect recognition of the equality of the sexes" (Magnuson 1977, 115).[7]

Before the elder Catherine died, she instituted a "Slum Sisters" program in London in which participants could be "as spiritual in sewing on buttons" as in preaching. Daughter Emma and (future) daughter-in-law Maud initiated the "Cellar, Gutter, and Garret Brigade." Maud took this program with her to America. In 1890 Slum Sisters ventured in pairs into the streets of New York. They performed mundane but necessary tasks: scrubbing floors, bathing babies, caring for the sick, cooking meals, changing beds, and washing and dressing the dead for burial. This practical ministry soon spread to other cities. By 1895 Brooklyn, Boston, Buffalo, Chicago, St. Louis, and Philadelphia all had Slum Sisters (McKinley 1995, 70).

The program lasted into the twentieth century. In New York in 1911 Slum Sisters were appointed in pairs and lived in the area they served. With "the Bible in their pocket and prayer on their tongue," Slum Sisters could march into brothels, saloons, opium dens, gambling halls, and lodging houses. "They grew accustomed to the worst aspects of life and quickly discovered that God's love, as shown by a helpful dustcloth or a scrub brush or a bar of soap or, more simply, a cup of hot tea, was usually more welcome than when expounded from a pulpit" (Chesham 1965, 138).[8]

While Slum Sisters took their mission into the streets, they also recognized that some of their intended converts needed to escape those streets. The following broadside appeared in an 1898 edition of their newsletter, *The War Cry.* Sung to the tune of "Throw Out the Life-line," it advertised the Army's work on behalf of fallen women and requested donations to keep its rescue homes open.

> Out in the darkness, out in the sleet,
> Outcast and homeless, walking the street,
> Sinful and wretched, friendless and poor,
> Somebody's girl we find close to our door.
>
> Yet, they are sisters, yes, every one,
> Reaping in sorrow the deeds they have done
> And whilst the world its anathema hurls,
> We mean to help them — somebody's girls.
>
> We have the Shelter, the Home, and the light,
> We long to bring to their lives something bright.
> We will find shelter, if you will give gold,
> Can you a little to help us withhold? (Chesham 1965, 72k)

Maud Booth played an important role in providing facilities for prostitutes and unwed mothers during the 1890s. The first recorded Salvation Army "rescue home for fallen or falling women" opened in 1886 in New York City as Morris Cottage. Others soon opened in East Oakland, California; Grand Rapids, Michigan; Boston; and Cleveland. In an 1893 address to a "well-dressed and prosperous looking" audience, Maud Booth requested funds for her homes by assuring those present that ninety-nine out of every one hundred women leading "the abandoned life" were doing so out of necessity rather than choice. Rescue homes were only one part of The Salvation Army's outreach to poor women. Nurseries and infant hospitals were opened in Brooklyn, Philadelphia, and Cincinnati between 1890 and 1895 (Abell 1962, 127, 128; MacLachlan, n.d.).

When Frederick and Emma Booth-Tucker took over command of The Salvation Army from Ballington and Maud in 1896, the work of rescuing women continued. Frederick Booth-Tucker's Christmas 1899 report of Army activities listed a total of fourteen rescue homes nationally with accommodations for 360. These homes apparently had extremely high turnover, for in one month they reported 11,095 beds occupied and 33,285 meals served. Demand was consistently high. Booth-Tucker estimated that "no less than 50,000 girls annually pass from the ranks of the fallen to a premature grave. Their places, alas, are quickly taken by others, so that there is no apparent diminution in the volume of vice which pours its Niagara of woe through our streets and homes." Girls stayed an average of four months and were expected to help meet their expenses by "various kinds of needle-work... bookbinding, chicken-raising, and other occupations." In 1899 the fourteen homes were caring for sixty babies as well as their mothers (Booth-Tucker [1899] 1972).

Commander Booth-Tucker's report blamed women's low wages for the necessity to provide homes, hotels, and boarding houses for women. Affordable lodging was necessary to keep virtuous girls from needing a rescue home, since opportunities for vice in the city were numerous:

> To pay for rent and food out of the $4 to $6 a week which their wages average, besides dressing with the neatness which their employers demand, is well-nigh impossible. To starve or sell their virtue becomes the painful alternative. At least the gateway of vice is dangerously near and wide open to those young and inexperienced feet. To help them after they have fallen is good — to prevent their fall is infinitely better. (Booth-Tucker [1899] 1972)

The Salvation Army, like the YWCA, tried to intervene before sinful behavior produced unwanted consequences. Unlike the YWCA, however, The Salvation Army took responsibility for sheltering the morally wayward. The Army liked to boast that from 70 to 85 percent of the girls were "restored to lives of virtue," and that successful "graduates" formed "Out of Loves" leagues that contributed to the upkeep of the homes. Its willingness to confront issues of sexual impropriety made The Salvation Army progressive for its time. It also tried to transcend prevailing sentiments regarding appropriate race relations, but was less successful.

Outreach to Blacks

When Commander Ballington Booth described himself in 1891 as one "who daily yearns for the salvation of the worst of our great cities" (McKinley 1986, 3), he no doubt included all races. Yet the predominance of European over black migration to major cities meant that the foreign-born were a larger proportion of the urban population in 1900 than blacks. Thus the vast majority of the poor for whom the Army provided shelter and services at the turn of the century were white.

Just as The Salvation Army subordinated its traditional beliefs about women's public role for the greater good of saving souls, it tried to overcome the conservative racial climate of the day in the name of evangelism. Shortly after establishing headquarters in Philadelphia, Commissioner Railton reported to General Booth,

> We have the honor today to be the only white people to whose company, to whose platforms, to whose operations colored people have had the same welcome as others. . . . If they will not join themselves with other races, we will go farther still, and there will be found officers ready to leave off association with their own race in order to rescue those of another. (Chesham 1965, 62)

Few details of Railton's efforts to break racial barriers are known, but one of his successors, Major Frank Smith, implemented specific plans to reach blacks. He announced the Army's "first colored station" in Baltimore in 1884, although it apparently never opened. The first commissioned corps band in America, formed in Grand Rapids, Michigan, in 1884, had at least one black male instrumentalist. During the summer of 1885 Major Smith launched the "Great Colored Campaign and Combined Attack upon the South." It was led by Captain W. S. Braithwaite of British Guiana, a black officer who had been saved at an Army service in New Jersey. Special meetings were held to raise funds and volunteers for the trip, and all who believed that "the colored race . . . was possessed of immortal souls" were asked for donations. The campaign soon produced black corps in Alexandria and Fredericksburg, Virginia. Two of its four pioneer officers were black: Captain Johnson of Maine (no first name given, providing no gender identification), and Lieutenant Minor, the daughter of Virginia slaves (McKinley 1995, 65).

Large black audiences at these first meetings encouraged The Salvation Army to expand further. Plans were made to open black corps in Washington, D.C.; Frederick, Maryland; Richmond, and Norfolk, Virginia. Black converts were often featured as "specials" at Army gatherings, providing entertainment in addition to testimony. The "colored jubilee singers," for example, performed for white groups in Chicago and Los Angeles. While some black participants were ridiculed, others were taken seriously as leaders of black corps (McKinley 1995, 66).

In 1894 Commander Ballington Booth took five black officers to the international congress in England to demonstrate the Army's endorsement of interracial evangelism. The following year the Army took an official stand against lynching and continued its campaigns to extend "Salvation Army work among the colored population of the Southern States." These efforts languished due to lack of funds and scarcity of black officers. The Army remained officially committed to black outreach, but did little to accomplish its goals. Despite their inadequacies, however, Booker T. Washington acknowledged the importance of The Salvation Army's efforts. He wrote in 1896, "I have always had the greatest respect for the work of the Salvation Army, especially because I have noted that it draws no color line in religion" (McKinley 1995, 67).

The new century produced little in the way of racial progress. The Army declared a continuing interest in preaching to blacks, but urged patience in pursuing this avenue. There were few black officers in the North and none in the South. Two of those in New York City worked in a rescue home in the early 1900s as "Sisters in Race, Sisters in Grace." In 1908 the regional Southern officer admitted in a private report that the Army's work was exclusively among whites because the "strong antagonistic feeling between the two races . . . made it practically impossible to do anything among the colored people." In 1912 a black corps was founded in Washington, D.C., and in 1913 yet another southern campaign was proposed, but again was accompanied by little action (McKinley 1995, 131). By that time the National Association of Colored Women had begun to create places for blacks parallel to those provided for whites by The Salvation Army.

As The Salvation Army was becoming more entrenched in its religious doctrine, other voluntary associations in which women worked were shifting their allegiance from the Social Gospel to municipal housekeeping. The College Settlements Association epitomized this transition. While the YWCA, NACW, and The Salvation Army provided lodging, settlement houses provided shelter of another sort. They offered an array of places in which immigrants learned middle-class American values and the English language through kindergartens, Boys' and Girls' Clubs, libraries, playgrounds, cooking classes, and public baths. They also gave college-educated women dedicated to urban reform socially acceptable alternatives to marriage (Crocker 1992; Davis 1967, 32).

The College Settlements Association (CSA)

Vida Scudder, an Episcopalian "Christian revolutionary" whose home displayed a Communist flag next to a crucifix, founded the College Settlements Association (CSA) in 1890. Scudder was a disciple of the English social reformer John Ruskin, a forceful critic of the industrializing city. Ruskin recommended in *Unto This Last* (1890) that the government should establish vocational schools for national standards of workmanship, a social security system, public works projects, minimum wage laws, public transportation, and affordable housing to improve the quality of city life. Ruskin believed a group of college men should live in the slums to most effectively address the conditions of poverty. Among Ruskin's followers were William Morris, Octavia Hill, Edward Denison, and Arnold Toynbee, for whom Toynbee Hall was named. Toynbee Hall, the original British settlement house, was located in the same Whitechapel district as the first Salvation Army facility.

Toynbee Hall became the inspiration for a generation of American reformers interested in bridging the gap between social classes. Robert Woods, who would become head resident at Boston's South End (formerly Andover) House, Jane Addams and Ellen Gates Starr of Hull House, and Vida Scudder all visited Toynbee Hall. Scudder heard Ruskin lecture when she was at Oxford in 1884. At a Smith College reunion in 1887 Scudder proposed the idea of a College Settlement to be located in New York City. Three years later she established the College Settlements Association. By 1892 there were five American settlement houses: Boston's Andover House and New York City's Neighborhood Guild were established by men, and Hull House, the CSA College Settlement in New York, and the St. Mary's Street CSA settlement in Philadelphia by women (Scudder 1892). Settlement houses founded and staffed by women soon outnumbered men's. Thus was the English model of the male university settlement effectively transformed to a female equivalent in America (Davis 1967; Weiner 1994).

John Ruskin and Toynbee Hall "kindled the flame of social passion" in Vida Scudder. Together with other graduates from distinguished women's colleges, Scudder rented a tenement building in 1889 at 95 Rivington

Street on the Lower East Side, named it the College Settlement, and appointed CSA member Jean Fine as its head worker. Their first visitor was supposedly a policeman who mistook them for prostitutes. The local press described their arrival in the neighborhood as "Seven Lilies... dropped in the mud" (Crocker 1992, 21; Davis 1967, 10, 11; Woods and Kennedy [1911] 1970, 2).

The College Settlements Association was formally organized in 1890 with chapters at Barnard, Bryn Mawr, Bucknell, Cornell, Elmira, Mount Holyoke, Packer, Radcliffe, Smith, Swarthmore, Vassar, and Wellesley. The organization's goals were to establish, support, and exercise general control over settlements, train women for social service, and accomplish educational work of a broad scope. By 1911 the CSA was making annual appropriations to the College Settlement in New York, the College Settlement of Philadelphia, Denison House of Boston, and Locust Point Settlement in Baltimore (based on dues and donations from members). Members of the CSA differed in religious faith but believed "that the higher life must draw joyfully close to the lower before the lower can be uplifted" (Scudder Papers, n.d.).

The first annual meeting of the CSA took place on May 12, 1890, at the Rivington Street Settlement. Graduates of Smith, Wellesley, Vassar, and Bryn Mawr served on the original electoral board with two noncollegiate members. Business items included amending Article III of the Constitution by substituting "person" for "woman" (in regard to qualifications for membership); deciding to allow electors to invite visitors to the settlement on Wednesday evenings, Sunday afternoons, and Fridays; and referring to the executive committee the "question of the amount of publicity desirable through the press" (Settlements File 1890).

The CSA's first annual report was filled with activities of the New York College Settlement. Sixteen women lived at 95 Rivington Street as resident workers during its first year of operation. They paid $6.00 per week in board and performed part of the housework to make the house self-supporting. Length of stay varied from one to eleven months, with an average of seven women in residence at any one time. The woman who stayed longest was Dr. C. F. Hamilton, a physician who healed sick neighbors and found work for those whose illness had cost them their jobs (Settlements File, 1890).[9]

Living as a volunteer at the College Settlement was like living in a college dormitory. The communal arrangements freed women from family responsibilities and provided safety, while the slum neighborhood provided a larger view of life. The CSA recognized the necessity for a delicate balance between such traditional and progressive roles for women. Vida Scudder emphasized this function in an article titled "The Relation of College Women to Social Need," presented to the Association of Collegiate Alumnae in 1890. Scudder identified settlements as a new vocation for women:

> It renders suitable, reasonable, and comparatively easy a mode of life which many women are most desirous of taking up, but upon which it would not be wise for them to enter singly. That a new vocation for our educated girls is sorely needed, can be doubted by no one who realizes the vast pressure on the teacher's profession from the crowds of new teachers who enter the ranks every year. And this new vocation thus offered is one . . . for which college women are quite peculiarly equipped, and which is thoroughly in line with the best effort of the times. (Scudder 1890, 13)

The CSA published a brochure for college undergraduates and alumnae explaining "What It Means to Be a Member of the College Settlements Association" (primarily, that "you claim your share of responsibility for bettering modern social conditions") and a fundraising pamphlet titled "What does the College Settlements Association mean to this little mother and to YOU?" with a picture of an immigrant child named Nicolina holding younger brothers and sisters. The tract illustrated how CSA membership fees of $5.00 per year were distributed among the four CSA Settlements to provide child care, classes, baths, and playgrounds (Settlements File, n.d.) (see figure 1.6).

In 1892 the CSA established two fellowships of $300 each to train promising women in social work. Scudder offered one of them to a Wellesley graduate, Sophonisba Breckinridge, who had returned home to care for her family after her mother's death. When Breckinridge asked her father's permission to accept the fellowship in New York City, he discouraged her with the observation that "Bowery boys can be found everywhere." She complied with his wishes and declined Scudder's offer. This missed opportunity was only a temporary setback for Breckinridge, however. She eventually attended the University of Chicago and founded (with Edith Abbott) the university's first graduate school of social work, the School of Social Service Administration (Fitzpatrick 1990, xii, 10). Breckinridge eventually wrote a research monograph titled

Women in the Twentieth Century: A Study Of Their Political, Social, and Economic Activities (1933).

The Russell Sage Foundation became a sponsor of CSA social investigations and the stipends were eventually raised to $400 each for three fellowships. Recipients of fellowships conducted studies of "occupations of girls who drop out of school in the grammar grades," the hours of working women, the illegal employment of school children, factory conditions, and occupational diseases and accidents (Woods and Kennedy [1911] 1970, 2, 3). Conditions of the training fellowships included a nine-month residence in one of the college settlements in New York, Philadelphia, Boston, or Baltimore; attendance at the local School of Philanthropy or Social Work; and field work in economics or sociology supervised by the head worker (Scudder Papers, n.d.; Woods and Kennedy [1911] 1970, 2).

Working within appropriately gendered expectations of the day, the settlement movement carved out a temporary niche for middle-class unmarried women. Nearly all settlement workers had attended college and more than one-half had attended graduate school, compared with only about one percent of all women nationally with college degrees.[10] The average length of stay in a settlement house was three years (Davis 1967, 33–39; Solomon 1985). Settlement houses provided the perfect place for young, single, highly educated women between school and marriage. According to Scudder, "There is a need for an instrument of social service, a center of social experience, which shall afford to people still on journey the opportunities they need for shaping conviction and discovering vocation" (Scudder 1915, 34).

This new group of demographically marginal women — highly educated and "sexually unemployed" (Davis 1967, 32) — created a threat to social order perhaps as serious as that of European immigrants. Female settlement workers were out of place. CSA women defied social conventions by choosing to live in poor neighborhoods instead of the middle-class homes to which they were entitled. They both rejected and criticized the system that had produced them at the same time they tried to incorporate immigrants into that system.

Scudder compared the settlement movement with medieval chivalry:

> The old impulse of knighthood shows itself, I think, in the new impulse
> to succor the oppressed, the battle against the monsters of crime,
> suffering, and industrial injustice. These monsters are fully as hard to

cope with as the monsters were of old; and if we want distressed damsels to succor, we can find plenty of them seized and enslaved in the tyranny of starvation wages. The economic emancipation of women is as great a cause as ever could have been fought for in past centuries. (Scudder 1896)

It is interesting that Scudder used this analogy when describing settlement work, because settlement houses shared similarities with the medieval *beguinage*. The beguinage was a communal living arrangement in which unmarried women established economic self-sufficiency through collective work; they were connected informally in an urban network throughout Europe. The beguinage developed as a secular institution comparable to the convent for women when the Crusades and monasteries created a shortage of men. As with many settlement houses, a wealthy benefactor often donated a city house to establish a beguinage (McDonell 1969, 69; Mizruchi 1983; Spain 1995).

Women known as Beguines occupied a social space somewhere between sacred and secular. Their liminal status gave Beguines independence otherwise impossible in medieval culture, just as settlement workers acquired atypical freedom for women of their era. Confusion existed about the position of both types of women. In 1274 a monk referred to the Beguines as women "whom we have no idea what to call, ordinary women or nuns, because they live neither in the world nor out of it" (Neel 1989, 323; Spain 1995). People were not sure what to call settlement workers either, since settlement houses allowed women to have both active public lives and well-nurtured private lives simultaneously (Matthews 1992). This ambivalence was reflected by a lack of consensus about whether settlement workers were reformers, missionaries, or municipal housekeepers. Their battles against poverty qualified them as all three.

Scudder seemed to be losing heart for the fight by 1909 when Jane Addams sent her a copy of her recently completed *Spirit of Youth*. Scudder praised the book, but lamented,

I rebuke myself, I grow heavy of heart as the years pass on, "save the children" was our cry when the settlements started twenty years ago. Those children are men and women now, fathers and mothers and still we raise the same cry and hold the new generation under the same stupid and criminal conditions as the old. How long, O Lord how long. (Davis 1973, 155)

It may have been Jane Addams's prodigious staying power in the face of such adversity that propelled her, rather than Scudder, to the forefront of the settlement movement.

Members of the YWCA, NACW, and The Salvation Army depended on familial imagery to justify their interaction with strangers: their clients were "daughters," "sisters," or "brothers." Although settlement workers abandoned the familial metaphor, they used domestic imagery to their advantage. Kitchens and cooking took on new significance as avenues of assimilation for immigrants. For example, *The Settlement Cook Book,* first published in Milwaukee in 1901, was compiled to help immigrant women "learn about American life and American ways" by reducing the time they spent copying recipes during cooking classes. *The Settlement Cook Book* included more than just recipes, though. It also had chapters on nutritional needs for all members of the family, directions for entertaining (such as how to set and clear the table properly), and tips on marketing, household management, and cleanliness (a stain removal chart appeared on pp. 648–49, right before the index) (Settlement Cook Book Company [1901] 1976).

African American Neighbors

The "Great Migration" of southern rural blacks to northeastern and midwestern cities began as the settlement movement was waning. Historian Allen Davis (1967) identifies the major settlement-house era as 1890 to 1914, while blacks did not begin competing with European immigrants for jobs and housing in the largest cities until after 1910. Demographic, political, and economic trends intersected with a discriminatory Jim Crow culture to reduce the benefits of settlement houses for blacks compared with those for European immigrants.

Settlement workers were well aware of the needs of newly arriving blacks. In 1905 a leading journal of philanthropy, *Charities* (later called *The Survey*), devoted an entire issue to "the negro city" that dealt with migration, shrinking industrial opportunities, and the lack of social services (Lasch-Quinn 1993, 12). Jane Addams, Louise deKoven Bowen, Mary White Ovington, and Frances Kellor were among settlement leaders who addressed the subject of race. Addams warned in 1911 that "a strong race antagonism is asserting itself." That same year Ovington published *Half a Man: The Status of the Negro in New York* and Bowen published *Colored People of Chicago* in 1913. Addams and Ovington were founding members of the National Association for the Advancement of Colored People in 1910 and contributed regularly to the black journals *The Crisis* and *Opportunity* (Lasch-Quinn 1993, 13, 14; Trolander 1975, 25).

Reformers' efforts on behalf of blacks often resulted in segregated facilities. Hull House benefactors helped start the black Wendell Phillips Settlement and the integrated Frederick Douglass Center, while their own summer club and cooperative boarding house for working girls (the Jane Club) were open only to whites during the first decades of the twentieth century. These inconsistencies led Bowen to observe that the few black women who attended Hull House functions "were not always received warmly" and that "the settlement seemed unwilling to come to grips with the 'Negro problem' in its own environs, yet Hull House was willing to be concerned with the same 'problem' elsewhere in the city" (Lasch-Quinn 1993, 15, 29).[11]

Other black settlement houses that existed at the end of the nineteenth century as branches of already established white settlements were Robert Gould Shaw House in Boston (a spinoff from South End House) and the Stillman Branch of New York's Henry Street Settlement. Others were opened specifically for blacks, but by whites or with white financing, and merely intensified racial segregation (Philpott 1978). Less common were settlement houses started by and for blacks, such as Janie Porter Barrett's Locust Street Settlement in Hampton, Virginia, and Lugenia Burns Hope's Neighborhood Union in Atlanta.

The Godman Guild House in Columbus, Ohio, introduced temporal segregation of its facilities as a way of reconciling black demand with white discrimination. Opened in 1898 in an immigrant factory neighborhood called Flytown, Godman Guild workers helped establish a library, the first free public bath and public gym, a kindergarten, playground, infant clinic, and summer camps. Blacks began moving into Flytown in the 1910s and by 1919 the director of Godman Guild instituted strict racial segregation of the facilities: blacks and whites could use the house on alternate days for classes, clubs, and teams; Sundays were open to both races; but the summer club was for whites only. Clinics, the employment bureau, and some other services were unrestricted (Lasch-Quinn 1993, 25).

Black settlement workers were conscious of their economic disadvantages relative to white settlements. Black organizations were more likely to depend on the accumulation of small sums from many poor blacks than on the philanthropic largess of a wealthy few. The 1915 annual report of the executive board of the Baptist Woman's Convention compared their efforts to those of Jane Addams:

> Do you wonder how Jane Addams built up that great Hull House? She has done it because her people have invested faith, money, and lives in it in response to her appeals. It is not large gifts that we need, but a large number of givers. We can do as much with small gifts from a large number of givers as Miss Jane Addams has done with large gifts from a small number of givers. (Higginbotham 1993, 175)

Common Goals, Different Paths

From their evangelical beginnings, the YWCA and NACW evolved into secular organizations "of women, for women" that simultaneously taught single working-class women *and* middle-class women volunteers how to fend for themselves in the city. The YWCA and NACW contributed significantly to the urban landscape through their boarding houses and vocational schools. In tribute to its importance, the YWCA was represented at the design event of the nineteenth century — the Columbian Exposition of 1893. (Ironically, the NACW was formed partially in response to the exclusion of black women from that same event.)

First for American-born girls, and eventually for immigrants, the YWCA tried to provide all the comforts of a middle-class home. The YWCA also offered concerts, classes, libraries, and summer retreats to compete with the dance halls and nickel movies that tempted young women. By the beginning of the twentieth century YWCA boarding houses included swimming pools, movies, soda fountains, and facilities for entertaining young men (Peiss 1986, 164–67; Wilson [1916] 1987, 100, 281–85).

Immigrant women received special attention from the YWCA after the turn of the century. Emissaries worked the docks to save hundreds of girls who were vulnerable because they spoke no English. The YWCA then taught them to speak and act like urban Americans. The YWCA formed the International Institute in New York City in 1910 to develop leadership skills and self-governing clubs among immigrant girls.

The NACW had a similar agenda for assimilating rural black women to the city, with an emphasis on cleanliness rather than the English language. The first Phillis Wheatley Home taught personal hygiene and neatness in addition to housekeeping skills. While the YWCA and NACW were providing shelter for women newcomers to the city, they were also laying the foundations for the emerging professions of sociology, social work, and city planning. Leaders defined their mission in sociological terms, conducted research, and took the kind of action that would soon be called social work. In their concern for housing the poor, for example, the YWCA and NACW preceded urban planners' interest in housing reform by sixty years (Birch 1989, 1994). A report from the second national conference of the YWCA in 1873 identified the organization's goal as "helping to solve the problem in social science, as to how to bridge the gulf that divides the favored from the less fortunate" (Sims 1936, 18, 19). These organizations were equally committed to analysis *and* action.

The Salvation Army's efforts to assimilate newcomers to the city differed in one important way from those of the YWCA and NACW: women of The Salvation Army took to the streets in search of the "floating population," while members of the YWCA and NACW conducted most of their work with women who came to them. The YWCA's and NACW's work of assimilation took place primarily in their own boarding houses and vocational schools, with trips to railroad stations and docks a smaller part of their mission. By contrast, Slum Sisters spent most of their time visiting homes, saloons, and the streets.

The Salvation Army did for the poorest urban men and women what the YWCA and NACW did for young single women: it tried to convert them to mainstream American Protestant religion, provided them with temporary shelter, and offered opportunities to meet others and learn how to survive in the city. Throughout its history The Salvation Army was one of "a large body of earnest evangelicals who entered the slums because of their concern for the souls of men and women" (Magnuson 1977, ix).

The Salvation Army and the YWCA shared the philosophy that dignity was preserved and character strengthened when the recipient of a service paid a nominal charge. Both organizations also tried to maintain self-supporting hotels that were minimally dependent on charitable contributions. Although neither was completely successful in this regard, the goal drove their fee structures and fundraising efforts.

Without redemptive places, living conditions in cities at the turn of the century would have overwhelmed newcomers arriving from farms, small towns, and foreign countries. Women volunteers in the YWCA,

NACW, CSA, and The Salvation Army provided networks of shelter that helped newcomers make the required transitions. At the same time, redemptive places served as abeyance structures that helped establish social order out of a chaotic flood of people surging into cities. Voluntary associations also opened productive outlets for a growing number of well-educated middle-class women. Bringing volunteers and their clientele into contact spatially made redemptive places an important link in the transformation of the social and physical fabric of cities.

II
Redemptive Places

CHAPTER FIVE

New York City Headquarters, Smaller City Branches

Edna St. Vincent Millay arrived in New York City at the absolute height of foreign immigration. In 1913, and again in 1914, 1.2 million immigrants entered the United States. So many earlier immigrants had disembarked in New York City, and stayed there, that 40 percent of the city's population was foreign-born in 1910. The Lower East Side, the district Jacob Riis immortalized in photographs and essays in *How the Other Half Lives* (1890), was their primary destination (U.S. Department of Justice 1997, 25; Ward 1971).

Voluntary associations established headquarters in New York City for the same reason immigrants stayed: it was the financial and cultural center of America. The consolidated YWCA set up its main offices in Manhattan, home of newly elected president Grace Dodge. The Salvation Army moved its headquarters to nearby Brooklyn (an independent city) in 1882, and the CSA opened its first settlement house on Rivington Street in the Lower East Side in 1889. Only the NACW established headquarters outside New York (in Washington, D.C.).

Their main offices may have been in New York, but the real strength of these organizations lay in their presence in smaller cities across the country. The Salvation Army and the YWCA had the greatest number of branches. Since administration was so decentralized, most affiliates operated independently. The CSA directly sponsored settlements in only three other cities in addition to the one in New York City (Baltimore, Boston, and Philadelphia), but its mission was replicated by autonomous settlements in dozens of other cities. The NACW affiliate in New York

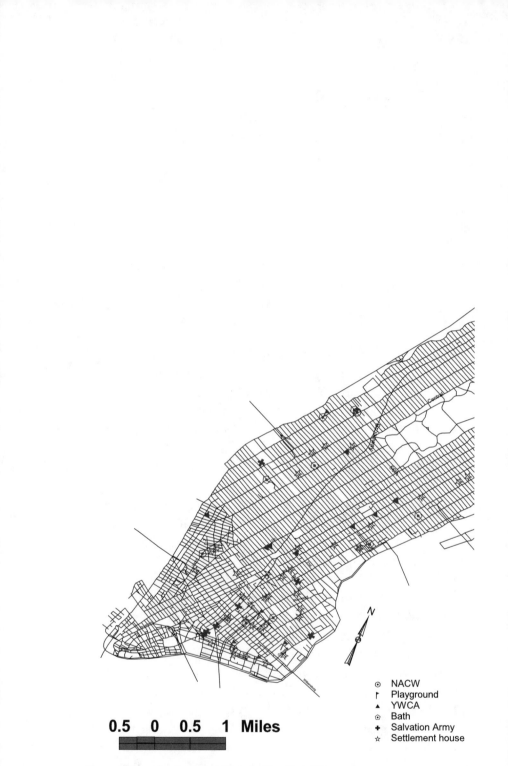

0.5 0 0.5 1 Miles

	NACW
⌐	Playground
▲	YWCA
⊚	Bath
✚	Salvation Army
☆	Settlement house

Map 5.1. Map of redemptive places in New York City, c. 1915.

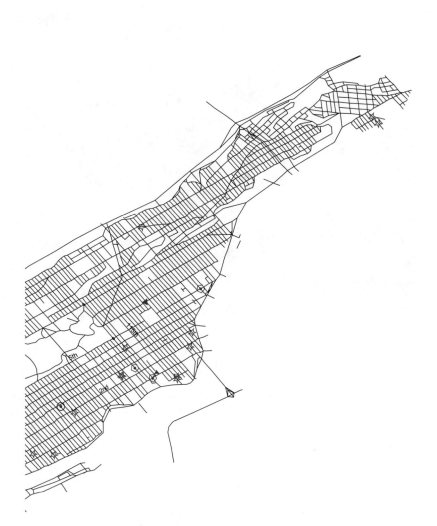

Map 5.1. *Continued.*

Figure 5.1. Aerial view of New York City, 1907. (Courtesy Library of Congress, 701585.)

City, the White Rose Mission, was the precursor to similar redemptive places for blacks in Cleveland and in Washington, D.C.

New York City

Two significant events related to parks and playgrounds occurred in New York City before the Civil War. In 1857 a group of lawyers and business-men announced a public competition for the design of a grand capital investment, Central Park. That same year a state legislative committee inquiring into tenement conditions recommended the construction of a playground for poor children (Rainwater 1922, 60; Schuyler 1986).

Frederick Law Olmsted and Calvert Vaux won the Central Park contest with their Greensward plan. Olmsted and Vaux started work in 1858 and the first stage of the park was completed by 1863. A tremendous amount of labor transformed the 840 acres of barren lowlands in rocky central Manhattan into the park admired for its "natural" beauty. The site was chosen partially because the location was less desirable than the water-front for commercial purposes and because its rough topography made it too expensive to incorporate into the rectangular street grid. Its de-velopment challenged even Olmsted, who found the site "filthy, squalid, and disgusting." His corps of workmen blasted tons of rock, moved cartloads of dirt, installed miles of underground drainage pipes, turned swamps into lakes, and planted thousands of trees. The entire effort cost over $10 million (Rosenzweig and Blackmar 1992, 18).

In contrast, the playground failed to materialize for more than forty years despite numerous subsequent commissions and legislation. Because playgrounds were small-scale rather than major capital projects, their political payoff was minor compared with Central Park's. In 1887 the state legislature authorized New York City to spend $1 million a year for "small parks." The two-and-one-half-acre Mulberry Bend was chosen as a site, but it took years to acquire, condemn, and raze the property. The site then sat empty for several more years. It was still barren when photojournalist Jacob Riis reported that he "came upon a couple of youngsters in a Mulberry Street yard . . . that were chalking on the fence their first lesson in 'writin'. And this is what they wrote: 'Keeb of te Grass.' They had it by heart, for there was not, I verily believe, a green sod within a quarter of a mile" (Riis [1890] 1957, 137). By the time Mulberry Bend Park finally opened in 1897, a field of grass had replaced the congested street (Alland 1993, 208–10; Rainwater 1922, 61–63; Zueblin 1902, 276–80).

Figure 5.2. Mulberry Bend in New York City, c. 1898. (*The Jacob A. Riis Collection*, 114. Courtesy The Museum of the City of New York.)

Seward Park took almost as much time to complete. Legislation in 1895 provided for at least two parks on the lower East Side to be finished as public playgrounds (Zueblin 1902, 281). Three acres of land were acquired for $1.8 million, land that contained five- and six-story tenement houses, which were demolished in 1898. Public funds soon ran out, but women in voluntary associations formed the Outdoor Recreation League to insure the playground opened. Plans for Seward Park (at Canal, Hester, Suffolk, and Division Streets) were ambitious. The facilities were to include a pavilion 138 by 50 feet in size, comfort stations, twenty-one baths for women and thirty for men, a cellar, and a playground with "merry-go-rounds or giant strides...teeter ladders...captive tennis balls...sand courts...and croquet sets" (Rainwater 1922, 78).

Residents of the neighborhood made thousands of contributions ranging from one to five cents each toward maintenance of the playground. The league provided equipment for children of "different ages, strength, sizes, and sexes;...sandbins for the children; and...good collections of domestic animals, common vegetables, and cereals" (Zueblin 1902,

Figure 5.3. Mulberry Bend Park, New York City, no date. (*The Jacob A. Riis Collection.* Courtesy The Museum of the City of New York.)

282). By 1903 Seward Park contained a stadium, gymnasium, play equipment, and public baths (Rainwater 1922, 63, 78). The histories of Seward Park and Mulberry Bend Park illustrate the difficulty of translating volunteer efforts into the same tangible results that the Central Park competition produced.

Another successful playground sponsored by the Outdoor Recreation League was Hamilton Fish Park at the intersection of Houston, Stanton, and Sheriff Streets.[1] Large by the standards of the day, it consisted of almost four acres. The 1902 annual report of New York's Department of Parks listed their plans for this recently acquired space to include "a running track, kindergarten, an ornamental iron fence around the playgrounds and a pipe iron fence around the lawns, the asphalting of the plaza in front of the building, remodeling of the public comfort station . . . and the laying out of a gymnasium and equipment of the same with parallel bars, swinging rings, vaulting horses, and other apparatus" (Rainwater 1922, 75).

In addition to their support for playgrounds, Jacob Riis and his disciples actively campaigned for municipal baths. New York's Association for Improving the Condition of the Poor commissioned a small bath-

Figure 5.4. Hamilton Fish Park playground, New York City, c. 1900. (Courtesy Library of Congress, LCB2-675-1.)

house with twenty-five showers and five tubs for the Lower East Side. In 1898 a mass meeting of Lower East Side residents at the University Settlement demanded that the mayor build more baths in compliance with the 1895 mandatory bath law. Years later, in midtown Manhattan about three hundred persons attended a West Side Neighborhood House meeting to urge the city to build a municipal bath on West Fiftieth Street (Williams 1991, 52, 58, 133). A few more charitable organizations built public baths during the 1890s, but it was not until water pollution forced the closure of floating baths in the East and Hudson Rivers around 1900 that the city seriously pursued the construction of public baths (Stern, Gilmartin, and Massengale 1983, 138).

Under the leadership of Dr. Simon Baruch, the "father of the public bath movement in the United States," New York City built nineteen baths in Manhattan by 1915; Brooklyn had six and the Bronx had one. They were so successful that committees from other cities visited New York before building their own public baths. New York City's baths were huge, with one hundred showers (and fewer tubs). They were modeled on Roman public baths with classical pilasters, columns, arches, and cornices. Construction materials included terra cotta, copper, and marble in addition to brick, with facades of ornamental ironwork and white Italian marble and granite. Two of the most imposing baths were the Milbank Memorial Bath (donated by Borden Condensed Milk Company heiress Elizabeth Milbank Anderson) built for $140,000 in 1904 to serve three thousand bathers daily, and the neo-Roman East Twenty-third Street Bath, built in 1908 for $225,000 by the architectural firm of Aiken and Brunner (Williams 1991, chapter 3).[2] Smaller cities seldom had the need or the resources to build baths as elaborate as New York's, but the ideals behind the buildings were quickly exported across the country.

The College Settlements Association

The Lower East Side was a logical choice for the first settlement house founded by the CSA. The neighborhood was home to thousands of Jewish and Roman Catholic immigrants when the College Settlement opened its doors at 95 Rivington Street in 1889. A resident observed in retrospect that it was "a wretched house" in a street that was a "blur of haunting filth." CSA founder Vida Scudder was more enthusiastic. She described the location as "unusually healthful," the house as "spacious and solidly built." The CSA moved in and converted the "vermin-rid and sin-be-

Figure 5.5. The College Settlement at 95 Rivington Street, 1889–1914. (Courtesy Sophia Smith Collection, Smith College, Northampton, Mass.)

grimed" building into a "happy house of vision" — "a vision of a city coming down from Heaven among the crowded pushcarts in the street" (Converse n.d.; Scudder Papers n.d.).

Residents hoped to implement their vision through a belief in the "power of friendship to shape character. The friend who lives 'around the corner,' next to the saloon, is obviously a potent influence. The residents of the College Settlement are the neighbors and friends of those about them, and seek through personal relations to give of the best that has been given to them." Although their goal was to make a long-term investment in the neighborhood, most residents stayed at Rivington Street only a short time. During the first year of operation, four permanent workers stayed all year, but three workers stayed only two to four months. Scudder was sufficiently unhappy with this turnover to consider requiring a three-month minimum residency for future applicants (Scudder and Hazard 1890).

Figure 5.6. Rivington Street interior, 1903. (Photographer unknown. Courtesy
Sophia Smith Collection, Smith College, Northampton, Mass.)

The College Settlement included a public bath in the basement and
a library with one thousand circulating volumes on the first floor; both
were eventually incorporated into the city's systems. The playground consisted of a paved backyard with "scups" (Dutch for swings) and a pile of
sand; it was open only on Saturdays. Women and children stood in line
to take tub baths for ten cents each. A considerable amount of socializing
occurred as bathers waited. During the summer an average of thirty-
five women a day talked with the housekeeper, and with each other, about
how to prepare meals, find jobs, and educate their children. Girls' clubs,
boys' clubs, and a club for older women all held meetings at the settlement. A Penny Provident Bank managed by the Charity Organization
Society accepted deposits on library night to teach children the value
of saving money (Settlements File 1890; Scudder and Hazard 1890).

The College Settlement provided a nursery, kindergarten, and music
school for youngsters; night classes were available for adults trying to
learn English. Residents of the house worked to improve the neighborhood by joining agencies, conducting studies of housing and sanitary
conditions, and educating the public about local conditions. Two former residents reminisced that the College Settlement had "offered an
incubating temperature to new and untried methods of furthering pub-

Figure 5.7. Library day at Rivington Street, c. 1900. From *Denison House College Settlement, Report for 1900*. (Courtesy Sophia Smith Collection, Smith College, Northampton, Mass.)

lic welfare" and that it had "assisted in the birth and rearing of sociological ideas which have gradually made over city life in America" (Irwin and Hopkins 1927).

By 1900 the College Settlement was attracting residents who stayed longer than they had in its first year of operation. Nearly all of the sixteen residents stayed from October to June, which was considered permanent since many volunteers took summer vacations or supervised neighborhood children at the settlement's summer home in Mount Ivy, New York. Rented rooms in a nearby tenement accommodated four of the residents. They learned first-hand about the conditions their neighbors endured every day: small, drafty windows that opened onto airshafts and conveyed the noise of babies crying all night. The rooms were so dark the gas lights had to be lit at three o'clock in the afternoon. The College Settlement residents lasted only seven months before pronouncing that "a house of this type was not a fit habitation for any one." They found it stifling, even though their six rooms would typically have housed two families who also cooked and washed in them (which the CSA workers did at the settlement) (Settlements File 1900).

The College Settlement outgrew its facilities quickly. In 1900 the kindergarten, music, and cooking schools had to turn away children. The music and cooking schools enrolled ninety students each. The kindergarten accommodated forty-eight children. Twenty boys' and girls' clubs counted between ten and thirty members at their weekly meetings, and eight clubs for adults had a combined membership of one hundred men and women. The College Settlement also cooperated with the Charity Organization Society to offset the worst problems in the neighborhood. The CSA took pride that the "Settlement resident is able, through the social activities of the house, to offer to the discouraged and discouraging applicants for relief a little brighter outlook and a respite from trouble" (Settlements File 1900, 6).

Two friends of the CSA started another settlement house in New York City that filled a special niche. In 1893 Lillian Wald and Mary Brewster opened Henry Street Settlement in the Lower East Side after graduating from nursing school. They lived initially with residents of the College Settlement on Rivington Street, then found rented rooms on Jefferson Street. Demand for home nursing multiplied so rapidly that they moved to 265 Henry Street in 1895 and eventually expanded to three three-story Federal-style homes at 299–301 Henry Street in 1905 (Woods and Kennedy [1911] 1970, 205).

The Henry Street, or Nurses', Settlement concentrated on delivering home health care, providing convalescent homes, treating tuberculosis, inspecting children in public schools, and educating mothers about the importance of pure milk and infant care. During the summer of 1900 the Nurses' Settlement sponsored a nurse in residence at the College Settlement on Rivington Street. Nurses used a variety of avenues to reach their clients, including the occasional roof-top shortcut (Wald 1915, 62).

Henry Street also provided meeting places for social events like weddings and for political organizations like the Women's Trade Union League. By 1911 Henry Street Settlement had branches on 232 East Seventy-ninth Street, in the Bronx, and the Stillman Branch for Colored People at 205 West Sixtieth Street. Forty-one women and five men were in residence at the Henry Street location and another seventy-seven women and twenty-three men volunteered their services (Woods and Kennedy [1911] 1970, 207–10).

The Henry Street Settlement, like the College Settlement, placed high priority on play space for children. Lillian Wald's memoir, *The House on Henry Street*, devoted a full chapter to the benefits of playgrounds for "the little hyphenated Americans [who] carry on their shoulders our

Figure 5.8. A visiting nurse from the Henry Street Settlement takes a shortcut over tenement roofs. (From Lillian Wald, *The House on Henry Street* [New York: Henry Holt and Company, 1915].)

hopes of a finer, more democratic America." At the same time Wald acknowledged the importance of mutual learning, hoping that "the good in their old-world traditions and culture shall be mingled with the best that lies within our new-world ideals" (Wald 1915, 66).

The Salvation Army

While the CSA tried to improve neighborhoods by crossing class boundaries, The Salvation Army tried to save transient men and women from sin and starvation. When The Salvation Army moved its headquarters from Philadelphia to Brooklyn in 1882, it joined prominent ministers like Henry Ward Beecher and T. DeWitt Talmadge in the "City of Churches" (Winston 1999, 32).[3] The new Brooklyn address conveyed more respectability than many of their earlier efforts. Some of The Salvation Army's first New York City meetings were held at the infamous Five Points Mission, site of Phoebe Palmer's revivalist work and object of Charles Dickens's scurrilous comments. Newspaper reporters had been aghast at the proceedings. The *New York Herald* reported,

A more motley, vice-smitten, pestilence-breeding congregation could seldom be found in a house of worship. There were Negroes, dancing girls, prostitutes and station-house tramps sandwiched between well-dressed visitors who had sauntered in out of curiosity.... The floors were as clean as the deck of a man-of-war, but in a few minutes they were frescoed with tobacco juice, the stench became overpowering, and a yellow-fever pest house could not have been less attractive.... But The Salvation Army did not seem to mind the air, and the ladies knelt on the floor and took turns in praying. (Chesham 1965, 59)

Ballington and Maud Booth moved The Salvation Army headquarters to Fourteenth Street in New York City in 1895. They constructed an elaborate nine-story fortress that the *New York Times* described as a "cross between a skyscraping office building and an armory." The building attracted plenty of attention with its turrets, tower, and huge wooden door surrounded by stone. Opening ceremonies were accompanied by a parade and a display of white and red electric lights outlining the Army's logo. The Salvation Army loudly announced its presence in the city with this edifice. According to historian Diane Winston, "While the Army's spiritual center, the cathedral of the open air, was an invisible canopy covering the entire city, its strategic base, the Fourteenth Street Headquarters, resembled a mighty fortress, an apt materialization of God's kingdom" (Winston 1999, 57).

The Fourteenth Street Headquarters represented the ceremonial side of The Salvation Army's influence on the urban landscape. More typical were the unassuming places that seldom elicited comment, like the hundreds of properties listed in the Army's historical record, the *Disposition of Forces*. These official sources are inevitably incomplete because the shelters changed location every few weeks or months depending on what happened with the rent or the officers in charge. It is impossible, therefore, to reconstruct all the properties occupied by The Salvation Army at the turn of the century due to the frantic pace of openings and closings (McKinley 1986, 39).

For institutions in New York City, however, the data are rich. The *Disposition of Forces* for March 1898 listed the Dry Dock at 118 Avenue D on the Lower East Side, the "Workingmen's Hotel," and a Salvage Brigade at 26 Cherry Street ("Social Wing" 1898). The Dry Dock had been built in 1896 to celebrate the Army's new era of social service. Beds for one

Figure 5.9. The Salvation Army Headquarters on Fourteenth Street in New York City, 1895. (Courtesy The Salvation Army National Archives and Research Center, Alexandria, Va.)

hundred men filled the top three floors of a four-story building; the street floor was occupied by a wood-veneering business. The Workingmen's Hotel was even larger. It had room for 140 guests. Beds rented for five, ten, or fifteen cents (the higher prices for single beds), reflecting the Army's "ladder principle" of social mobility within the hotel (McKinley 1986, 36, 37).

Figure 5.10. The Memorial (Workingmen's) Hotel at 21 Bowery, New York City, c. 1900. (Courtesy The Salvation Army National Archives and Research Center, Alexandria, Va.)

The December 1900 *Disposition of Forces* recorded, in addition to the Workingmen's and Dry Dock Hotels, the Ardmore Hotel for 170 men at 83 Bowery and a Women's Shelter at 243 Bowery that included a food depot. In the interim a food depot had been added to the Dry Dock; the Salvage Brigade on Cherry Street had disappeared. The January 1905 *Disposition of Forces* included "A. Hotel" (later called the "Braveman") at 18 Chatham Square for 437 guests in addition to the Dry Dock, Ard-

Figure 5.11. Commander Evangeline Booth of The Salvation Army with William Peart and Edward Justus Parker in front of Memorial Hotel, 1912. (Courtesy The Salvation Army National Archives and Research Center, Alexandria, Va.)

more, and Workingmen's Hotels ("Department of the Metropolis" 1905; "Social Wing" 1900).

The Salvation Army's first women's shelter was opened in rented quarters on Bayard Street in the Bowery by Frederick and Emma Booth-Tucker in 1896. "Women sleeping in hallways and on steps on the Bowery, looking dirty, ragged, neglected and alone" were invited to sleep free of charge in the building. The home was soon moved to 243 Bowery Street, where it became "the Glyndon." The building was equipped with "clean comfortable beds in large dormitories" on three floors; prices ranged from ten to fifteen cents per bed: "The higher you went, the cheaper the bed" ("National and Territorial Manual" c. 1940s).

The Glyndon's purpose was to keep women from the streets, and to "strive to instill in each a desire to improve their methods of living.... Great effort was made to lead them to Christ who could break every fetter, and set the prisoner free." Salvation Army female officers were responsible for this task. Ensign Bisbie was the first woman in charge of

Figure 5.12. The Dry Dock Hotel at 118 Avenue D on the Lower East Side, c. 1900. (Courtesy The Salvation Army National Archives and Research Center, Alexandria, Va.)

the Glyndon, followed in quick succession by Ensign Rawson and then Adjutant Cordill. Cordill managed the Glyndon for twenty years and "enjoyed every minute of it" despite a clientele that was mostly quarrelsome and drunk ("National and Territorial Manual" c. 1940s).

Figure 5.13. First Women's Shelter in New York City sponsored by The Salvation Army, on Bayard Street between a pool room and a building with a sign in Chinese characters, c. 1900. (Courtesy The Salvation Army National Archives and Research Center, Alexandria, Va.)

Figure 5.14. The Salvation Army Rescue Home at 316 East Fifteenth Street in New York City, c. 1900. (Courtesy The Salvation Army National Archives and Research Center, Alexandria, Va.)

Ensign Rawson was singled out for praise as "very competent and re-liable" in an internal Army memo about facilities. According to this memo, the Glyndon had "never paid before, but we raised the prices a couple of cents so it is doing better than ever now. The place needs paint-ing and kalsomining and I understand that Adjt Welte [of the Braveman] has paint enough to paint this place" ("Brief: Re the Shelters" 1904).[4]

The Glyndon was for respectable women only. Women who had lost their virtue and needed shelter were sent to rescue homes for "fallen or falling women." The first rescue home in New York City was Morris Cottage, opened in 1886. Subsequent homes for unwed mothers or former prostitutes were located in rowhouses and other unobtrusive facilities (MacLachlan n.d.).

A candid internal Salvation Army brief dated March 1904, not identified by author but apparently written by the regional director to his or her supervisor, reveals some of the problems associated with managing all these facilities. The Braveman at 18 Chatham Square, for example, was "a first class hotel in every sense of the word, but it has one weak point—it does not pay. It is a dead loss to the Army. If it wasn't for that hotel, we could run the rest of the shelters with a nice weekly surplus. It runs full now nearly every night, but I do not know what to do to make it pay" ("Brief: Re the Shelters" 1904).

Other shelters helped support the Braveman. The Workingmen's Hotel at 21 Bowery was "a very good paying institution" that was undergoing "a few alterations so we can do away with the double deckers on one of the floors." The Ardmore at 83 Bowery was likewise a profitable venture, and "in every sense of the word an honor to the Army." Captain Henrichson was "competent . . . and thoroughly reliable," keeping the shelter "nice and clean . . . more like the spirit of a home." Apparently Captain Henrichson was being recruited by others, but the supervisor was advised to "insist on keeping him, as you will find it difficult to get another man like him again" ("Brief: Re the Shelters" 1904).

Maintaining presentable surroundings was a challenge often met by sharing resources among shelters. But sometimes even the best efforts at cleanliness were insufficient. The Dry Dock at Avenue D, built with such flourish in 1896, had sunk low by 1904:

> The Dry Dock Hotel, 118 Ave. "D," City, is a dirty house; has dirty guests, and the manager Capt "Scotty" Wallace, is not one of the cleanest himself, but "Scotty" is doing very well, and it pays a nice surplus every week, and I would not change him if I were you, as you would have difficulty in getting any one to go into that dirty place, and "Scotty" wont [sic] do for any cleaner place. ("Brief: Re the Shelters" 1904)

This tolerance for dirt partially explains the response of main-line religion to The Salvation Army. Religious leaders, especially those espousing the Social Gospel, wanted to clean up cities. Much of their ministry emphasized clean bodies, souls, and surroundings. The Salvation Army, by contrast, accepted people as they were. Of the three parts of their motto, "Soup, soap, and salvation," soap was the least important.

The YWCA and NACW

The Salvation Army was the voluntary organization most likely to shelter transients, but the YWCA also created facilities for an increasingly mobile population of women workers. The YWCA first provided lodging for young women in New York City in 1860 at a home on Amity Street. About one-third of the rooms remained empty that year, but demand increased rapidly and required two moves to accommodate more than two hundred residents by 1868. Boarders had to be unmarried, self-supporting or pursuing an education, and respectable (i.e., white members of a Protestant church). Weekly rent was $3.00 to $4.00 in 1865 (Bittar 1979, 19).

The first YWCA hotel strictly for transient guests, the Margaret Louisa, was built in New York City in 1891 at 14 East Sixteenth Street. It included seventy-eight sleeping rooms, several parlors, a laundry, and a restaurant. One room was reserved for the travelers' aid department to process applications for lodging and employment from women referred by YWCAs in other cities. The building was donated and entirely furnished by Margaret Louisa Vanderbilt (Mrs. Elliot F.) Shepard. Room, laundry, and restaurant receipts usually covered expenses well enough to make the enterprise self-supporting under Mrs. Shepard's management (Bittar 1979, 137–40, 224–28; Wilson [1916] 1987, 82).

The Margaret Louisa was intended as a temporary home for women who earned less than $15 a week and had either just arrived in New York or moved from one residence to another. The original four-week limit, however, was lifted in 1911, and many guests stayed for several months. The Margaret Louisa was New York's first cooperative residence for young women. It proved to be financially sound because boarders paid between fifty and ninety cents daily and contributed twelve hours of housekeeping weekly. These rates were moderate for working women, but much higher than clients of The Salvation Army facilities could afford. During 1911 the Margaret Louisa was the only profitable YWCA facility in New York City. That year it admitted 10,350 women boarders, provided 60,000 nights of lodging to transient guests, and served 302,250 meals (Bittar 1979, 53).[5]

Like the residents of the first YWCA lodging house on Amity Street, residents of the Margaret Louisa were required to be self-supporting, and, until 1915, Protestant (it went without saying they had to be white).

The unemployed traveler just passing through New York was charged double the usual rates. Women who dined at the restaurant were welcome regardless of religious affiliation, and the large majority of lunchtime clients were working women from the neighborhood. Demand for hot lunches was so great that the restaurant expanded in 1908. By then 500,000 meals a year were being served, 80 percent of them to nonboarding women from the immediate manufacturing district (Bittar 1979, 145–226).

An earlier effort by millionaire dry goods merchant A. T. Stewart to run a hotel for working women in New York City was met with derision by the women of the YWCA. Stewart opened the "Women's Hotel," "a home for women who support themselves by daily labor" in 1878 on Fourth Avenue. The Women's Hotel charged $6.00 to $7.00 per week (twice what the YWCA charged), rates too high for most women and therefore too high for it to be a financial success. The Women's Hotel was converted to commercial use within two month of its opening (Bittar 1979, 20; Hayden 1981, 168). An article in an 1878 edition of the YWCA's magazine, *Faith and Works*, declared that men were not up to the task of providing suitable housing for working women. Titled "A

Figure 5.15. Postcard of restaurant waiting room in the YWCA's Margaret Louisa Home at 14 East Sixteenth Street in New York City. (Courtesy Archives of the National Board of the YWCA of the USA.)

Gigantic Failure," the article outlined how A. T. Stewart had gone wrong: the fittings and carpets were too elaborate, making working women feel shabby by comparison; the stringent rules were more like an asylum than a home; the residents were not allowed to have pictures, plants, or sewing machines; and, finally, the hotel had been opened in the spring when women were already committed from fall until summer to their boarding houses (Sims 1936, 88).

In 1906, when the American Committee and the International Committee merged into a national YWCA, the National Board established headquarters in New York City and began a trajectory of growth independent of the local New York City YWCA. The first twenty members of the National Board rented rooms 801–815 at the Hotel Montclair, 541 Lexington Avenue at Forty-ninth Street. In 1908 Mrs. William Dodge and Mrs. Russell Sage donated the money to build a new YWCA headquarters at 125 East Twenty-seventh Street. At the same time the National Board rented a five-story private house at No. 3 Gramercy Park as the training school for YWCA professional workers. The school opened with a dean, Bible teacher, eleven students, and equipment shipped from the American Committee's old Training Institute in Chicago (Norris 1981).

The school expanded to another building at Gramercy Court on Twenty-second Street to accommodate an overflow of students. Administrative offices were shifted back and forth between 125 East Twenty-seventh Street and No. 3. Administrators, faculty, students, and maids eventually all moved to a new building at 135 East Fifty-second Street and Lexington Avenue in 1912. That was only a temporary solution to the crowding problem, however. Later that year the YWCA opened the doors of its premier headquarters, training school, and residence at 600 Lexington Avenue. The land was donated by Helen Gould, the building was a gift from Grace Dodge, and the equipment was financed by contributions from hundreds of local YWCAs and their friends (Norris 1981).

The architect of "600 Lexington," Donn Barber, was instructed by the National Board to keep "simplicity and harmony in construction and furnishings" uppermost in mind. Barber designed the administration building to house a reception hall, eighty-nine offices, a large assembly room, exhibit areas, boardroom and committee areas, lounges, restrooms, a library, and a cafeteria to serve 125 people. The Training School was adjacent (entered around the corner from Fifty-second Street)

Figure 5.16. Postcard of National Headquarters and Training School of the YWCA of the USA, New York City, c. 1912. (Courtesy Archives of the National Board of the YWCA of the USA.)

and featured a reception hall, lecture hall, a library with over ten thousand volumes, offices, kitchen, roof garden, study alcoves, and 112 bedrooms. The living room for Training School students featured a fireplace, bookcases, grand piano, mirrored doors, and floor-to-ceiling windows (YWCA of the USA 1982). Although the Training School admitted four black women to attend summer classes in its first year, they were excluded from the residence hall (Jones 1997).

Figure 5.17. Postcard of reference library at the National Headquarters of the YWCA of the USA, New York City, c. 1912. (Courtesy Archives of the National Board of the YWCA of the USA.)

A black woman who emerged as a leader without any help from the YWCA was Victoria Earle Matthews. Matthews was the daughter of Caroline Smith, a slave who escaped from her Georgia owner during the Civil War. When Smith returned after the war to claim her children, she found Victoria and her sister Anna being raised in the former master's home as his children (whom they supposedly were). Smith took her girls to New York City, where Victoria attended Grammar School 48 before dropping out to work as a domestic. At age eighteen she married William Matthews, a carriage driver, and began a career as a freelance writer. She contributed articles to the *New York Times,* the *New York Herald,* and the *Brooklyn Eagle.* Matthews also wrote regularly for black newspapers around the country like the *Boston Advocate,* the *Washington Bee,* and the *Cleveland Gazette* (Cash 1992b).

In 1892 Matthews organized a testimonial for antilynching crusader Ida B. Wells. More than two hundred women attended and raised $700 to support Wells's work. Josephine St. Pierre Ruffin was also at that event. After the meeting Ruffin went back home and founded Boston's Woman's Era Club, Matthews established the Woman's Loyal Union of New York City and Brooklyn, and Ida B. Wells opened a woman's club in Chicago. The Woman's Loyal Union attracted seventy members, among whom were journalists, artists, businesswomen, teachers, and homemakers. Their mission was to promote social and political improvement for the race in schools and jobs. Matthews attended the organizing conference for the NACW and served as an officer from 1897 to 1899 (Cash 1992b).

Although New York's Woman's Loyal Union shares center stage with Boston's Woman's Era Club as one of the first black women's clubs, Matthews became best known as the founder of the White Rose Mission. Matthews visited Booker T. Washington's Tuskegee Institute in Alabama in search of a purpose after the death of her only son. She returned to New York and began to work with poor black families who had been displaced when Italians moved into the Bleecker Street neighborhood. She formed a mother's club that held meetings at various members' homes. At one of these meetings they "prayed especially for a permanent home where we might train the boys and girls and make a social center for them where the only influence would be good and true and pure. Almost immediately Mr. Winthrop Phelps, who owns an apartment house, offered us one of its flats" (Brown [1926] 1988, 211).

The White Rose Mission and Industrial Association opened its doors on February 11, 1897. Initially it conducted settlement work among children. Volunteers offered classes in cooking, sewing, and dressmaking to girls training to go into domestic service. One of the volunteers who taught kindergarten was Alice Ruth Moore, the future wife of the poet Paul Laurence Dunbar. The mission eventually evolved into a home for "the protection of self-supporting colored girls who were coming to New York for the first time" (Best n.d.). One of those girls had been a friend of Mrs. Matthews from the South whom she had agreed to meet at the dock. Mrs. Matthews arrived too late to save her from "one of those unprincipled men who haunted the incoming ships and lured her far away." By the time she was found several days later she was "a perfect wreck of her former self" and had to be sent back home (Brown [1926] 1988, 213).

This experience prompted Matthews to form a travelers' aid department of the mission in 1900. Volunteers met trains and ships bringing "strange Negro girls to New York" from the South, the West Indies, and Africa. These newcomers, many of whom came "wholly unprepared to grapple with the problems of the great city," received advice, a temporary home, and sometimes employment (Best n.d.; Brown [1926] 1988, 214). Mrs. Matthews's reputation for charitable work spread, and "a series of services, like a perfect chain of white roses, was established from Norfolk to New York," thus the name White Rose, which Matthews hoped would inspire girls to lives of purity, goodness, and virtue (Cash 1992b). YWCA president Grace Dodge shared a dedication to travelers' aid and funded Matthews's efforts before founding an independent Travelers' Aid Society in 1907. Dodge supported the work of the White Rose Mission until her death (Best n.d.).

The White Rose Home and Industrial Association for Working Girls and Women (as it became known) had an outstanding library on black history. All the prominent black intellectuals of the day delivered lectures at the Home, including Booker T. Washington, W. E. B. Du Bois, Mary Church Terrell, Hallie Q. Brown, and Paul Laurence Dunbar. The White Rose was funded entirely by voluntary donations. Most of the contributions came from the black community (Du Bois and Adam Clayton Powell Sr.) and from a few white philanthropists (Andrew Carnegie, Grace Dodge, and Seth Low) (Weisenfeld 1996).

Victoria Earle Matthews died from tuberculosis in 1907 at the age of forty-five. Her accomplishments had been so remarkable that she was once described by a newspaper reporter as "a Salvation Army field officer, a College Settlement worker, a missionary, a teacher, a preacher, a Sister of Mercy, all in one, and without being in the least conscious of it" (Brown [1926] 1988, 215). One contribution that she may have been unaware of was her influence in Cleveland, where her early articles for the *Cleveland Gazette* may have inspired Jane Edna Hunter to create the Phillis Wheatley Association. Hunter became known as a pioneer in the settlement movement who "held to her purpose with the same fortitude which characterized Jane Addams" (Hunter 1940, 8).

Smaller Cities

Cleveland, Ohio

Jane Edna Hunter was born on a farm in South Carolina. Her earliest memories were of running around the barn to catch chickens and wring their necks when company came for dinner. Hunter's father died when she was ten years old and she went to work for another family. She held a series of jobs, completing schoolwork when she had the time, and eventually found a job as nursemaid to a wealthy Charleston family. Hunter pursued a career in nursing and earned her degree from the Hampton

Institute's Dixie Hospital and Training School for Nurses in Hampton, Virginia. She met friends in Richmond after graduating and moved with them to Cleveland (Hunter 1940).

Hunter arrived in Cleveland in 1905. Despite her professional training, she had to take a job cleaning downtown office buildings because she could not find work with white physicians. Her search for housing involved trudging "up one dingy street and down another, ending with the acceptance of the least disreputable room" (Hunter 1940, 85). Although Hunter's plight was similar to that of young white women migrating to Cleveland, the YWCA residence that met their needs was closed to black women.

Hunter took various temporary jobs before she was introduced to Dr. H. F. Biggar, John T. Rockefeller's personal physician (Hunter and the doctor's secretary attended the same church). Dr. Biggar referred her to a family on Euclid Avenue, Cleveland's "millionaire's row," and Hunter's financial situation improved dramatically. Her association with Dr. Biggar sent her "stock in the profession bouncing upward." During these prosperous days Hunter's mother died unexpectedly. The loss affected her deeply and gave her the inspiration to establish a home for young African American women seeking work in Cleveland. While riding on a streetcar she imagined she heard the spiritual "Ah Feels Like a Motherless Child"; "and it was borne in upon me that here was my work, my salvation; here was the supreme task for which God had designed me, the one which would take up the discords of my early life and resolve them in harmonious music" (Hunter 1940, 72, 83).[6]

Hunter met with a group of friends in 1911 to put her vision into action. They discussed the housing problems of poor working women, trading stories of their own experiences about the lack of places to entertain friends or cook a meal. The women agreed they would have to solve the problem themselves since white women would not understand the problems faced by hundreds of girls who lived in squalid surroundings. The group pledged to each raise a nickel per week and recruit new members to build a home "for all the other poor motherless daughters of our race." They chose the name Working Girls' Home Association for their project (A. Jones 1990, 43).

Hunter soon became part of a local controversy. As she was establishing the Working Girls' Home Association, an NACW club announced the opening of a settlement house on Central Avenue. The NACW, of which Hunter was not yet a member, received great initial support for its project, but the settlement house closed in 1913 for lack of funding (A. Jones 1990, 57; Lerner 1972, 452).[7]

By comparison the Working Girls' Home Association was just hitting its stride. The constitution stated its purpose as "establishing a home of good repute, where good, honest, upright working girls can have pure and pleasant surroundings, where they can be taught the art of housekeeping, techniques of hygiene, importance of loyalty, the beauty in neatness and dispatch" (Phillis Wheatley Association 1913). The Working Girls' Home Association was renamed the Phillis Wheatley Association in 1912, with a slightly modified constitution: its purpose would now be to "maintain a home with wholesome surroundings that will afford girls and women an opportunity for fuller development, and promote growth in Christian character and service through physical, social, mental, and spiritual training" (Phillis Wheatley Association 1912).[8] In 1917 another sentence appeared at the end of this description: "It seeks to protect and shelter them from the evils of city life" (Phillis Wheatley Association 1917).

Hunter never acknowledged either Elizabeth Davis's Phillis Wheatley Home for Girls established in Chicago in 1907 or the Phillis Wheatley Home for "aged colored women" established in Detroit in 1897, but she probably knew about them through her connections with the Hampton Institute. Whether Hunter knew of their work or not, they were soon to know of hers. By proposing a separate home for black women, Hunter joined the national debate over Booker T. Washington's leniency toward temporary racial segregation versus W. E. B. Du Bois's demands for immediate integration.

The $1,500 needed to open the association's home was raised quickly. The location was a house adjacent to St. John's A.M.E. Church at 2265 East Fortieth Street. The house had rooms for fifteen boarders, Hunter, and a matron, as well as a kitchen, laundry facilities, and space to entertain guests. A dining room was added later, and furniture and labor for cleaning and painting were donated. Residents were encouraged to attend weekly lectures and religious services conducted at the home. The home received more requests for lodging than it could fill as soon as the doors opened (A. Jones 1990, 61).

During this time the Phillis Wheatley Association was, first and foremost, concerned with lodging for black women. In 1917 the Boarding

Department recorded 225 girls in the home for one month or more and 142 transients. Weekly room rates were $1.50 for a double and $2.00 for a single. Three meals a day were provided for $3.50 a week. The employment aspect became a larger part of the association's mission as the century progressed. The association added an employment bureau that received four thousand requests during 1917 and the bureau found work for two thousand of those girls (Phillis Wheatley Association 1917).

Hunter received financial support from the president of the Sherwin-Williams Paint Company on the condition that whites be included on the governing board. Hunter then approached Elizabeth Scofield, president of the YWCA board, who agreed to serve if she could choose the other executive committee members. Soon the Phillis Wheatley Association was under the control of white women, with Jane Edna Hunter, as executive secretary, the only black member of the board of trustees of the organization she had created. In effect the Phillis Wheatley Association became the black branch of the YWCA, relieving the YWCA from pressures to integrate (A. Jones 1990, 52–55, 64).

The National Board of the YWCA soon took an interest in the Phillis Wheatley Association. Florence Simms, the industrial secretary of the New York City YWCA, was sent to Cleveland to explore the possibility of making the home a formal branch of the local YWCA with the idea of making it a model for other cities. Protracted negotiations ensued because Hunter was ambivalent about the merger. Eva Bowles, national secretary for colored work of the YWCA, traveled to Cleveland several times between 1915 and 1917 to assess whether a merger was feasible. In 1916 Hunter declared her intent to keep the Phillis Wheatley Association independent and she raised additional funds for an expanded facility. In 1917 the Winona Apartments at the corner of Central Avenue and East Fortieth Street became the association's new location. With seventy-two rooms, it tripled the capacity of the association and required an increase in staff from two to twenty. A campaign among blacks resulted in enough money to purchase an adjacent two-story building that provided activity and meeting rooms for the local community. Continued pressures from Cleveland's Welfare Federation to affiliate with a national organization were alleviated when Hunter chose to join the NACW rather than the YWCA (A. Jones 1990, 66–71).[9]

The Cleveland YWCA had been in existence for nearly half a century by the time Jane Edna Hunter founded the Phillis Wheatley Association.

The Women's Christian Association (WCA), as it was called, was established in 1868 to protect the "spiritual, moral, mental, social, and physical welfare of Woman in our midst." Within the year it had opened a boarding home for working women and a shelter for "tempted and betrayed [i.e., pregnant unmarried] women." By 1893 the WCA also had opened a Home for Aged Women, the Eliza Jennings Home for Incurables, five nurseries, six kindergartens, and an Educational and Industrial Union (Women's Christian Association 1893).

The Working Women's Home at 16 Walnut Street was purchased by businessman Stillman Witt for $5,000 in 1869 and donated to the WCA.

Figure 5.18. Women's Christian Association boarding home at 16 Walnut Street in Cleveland. (From *Manual of the Women's Christian Association of Cleveland*, 1879. Courtesy Western Reserve Historical Society, Cleveland, Ohio.)

Figure 5.19. Women's Christian Association Home for Aged Women on Kennard Street in Cleveland. (From *Manual of the Women's Christian Association of Cleveland,* 1879. Courtesy Western Reserve Historical Society, Cleveland, Ohio.)

It was a two-story brick house, originally twenty-two by forty-four feet, enlarged and renovated for its new use. The basement was divided into an office and sewing rooms, furnace room, coal bin, vegetable cellar, and laundry. The first floor had two parlors for visitors, a sitting room for boarders, a matron's room, dining room, and kitchen. The second floor contained seven sleeping rooms, and the attic five more. The house was furnished with donations from twelve churches and several individuals (Women's Christian Association 1870, 19–23, 42). This home filled so quickly that Mr. Witt bought the adjacent lot and more than doubled the number of rooms. The price of room and board was $3.00 to $4.50 per week, depending on the room's location (Women's Christian Association 1879, 6–7).

The Working Women's Home must have been somewhat controversial because the author of the annual report went to great lengths to defend it. She confusingly described it as "an institution so recently established in Cleveland that some of the details of its arrangement may not be unacceptable to the public." Its purpose was clear, however:

The necessity which prompted its establishment will not cease to exist so long as a prosperous city calls to its various pursuits the sisters and daughters of more distant homes. It is to meet the yearnings of the homeless that the "Working Women's Home" has set an open door, and invites now to its friendly and its Christian protection those who count such advantages as safe-guards, with which a friendless woman does well to surround herself.

Daily worship service was mandatory, and visiting on the Sabbath was prohibited (Women's Christian Association 1870, 22; 1879, 19).

Truly friendless women with no economic resources were also a concern of the WCA. Those who had lost their virginity were housed at the WCA's Retreat at 267 Perry Street, while older women could apply to live in the Home for Aged Women on Kennard Street. Twenty Protestant (white) elderly women of good character were "inmates" at the Home for Aged Women in 1879. Women who had any property or cash income had to give it to the home, and everyone was placed on a three-month probation before being accepted for residency (Women's Christian Association 1879, 27).

The Retreat sheltered twenty-six women in a "refuge from the fearful associations" that had produced their "wrecked and stranded" lives. Because of the necessity for discretion, the WCA had trouble funding the Retreat. Donations came mostly from individuals in small amounts of cash ($1 to $50), blankets, furniture, kitchen utensils, framed copies of the Lord's Prayer, and various fruits and vegetables. The city must have recognized the Retreat's value, and its own reliance on it, because the Cleveland City Council was the largest single cash donor ($200) in 1868. The Retreat expanded and moved to quarters at 934 St. Clair Street ten years later. Destitute women were admitted free, but those with the ability to pay were charged $25. House rules were strict for the "inmates," as they were called. Girls were required to stay for six months; they could not leave the Retreat unchaperoned, nor could they entertain visitors alone. Worship services were mandatory and mail was censored (Women's Christian Association 1870, 37–41; 1879, 24).

By 1899 the WCA, which had become the YWCA, was somewhat defensive about the Retreat (now at 1450 St. Clair Street). Officers believed it was subject to "unreasoning prejudice" by those who misinterpreted the secrecy surrounding it in sinister terms. Potential donors who thought the regulations were too harsh were reminded that the average resident was only seventeen years old and that many were much younger. These

Figure 5.20. The Retreat of the Women's Christian Association at 934 St. Clair Street in Cleveland. (From *Manual of the Women's Christian Association of Cleveland,* 1879. Courtesy Western Reserve Historical Society, Cleveland, Ohio.)

girls had to stay for six months because they were "paying the penalty of violated virtue." They were also required to learn some branch of domestic science, take care of their new babies (including making all their clothes), and share in the household work of the Retreat (YWCA of Cleveland 1899).

The YWCA erected a new building in 1908 to house the Association and accommodate more lodgers.[10] The Stillman Witt Boarding Home at the corner of Prospect Avenue and E. Eighteenth Street was an eight-story structure of brown stone and Darlington brick. It contained a library, administrative offices, gym, departments of domestic science, domestic arts, and commercial skills (e.g., stenography, typewriting, and bookkeeping), chapel, dining room, and bedrooms for 220 boarders (Geary 1913).

The annual report for 1910 reveals that the Stillman Witt Boarding Home housed over two hundred women, the Home for Aged Women cared for thirty-nine, and the Eliza Jennings Home for Incurables took care of twenty-four women. The Retreat provided shelter for almost fifty women and recorded thirty infants born in the home.

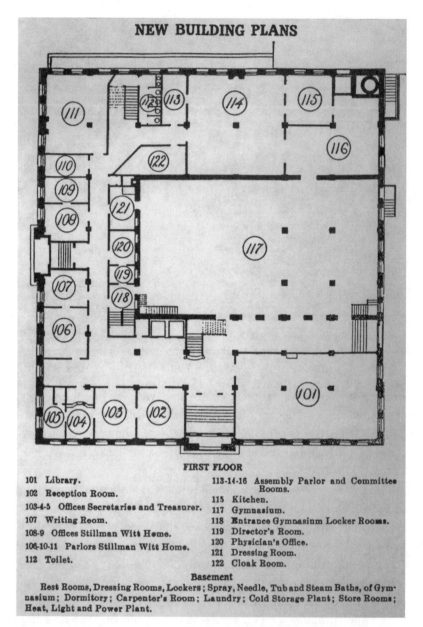

NEW BUILDING PLANS

FIRST FLOOR

101 Library.
102 Reception Room.
103-4-5 Offices Secretaries and Treasurer.
107 Writing Room.
108-9 Offices Stillman Witt Home.
106-10-11 Parlors Stillman Witt Home.
112 Toilet.

113-14-16 Assembly Parlor and Committee
Rooms.
115 Kitchen.
117 Gymnasium.
118 Entrance Gymnasium Locker Rooms.
119 Director's Room.
120 Physician's Office.
121 Dressing Room.
122 Cloak Room.

Basement

Rest Rooms, Dressing Rooms, Lockers; Spray, Needle, Tub and Steam Baths, of Gymnasium; Dormitory; Carpenter's Room; Laundry; Cold Storage Plant; Store Rooms; Heat, Light and Power Plant.

Figure 5.21. First-floor plan for new Cleveland YWCA Stillman Witt Headquarters and Boarding Home, c. 1908. (Courtesy Archives of the National Board of the YWCA of the USA.)

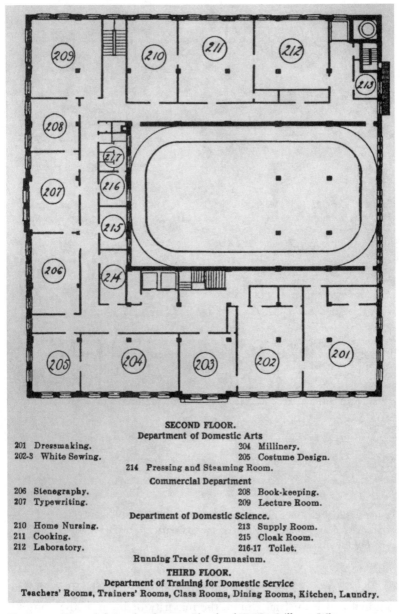

SECOND FLOOR.
Department of Domestic Arts

201 Dressmaking.	204 Millinery.
202-3 White Sewing.	205 Costume Design.

214 Pressing and Steaming Room.

Commercial Department

206 Stenography.	208 Book-keeping.
207 Typewriting.	209 Lecture Room.

Department of Domestic Science.

210 Home Nursing.	213 Supply Room.
211 Cooking.	215 Cloak Room.
212 Laboratory.	216-17 Toilet.

Running Track of Gymnasium.

THIRD FLOOR.
Department of Training for Domestic Service
Teachers' Rooms, Trainers' Rooms, Class Rooms, Dining Rooms, Kitchen, Laundry.

Figure 5.22. Second-floor plan for new Cleveland YWCA Stillman Witt Headquarters and Boarding Home, c. 1908. (Courtesy Archives of the National Board of the YWCA of the USA.)

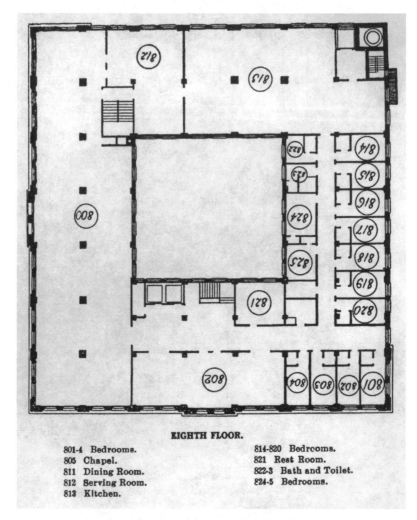

EIGHTH FLOOR.

801-4 Bedrooms.
805 Chapel.
811 Dining Room.
812 Serving Room.
813 Kitchen.

814-820 Bedrooms.
821 Rest Room.
822-3 Bath and Toilet.
824-5 Bedrooms.

Figure 5.23. Eighth-floor plan for new Cleveland YWCA Stillman Witt Headquarters and Boarding Home, c. 1908. (Courtesy Archives of the National Board of the YWCA of the USA.)

More than one thousand women took classes from the YWCA's Educational and Industrial Union, the majority of them in the domestic arts of sewing, millinery, and cooking. Travelers' Aid recorded contact with more than three thousand girls (YWCA of Cleveland 1911). By assuming responsibility for women adrift during an era of extremely rapid change, the Cleveland YWCA helped to shape the future of the city as well as the lives of individuals.

Like the YWCA, the NACW recognized that women needed both lodging and vocational education. One of the NACW's most successful efforts was the National Training School for Women and Girls, founded in Washington, D.C., by Nannie Helen Burroughs. Like black women who read the *Cleveland Gazette,* Nannie Helen Burroughs may have seen Victoria Earle Matthews's byline on articles about racial uplift in the *Washington Bee.*

Washington, D.C.

Nannie Helen Burroughs was born in rural Virginia in 1879 and moved to Washington, D.C., with her mother when she was a child. By the time Burroughs died in 1961, she had founded the Woman's Convention of the National Baptist Convention, become an officer in the National Association of Colored Women, established the National Training School for Women and Girls, organized a union for domestics, and been a national speaker for the Republican Party.

Burroughs's accomplishments were atypical for a black woman of her day, but then so were her origins. She was the granddaughter of slaves, whose father attended college and was an itinerant preacher. Her mother moved to Washington, D.C., without her husband, to find work for herself and schools for Nannie Helen and her sister (who died in childhood). Nannie Helen Burroughs attended the District's Colored High School and joined the Nineteenth Street Baptist Church. After graduation Burroughs was denied a position she coveted as assistant to her former domestic science teacher, ostensibly because of her dark skin color and lack of social connections. This disappointment shaped Burroughs's lifelong commitment to creating opportunities for poor black women (Higginbotham 1993).

Before finding her niche with the National Training School, Burroughs graduated from the Washington Business College and moved to Louisville, Kentucky. There she organized a women's industrial club with evening classes in bookkeeping, sewing, cooking, and typing. She was living in Louisville when she made the trip to the National Baptist Convention in Richmond, Virginia, in 1900. That was the convention at which she delivered the speech on "righteous discontent" that gave birth to the Woman's Convention. Burroughs returned to Kentucky and attended Eckstein Norton Institute while living as a boarder at Reverend C. H. Parrish's home. She graduated in 1904 and became a member of

the Theological Faculty at Louisville's State University, "an institution
for the training of colored young men and women." Burroughs was
teaching at State University (soon renamed Simmons Bible College after its first president) the year preceding her move back to Washington,
D.C. (*Caron's Directory of the City of Louisville* 1901; Higginbotham 1993;
Simmons Bible College Records, n.d.).

Nannie Helen Burroughs spoke to — and for — thousands of black
women about the importance of racial and gender equality at the same
time Booker T. Washington and W. E. B. Du Bois were debating whether
black progress depended on vocational education for the masses or on
the cosmopolitan example set by the most "talented tenth" of the race.
Burroughs rejected Du Bois's emphasis on the talented tenth. She believed that "teachers, preachers, and 'leaders' cannot solve the problems
of the race alone. The race needs an army of skilled workers, and the
properly educated Negro woman is the most essential factor" (Higginbotham 1993, 212).

Burroughs had a radical understanding of the conflict of interest between black women workers and white middle-class women. During debates over the Nineteenth Amendment Burroughs advocated the union-
ization of domestics because "the women voters will be keen to see that
laws are passed that will give eight hours a day to women in other in-
dustries, but they will oppose any movement that will, in the end, prevent them from keeping their cooks and house servants in the kitchen
twelve or fifteen hours a day" (Higginbotham 1993, 218). Burroughs proceeded to launch the National Association of Wage Earners in 1920 to
improve living and working conditions for domestics; members of the
NACW and the WC were on its governing board.[11]

Nannie Helen Burroughs occupied a pivotal position within the
Woman's Convention, one that helped her make connections to the
NACW and allowed her to mobilize both organizations to support her
vocational school. Burroughs's greatest achievement was the National
Training School for Women and Girls, a redemptive place she created
for women who were new to Washington, D.C., just as her mother had
been two decades earlier.

The National Training School for Women and Girls opened in 1909
in a dilapidated eight-room farmhouse outside Washington, D.C. The
school's curriculum and discipline attempted to professionalize domestic service by offering vocational courses in housekeeping, laundering,

and household and dining-room management for its first thirty-one students.

The school was located in a community called Lincolnville that had fewer than a dozen houses and no paved streets, water, or electric lights. The purchase price of $6,500 was funded almost entirely by donations from blacks, mainly through the Baptist Woman's Convention. Whites were solicited for donations after the first buildings were constructed, but at no point did the school's existence depend on white funding. Students lived, learned, and worked at the school. Burroughs required the girls to fetch coal from the bottom of the hill (where it was dumped by a freight train) and to tend to the garden, pigs, and chickens (Hayes 1997).

Two of the reasons the school was located in Washington were the large number of black female migrants to D.C. and the opportunities for employment with government officials. Burroughs fought to redefine domestic service as skilled rather than menial labor, urging women to do "ordinary things in an extraordinary way." Burroughs thought liberal arts education for the majority of blacks was in the distant future, and

Figure 5.24. National Training School for Women and Girls in the Lincolnville neighborhood of northeast Washington, D.C., c. 1912. (Courtesy Library of Congress, USZ62-92834.)

her pragmatism translated into the homily that "[u]ntil we realize our ideal, we are going to idealize our real" by insisting that "first-class help must have first-class treatment" (Higginbotham 1993, 211–14; Hine 1990).

A model house at the school was named after benefactor Maggie Lena Walker, the first black woman bank president (of the Penny Savings Bank in Richmond, Virginia). This "practical house" offered instruction in food preparation, cleaning, answering the doorbell and telephone, and other tasks most employers expected. Soon a laundry and several other buildings supplemented the original farmhouse and barn. Students also could take classes in missionary work, nursing, bookkeeping, and nontraditional subjects like printing, barbering, and shoe repair (Higginbotham 1993, 215, 220; Hine 1990).

Burroughs opened the combination boarding home and vocational school because she recognized that "two-thirds of the colored women must work with their hands for a living, and it is indeed an oversight not to prepare this army of breadwinners to do their work well" (Hine

Figure 5.25. Library of National Training School for Women and Girls, c. 1912. (Courtesy Library of Congress, USZ62-113208.)

Figure 5.26. Laundry of National Training School for Women and Girls, c. 1912. (Courtesy Library of Congress, USZ62-104412.)

1990, 75). The school's motto was "Work. Support thyself. To thine own powers appeal." Equal emphasis was given to good conduct, manners, and dress. Burroughs referred to her school as the "School of the 3 Bs," since the Bible, bathtub, and broom symbolized "righteous lives, clean bodies, and clean homes." Burroughs noted in 1912 that several girls failed to get their diplomas because of untidiness and careless attire (Higginbotham 1993, 216, 293).

The National Training School, like the NACW and WC, recommended domestic virtue as an avenue of acceptance into white society. It encouraged students to be clean and orderly to combat racial stereotypes that blocked their upward mobility, and to adopt Booker T. Washington's "Gospel of the Toothbrush." Not surprisingly given the similarity of their educational philosophies, Burroughs was known among her contemporaries as the "female Booker T. Washington."[12]

Washington, D.C., was one of only several southern cities in which women volunteers created redemptive places. Although many blacks migrated to northern cities, many also stayed in southern cities. The NACW's emphasis on cleanliness influenced local building agendas in cities throughout the South.

Figure 5.27. Graduates of the National Training School for Women and Girls, c. 1912. (Courtesy Library of Congress, USZ62-92858.)

Hampton, Virginia

Janie Porter Barrett, president of the Virginia State Federation of Colored Women's Clubs, invited girls playing in the street into her own home, thereby establishing the Locust Street Social Settlement at 320 Locust Street in Hampton, Virginia, in 1890. Activities took place in Barrett's home until a clubhouse was erected in 1902. The down payment for the clubhouse came from money Barrett and her husband had saved to add a bathroom to their home. Barrett justified the investment because it "helped the people to whom I preached cleanliness, cleanliness, cleanliness all day and every day to know that I had exactly the same inconveniences that they did" (Lattimore 1915, 10).

Programs expanded with the facilities: soon the settlement provided a library, playground, cooking and sewing classes, lectures, and girls' and boys' clubs. The settlement was staffed by head resident Mrs. Barrett and twenty volunteers (sixteen women and four men). The goals of Locust Street stressed economic self-sufficiency, personal dignity, and municipal housekeeping:

We are teaching through the efforts of the settlement house, how to have more attractive homes, cleaner back yards, more attractive front yards, cleaner sidewalks, how to have better gardens, how to raise poultry successfully, the proper food for the family, care and feeding of infants and small children. Through the efforts of the house much has been done to improve the social life of the community. (Woods and Kennedy [1911] 1970, 298)

Atlanta

Lugenia Burns Hope added children's well-being to a municipal housekeeping agenda in Atlanta, Georgia. Hope had spent time at Hull House before she moved to Atlanta as the wife of the president of Morehouse College. W. E. B. Du Bois invited Hope to an Atlanta University conference on "The Welfare of the Negro Child," out of which grew the Gate City Free Kindergarten Association. As a result of her involvement with that group, Hope founded the Neighborhood Union in 1908 "to raise the standard of living in the community and to make the West Side of Atlanta a better place to rear our children" (Lasch-Quinn 1993, 122).

Eight women met in Hope's home to decide whether settlement work was needed. Each member was sent on "friendly visits" to find out the names and ages of neighbors, especially girls between the ages of eight and twenty-two. One of the Union's first steps was to establish a playground on the Morehouse College campus because the neighborhood lacked playground facilities; the women themselves supervised the children and raised money for equipment. Members also organized holiday celebrations, community cleanups, gardens, and summer vacation Bible schools. In 1912 the Neighborhood Union investigated conditions in Atlanta's black public schools and in 1915 it established a health clinic. Between 1917 and 1921 its Home Investigation Committee documented the extent of substandard housing conditions, unpaved and unlighted streets, inadequate trash and garbage removal, contaminated water, and scarcity of indoor plumbing. Neighborhood Union's study resulted in the repair of forty houses, street paving and lighting, installation of sewers and plumbing, and the reconstruction of streets (Lasch-Quinn 1993, 114–24; Lerner 1974).

The CSA was also represented in the South. In addition to settlements in New York City, Boston, and Philadelphia, the CSA sponsored a house in Baltimore, Maryland.

Baltimore

Baltimore's Locust Point Settlement opened on Hull Street in 1896 and moved to 1504 East Fort Avenue in 1904 in a German neighborhood on the outskirts of the city. The earliest annual reports list events cosponsored with the YMCA and the WCTU. The Locust Point Settlement engaged in relief work, distributing more than one thousand pieces of donated clothing and recording more than thirteen hundred visits to deliver clothes, food, or medicine to the poor during 1899 (Locust Point Social Settlement Association 1900).

The 1904 annual report listed the settlement's accomplishments for the year: sewing classes, fifteen boys' and girl's clubs, mothers' meetings, kindergarten, library, garment rummage sales, home visits, and Christmas entertainment. More than six thousand people attended one or more of these programs during 1904. The settlement was just barely self-sustaining. The treasurer's report identified donations and subscriptions as the largest single source of income ($543 out of total receipts of $2,241) and salaries for the residents as the largest single disbursement

Figure 5.28. The College Settlement of Philadelphia, 423–425 Christian Street, established 1892. (Photographer unknown. Courtesy Sophia Smith Collection, Smith College, Northampton, Mass.)

Figure 5.29. Roof garden at the College Settlement of Philadelphia, c. 1900. (From *Denison House College Settlement Report, 1900.* Courtesy Sophia Smith Collection, Smith College, Northampton, Mass.)

($896 out of $2,116). Residents may have been acknowledging this slim surplus when they composed the theme song whose chorus ended with "God keep us all, and heaven bless, the Settlement House forever" (Locust Point Social Settlement Association 1904, 9).

Philadelphia

Philadelphia's College Settlement inherited its building at 617 St. Mary Street from the St. Mary Street Library Committee in 1892. It was located in a neighborhood known as one of the worst in the city: the square bounded by Lombard and South, Sixth and Seventh Streets that housed Jewish, Negro, German, Polish, and Italian immigrants. A CSA member described the district as a "badly-lighted overcrowded quarter with the most frightful sanitary conditions, the people ignorant and lawless." The settlement operated as a refuge for the children of the neighborhood. A kindergarten and rooftop playground served children's educational and recreational demands, while a resident nurse met their health needs (Farrington 1898).

One of the settlement's first projects was to repave streets, clear out a dump, and tear down rookeries (tenements) to make room for a new park. They accomplished this by becoming active in local politics. Volunteers also established a public kitchen that provided moderately priced food to neighborhood residents. The Philadelphia Settlement soon in-

Figure 5.30. "We play in a crack on Christian Street, 435 Play Yard." (From *News of the College Settlement of Philadelphia* 3, no. 8 [September 1912]. Courtesy Sophia Smith Collection, Smith College, Northampton, Mass.)

cluded a bank, library, carpenter shop, sewing club, cooperative coal club, and English classes. Like the library at the College Settlement in New York, the library at Philadelphia College Settlement eventually merged with the city's system. The Settlement cooperated with the city in other ways as well. It acted as a relief station during the economic crisis of 1893–94 by dispensing food to the needy. It also paid the salaries of two juvenile probation officers for six years (Farrington 1898; Woods and Kennedy [1911] 1970, 263).

Vida Scudder cited the settlement's efforts to clean heaps of garbage off neighborhood streets as an example of their tenuous relationship with city officials. Residents of the settlement and their neighbors attacked the problem with "Ruskinian ardor." They swept the road, scrubbed stoops, and stacked rubbish in neat piles so that "one could walk in the street without rubbers." The piles remained on the street for three days. When settlement workers complained to the city about the lack of scheduled pickup, they were told the budget for 1893 was not yet in place. Nothing could be done until the city leaders met in another ten days. Rather than let the trash sit, residents decided to put it in barrels. Then they realized their "rubbish" was technically "garbage" and the street cleaners would not touch anything in barrels. Neither would the ashman remove it because his job was to remove only ashes.

In mock despair, Scudder complained of the "Enchanted rubbish! Sacred rubbish! What shall move thee from thy place?" Eventually a boy from one of the settlement's clubs hauled it away, leaving Scudder to muse, "The street is clean, for today, and, while waiting new developments, we meditate on the substantial reality of dirt and the peculiar nature of city action" (Scudder 1893, 231).

The most important CSA settlement house, after the original one in New York City, was Boston's Denison House. Vida Scudder left the Rivington Street Settlement to her colleagues' management and established Denison House with Helena Dudley in 1892. Dudley served as head resident for many years while Scudder taught at Wellesley. Denison House and Wellesley remained Scudder's homes for the rest of her life.

CHAPTER SIX

Boston, the Cradle of Redemptive Places

Boston was the destination of America's first immigrants. Like New York City's Ellis Island, Plymouth Rock was Boston's symbol of immigration. Boston was small by comparison with New York, and it lacked the fame Chicago generated for hosting the World's Columbian Exposition. Yet the city had something New York and Chicago could never possess: History with a capital *H*. The elite residential Beacon Hill and Back Bay became distinctive features of Boston's rich cultural terrain by the end of the nineteenth century, setting it apart from the newer commercial landscapes of Chicago and New York (Domosh 1996).

In addition to its centrality in America's heritage, Boston is important to the history of domestic reform movements. The city is filled with sites where women taught other women to convert housekeeping skills into marketable wage labor. The most important of these was the Women's Educational and Industrial Union (WEIU), an organization that sponsored laboratory kitchens, food companies, and schools of housekeeping (Spencer-Wood 1987). Boston was a pioneer in the playground and public bath movements as well, and three of the four organizations discussed in this book began in Boston. The first formal YWCA was founded in Boston (in 1866), as was the precursor to the NACW (Josephine St. Pierre Ruffin's Woman's Era Club in 1893). Denison House in the South End, Vida Scudder's home for most of her adult life, connected Boston directly with CSA settlements in New York City, Baltimore, and Philadelphia. With the exception of The Salvation Army fa-

Figure 6.1. Aerial view of Boston, 1905. (Courtesy Library of Congress, 701585.)

cilities first established in Philadelphia, the entire range of redemptive places originated in Boston.

Boston's South End illustrates the depth of coverage a thick web of redemptive places could create. In fact, this neighborhood was recognized at the time as one of the most intensely "charitied" districts in the country. Maps at three different scales illustrate Boston's redemptive net. The first map for the entire city includes locations of redemptive places in the North End, West End, and South End. The second map is adapted from a book written in 1898 by Robert Woods, head resident of South End House settlement. This map reveals the social scientific contributions of the settlement movement. Like Jane Addams of Hull House, Woods documented countless neighborhood conditions that needed reform. The third map is an adaptation of a 1909 Sanborn Fire Insurance Map for the South End streets immediately surrounding Denison House.

Beginning in 1867 the Sanborn Map Company of Pelham, New York, produced large-scale maps for thousands of cities to assist fire-insurance agents in determining the degree of risk associated with a particular property. The maps identify commercial, industrial, and residential land use and show the size, shape, and construction material of individual buildings, including the presence of fire walls, sprinkler systems, loca-

1   0   1   2 Miles

Map 6.1. Map of redemptive places in Boston, c. 1915.

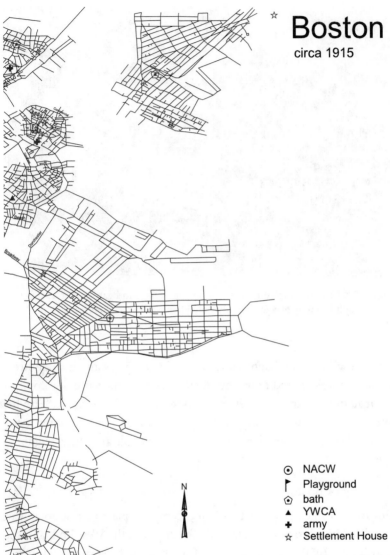

Boston

circa 1915

⊙	NACW
⌐	Playground
⬠	bath
▲	YWCA
✚	army
☆	Settlement House

N

Map 6.1. *Continued.*

Figure 6.2. Children stuffed into one of Boston's early sand gardens for a photograph taken by playground advocate Ellen M. Tower. (Reprinted from Rainwater 1922.)

tions of windows and doors, and types of roofs. They also include street names and block and house numbers. Sanborn maps provide copious information about the streetscape at the turn of the century ("Fire Insurance Maps" 1981). Combined with city directories and voter registration lists, I use them here to describe the people and their neighborhood.

The City of Boston

Boston had an extensive network of redemptive places, most notably in the three immigrant districts of the North End, the West End, and the South End. By the second decade of the twentieth century Boston had thirty settlement houses, dozens of playgrounds and gymnasiums, and twelve public baths.

The North End was the closest neighborhood to the wharves where immigrants entered the city. It was a tiny peninsula extending into Boston Harbor, smaller than New York City's Central Park. The immigrant population was mainly southern Italians and grew from 28,000 to 40,000 between 1900 and 1920. All these people were crammed into two- and three-room apartments in stuffy tenements with shared (or no) plumbing facilities. Boston's Associated Charities was formed in the late 1870s to alleviate some of their misery. Its purpose was to improve the life of immigrants and to inoculate Boston "against plagues like tuberculosis, crime, and rioting [by spreading] the gospel of hygiene and hard work" (Henry and Williams n.d.).

In 1879 a group of fifty women volunteers from Associated Charities rented a large four-story brick building at 39 North Bennet Street to teach immigrant women how to earn a living. Sewing classes at the North End Industrial Home were open to widows, women abandoned by their husbands, or those supporting sick husbands. They learned how to sew and were paid wages for piecework. Classes did more than just prepare students for work, however. In the 1880s sewing symbolized moral worth, family values, industriousness, and a route to social integration (Henry and Williams n.d., 10).

The North End Industrial Home expanded dramatically with the assistance of Pauline Agassiz Shaw. Shaw, born into a family with impeccable educational credentials, was a pioneer in the public kindergarten movement. Her father was a Harvard professor and her stepmother founded Radcliffe College. Pauline married a wealthy businessman, raised five children, and became the spiritual and financial "angel" for the home when she opened a kindergarten and day nursery there. Shaw donated money to pay the rent for five years. By the time the lease expired in 1885, the board of managers had raised enough money to purchase the building; the home was incorporated as the North Bennet Street Industrial School. Shaw served as president of the board from 1885 until her retirement in 1915 (Henry and Williams n.d.).

In 1885 Shaw contracted with the Boston public schools to provide manual training classes for three hundred grammar-school students. The "prevocational" curriculum helped keep children in school longer while it provided them with work skills for the future. Girls took cooking classes and boys learned woodworking through the *sloyd* method, which emphasized an appreciation for fine craftsmanship.[1] By 1891 public schools required manual training and continued to hold classes at the North Bennet Street Industrial School. Enrollment in the prevocational classes reached nine hundred students by 1902 (Henry and Williams n.d.).

In that same year the board decided the school's social service work had grown beyond the ability of its volunteers. They hired Zelda Brown, a "scientifically trained" head resident, to live at the school with other residents. The board recognized that their mission was still to "instruct this alien procession in the best American ideals and to hold steadily before the young, high standards of skill, taste, and citizenship" while "retaining [the] industrial and educational features at their best." They also understood that the school was increasingly involved in settlement work, so they established a Social Service House behind 39 North Bennet Street. In 1907 it transferred responsibility for administering the school from volunteers to a trained professional, Alvin Dodd. By 1911 Dodd's annual report boasted more than one thousand students enrolled in classes taught by twenty-eight salaried teachers and fifty-five volunteers (Henry and Williams n.d., 25, 29).

The North Bennet Street Industrial School provided a vast array of opportunities to immigrants before the city was organized to deliver social services. Classes, vocational guidance and placement, a day nursery, kindergarten, and a branch of the Boston Public Library were all part of the school's original mission. Boys at the school's Social Service House planted a garden in an adjacent lot acquired from the city in 1906; it was eventually turned over to the Boston School Gardens Committee. The school also opened public baths for children at 30 North Bennet Street in 1888 and expanded its facilities in 1907 to accommodate adults before the city financed it (Woods and Kennedy [1911] 1970, 105–35).[2]

The West End also hosted numerous redemptive places. The Frances E. Willard Settlement at 24 South Russell Street was a truly hybrid institution, established in 1898 by Caroline Caswell under the auspices of the YWCA and the WCTU. It began as a social center for factory girls and expanded into a boarding home for working women earning very low wages, those training for self-support, and "strangers" who needed assistance. In 1919 sixteen young women, each of whom earned approximately $5.00 per week, paid $3.00 a week for room, board, and washing. The girls had to be "good and worthy and have references" to qualify for residence (Geary 1919). The Willard Y, as it was first called, offered religious and secular classes in addition to a playground for neighborhood children. Its mission statement was similar to that of other YWCA boarding houses, stressing the extension of home life to young working women and "aggressive Christian work." It was supported solely by private donations and depended on the volunteer work of thirty-one women and twelve men to supplement that of the seven women in residence (Woods and Kennedy [1911] 1970, 125, 132).

Another prominent West End settlement was the Elizabeth Peabody House at 357 Charles Street. Established in 1896 by friends of Elizabeth Palmer Peabody to honor her volunteer work in the district, its special mission was municipal housekeeping.[3] Nine female and two male residents of the house made special efforts to ensure proper street-cleaning and sanitary services for the neighborhood. They also publicized the district's overcrowded housing and corrupt political life. Much like members of the Hull House Women's Club in Chicago, members of the Elizabeth Peabody street-cleaning brigade collected garbage to shame city officials into providing better services.

The house took care of other details that would eventually be assumed by the city: a kindergarten, library, nursing services, and playground. During the summer the Elizabeth Peabody House sponsored vacant-lot and windowbox gardening. A friend, Edward Ginn, donated and fenced vacant adjacent land for the creation of a large garden with 220 individual children's plots (Spencer-Wood 1994; Woods and Kennedy [1911] 1970, 112).

The five-story building contained rooms for industrial, educational, and social work in addition to a theater and an apartment for the workers. Part of the basement was reserved for men and boys to play billiards in a room they could enter from a rear alley. The front of the basement was used for a nurse's station and milk dispensary, also accessible from a separate door. The rest of the basement contained heating equipment and a fifty-ton coal-storage bin.

A kindergarten for thirty children was on the third floor. After morning classes the space was cleared for use in the afternoon and evening as a library and reading room. A carpentry shop was on the high-ceilinged fourth floor, along with two rooms for the male residents. The girls' department occupied the entire fifth floor. It included a complete suite of kitchen, pantry, dining room, bedroom, and sitting room for homemaking classes. There was a dressmaking room and three clubrooms, one of which was used for large group instruction (Geary 1919).[4]

Boston was a pioneer in creating playground and gymnasium facilities. A local physician, Dr. Marie Zakrsewska, visited Berlin and observed children playing in heaps of sand in the public parks, after which she

Figure 6.3. Garden of Elizabeth Peabody House, no date. (Courtesy of the Schlesinger Library, Radcliffe Institute, Harvard University.)

suggested to the Massachusetts Emergency and Hygiene Association (MEHA) that similar facilities should be supplied for poor children in Boston. Large hills of sand were piled in the yard of Parmenter Street Chapel (soon to become the North End Union) and at the West End Nursery during the summer of 1885.[5] Boston followed up the experimental sand gardens in 1889 with construction of the ten-acre Charlesbank Outdoor Gymnasium for boys and men and added a section for girls and women in 1891. Designed by Frederick Law Olmsted's sons, Charlesbank was Boston's first small space intended primarily for play. It included swings, ladders, see-saws, a running track, sand garden, and rowing and bathing facilities, all free to the public. Most of the playgrounds were not this large, however. The Metropolitan Park Commission plan stipulated the provision of numerous small squares, playgrounds, and parks in the most congested neighborhoods. The sand garden and Charlesbank examples, combined with evidence that other cities adopted Boston's model, establish Boston as the home of the play movement in America (Rainwater 1922, 28; Spencer-Wood 1994).[6]

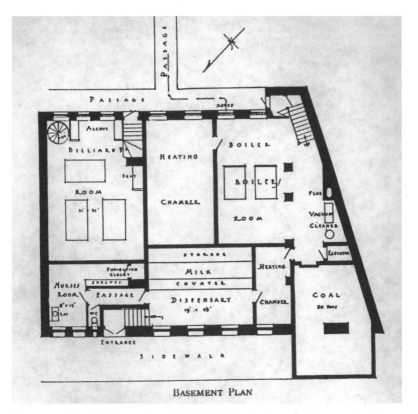

BASEMENT PLAN

Figure 6.4. Basement floor plan of Elizabeth Peabody House in Boston, showing front entrance to nurses station and rear-alley entrance to billiards room. (Courtesy Archives of the National Board of the YWCA of the USA.)

The history of the sand-garden experiment in Boston is a textbook example of the evolution of voluntary activities into municipal responsibility. Between 1885 and 1900, along with their growth in numbers, playgrounds (1) underwent a transition from philanthropic support to annual public subsidies, (2) expanded their hours of operation and number of children served, (3) moved from tenement courts and mission yards to schoolyards and parks, and (4) replaced volunteers with trained supervisors (Rainwater 1922). The summers of 1898 and 1899 were critical years. In 1898 Mayor Josiah Quincy opened twenty schoolyard playgrounds to supplement the dozen sponsored by the MEHA. These efforts were a failure, reportedly due to lack of appropriate supervision, and the playgrounds remained deserted. The next summer Mayor Quincy

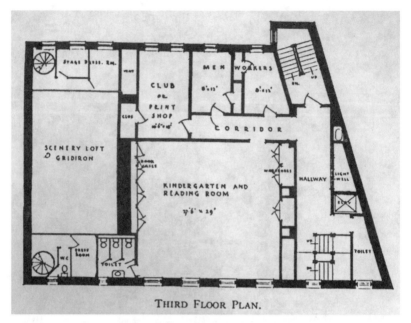

THIRD FLOOR PLAN.

Figure 6.5. Plan of the third floor of the Elizabeth Peabody House, with large room for morning kindergarten and afternoon reading room and auditorium with stage. Courtesy Archives of the National Board of the YWCA of the USA.

Figure 6.6. Floating baths at North End Park in Boston, c. 1900. (Frank B. Conklin, photographer. Courtesy of the Boston Public Library, Print Department.)

directed the schools to appropriate money for the support of play-grounds, but to spend it under the direction of the MEHA. Twenty-one playgrounds were managed under this system, employing sixty super-visors and serving four thousand children daily at an annual cost of $4,000. The experiment was repeated in 1900 with more supervisors, a larger budget, and greater attendance. By 1901 the transition from phil-anthropic to public control was complete. The school system severed its ties with the MEHA and established its own budget and administra-tion for summer playgrounds; the MEHA continued to sponsor its own playgrounds (Rainwater 1922, 32).

Boston's cold climate meant that playgrounds were a seasonal luxury. Children's need for physical activity lasted into the winter, however, so gymnasiums were built to provide exercise opportunities throughout the year. Boston is credited as the first city to open an "establishment solely for physical training by up-to-date systematic methods" in 1897 (Mero 1909). Mayor Quincy was an ardent supporter of gymnasiums as well as playgrounds, believing that both were part of a year-round public health system for which the city should assume responsibility. Mayor Quincy considered it "but a step from the open-air playground to the indoor gymnasium, and the same considerations which warrant the expenditure of public money for the former justify it for the latter purpose" (Quincy 1898).

Mayor Quincy was also a strong advocate for year-round public baths, which often occupied the same building as a gymnasium. The poor in Boston first had access to outdoor floating baths in 1866 at five differ-ent river sites and one beach site (the L Street Bathing Beach). Floating baths were wooden, docklike structures about the size of a modern swimming pool, filled with river water and surrounded by dressing rooms around the sides. They were extremely popular their first sum-mer of operation and recorded over 400,000 bathers at a time when the city's entire population was only 200,000. The Commonwealth of Massachusetts passed a bath law in 1874 enabling towns to appropriate money for the construction of public baths, but it took Boston another two decades to open its first indoor bath. In October 1898 the Dover Street Bath in the South End became the city's first year-round bath house (Williams 1991, 18, 68).

The Dover Street project began with Mayor Quincy's formation in 1896 of the Advisory Committee on Public Baths, chaired by South End

Figure 6.7. Interior of North Bennet Street Gymnasium and Bath House in Boston. (*The American City*, October 1909.)

head resident Robert Woods. Mary Morton Kehew, president of the Women's Educational and Industrial Union, was also a member of the mayor's advisory committee. After visiting New York City's People's Bath, the Boston committee recommended building the first free, all-year-round public bath in the South End. Construction began in 1896 on the 43- by 110-foot, two-story Dover Street Bath House, designed by the architectural firm of Peabody and Stearns. When it was finished in 1898, the bathhouse had fifty showers that could accommodate fourteen hundred people per day. The mayor then created a Department of Baths consisting of five male and two female volunteers to supervise the Dover Street and floating baths (Stewart 1902; Williams 1991, 72, 74, 80; Woods 1898, 286).[7]

Debate ensued about whether the baths should be free or subject to a small fee. Proponents of the fee system wanted to avoid the appearance of charity, while advocates of free baths pointed out that other public services like parks, schools, and libraries were already free. In the end the baths were made free out of fear that even a small charge might keep away the very people who most needed them. A patron could purchase soap and towel for a penny, and a bathing suit for five cents; children's suits were free. The city maintained a huge inventory of supplies. In 1902 the city owned nearly 9,000 bathing suits: 1,200 girls' one-part suits, 1,200 women's suits in two parts, 1,800 men's two-part suits, 1,200 men's trunks, and 3,600 boys' trunks. The rental of all these suits and another 15,000 towels generated $3,500 during the summer of 1901, one-tenth of the city's bath budget (Stewart 1902; Williams 1991, 74).

Mary Morton Kehew's involvement in the public bath movement was typical of the municipal housekeeping projects undertaken by the Women's Educational and Industrial Union (WEIU). The WEIU was founded in 1877 by Dr. Harriet Clisby for women who wanted to escape the "immense imprisonment of life which was stifling them," a feat possible only through education and training in marketable skills. Clisby's idea sprang from regular Sunday afternoon religious meetings with women who gathered to discuss ethical, moral, and spiritual issues. They recognized the necessity of narrowing the increasing distance separating ethnic, racial, and class groups. The WEIU became a class-bridging organization with philanthropic roots, simultaneously delivering charity, promoting new careers for women, and establishing a strong female presence in the city. Although many of the original members belonged to Boston's elite, the WEIU actively recruited women from other circles. Josephine St. Pierre Ruffin and Mary Kenney O'Sullivan, an Irish-Catholic labor organizer, both held office in the WEIU. Its inclusive membership strategy worked. Having begun with only forty-two women in 1877, the WEIU boasted forty-five hundred members by 1915 (Blair 1980; Deutsch 1992).

The WEIU announced its presence by staking out space for itself in the heart of commercial Boston. First in rented rooms and then in purchased buildings, the WEIU opened a clinic, employment bureau, pure milk station, laboratory kitchen, food supply company, and a salesroom (called an Exchange) where women sold homemade handicrafts and baked goods. Their lunchroom was staffed by volunteers who provided inexpensive meals for women who were working or shopping downtown. In 1900 WEIU lunchrooms served almost 45,000 dinners to middle-class and wage-earning women; profits from the lunchroom supported less lucrative projects (like the salesrooms). Ellen Swallow Richards, the first woman to earn a Ph.D. from MIT, established the New England Kitchen in Boston's South End through the auspices of the WEIU; it provided 9,500 lunches daily to public school children by 1912. The WEIU turned Boylston Street into a "woman's mile" where women's "proximity to the corridors of power, the state legislature and city hall, coincided with [their] increased lobbying efforts to change the city and their own condition" (Blair 1980; Deutsch 1992, 390; Goodrich n.d.).[8]

Mary Morton Kehew became president of the WEIU in 1891. Kehew was born into a wealthy family, married a Boston oil merchant, and remained childless. All of her time went into reform work. In addition to her duties for the WEIU, Kehew was a member of numerous women's organizations, including the College Settlements Association and Denison House. She also was president of the National Women's Trade Union League. Kehew's progressive labor activities within the WEIU took the form of chairmanship of the Domestic Reform League organized in 1897. The purpose of the Domestic Reform League was to insure that workers were treated fairly and that they delivered efficient service in exchange for decent wages (Hersey 1903).

One of the members of the Domestic Reform League, Josephine St. Pierre Ruffin, was as well connected in the world of women's organizations as Mary Morton Kehew. Ruffin's Woman's Era Club never had the same impact on the city's landscape as the WEIU, however. A building campaign produced insufficient funding for new quarters, and the club and its newspaper remained in Ruffin's home at 103 Charles Street in a black elite neighborhood near the West End (Boston 1900; Deutsch 1994, 214).[9]

Josephine St. Pierre was born in Boston in 1842. She was the daughter of an English mother and black father. Sent away to school because Boston's public schools were not yet open to blacks, she returned home and married George L. Ruffin from Virginia.[10] The Ruffins moved to England to avoid raising a family in a slave-holding nation, but came back to America following the abolition of slavery. George eventually became the first black judge in the North (in Charlestown District Court in 1883) and Josephine eventually founded the Woman's Era Club and the National Association of Colored Women (Pleck 1979, 30).

Ruffin organized the Woman's Era Club in 1893 with her daughter, Florida Ridley, and Maria Baldwin, principal of a Cambridge high school. Its purpose was to promote all activities "uplifting to the race." Membership was open to all women regardless of race. The first meeting was attended by white suffragist and abolitionist Lucy Stone Blackwell and the club's motto, "Make the World Better," were reportedly Black-well's dying words. The club's name was borrowed from another suffragist, Frances Ellen Watkins Harper, who declared the end of the nineteenth century to be the "woman's era" (Cash 1992a; White 1993, 250).

The Woman's Era Club awarded scholarships to deserving students, provided aid to a hospital for black women, and supported a kindergarten in Georgia. By 1895 the club had 133 members who met twice a month and paid membership dues of one dollar per year. Ruffin and her daughter founded a monthly illustrated magazine for clubmembers called *Woman's Era,* the first American newspaper to be owned, managed, and published by black women (Cash 1992a).

Josephine St. Pierre Ruffin's life was devoted to women's issues. Because of her light skin color, she moved more easily between black and white women's organizations than a darker-skinned woman might have. Ruffin, for example, was the only black member of the Women's Press Club of Boston. She was a pioneer of integration, forcing the General Federation of Women's Clubs to confront their racially exclusionary policies. Ironically, although Ruffin was the undisputed founder of one local and one national black voluntary organization, she was admitted to the GFWC only as a member of the white Women's Press Club.

The South End

Dr. Edward Everett Hale, noted nineteenth-century minister and author, identified Boston's South End as the "most 'charitied' region in Christendom." The district's origins could not have predicted the need for such help. The centrally located South End once had been in competition with the prestigious Back Bay as the residential preference of elites. By 1898, however, the region had become "a fit haunt for the depraved and vicious," where "evils of all kinds find congenial soil and produce a rank growth" in "dreary and depressing" streets and "dark squalid courts and alleys" (Woods 1898, 2).

The area described by settlement worker Robert Woods in *The City Wilderness* (1898) covered about half a square mile between Eliot and Kneeland Streets to the north and the wharves of Fort Point Channel on the east. Tremont and Ferdinand Streets on the west and Brookline Street on the south formed the other boundaries. Railroad tracks for the Boston and Albany Station bisected the district of tenements, shops, and factories. This area was home to about forty thousand people in

1895. Most were Irish, joined by a few blacks from the rural South, and Jewish, Italian, Greek, Chinese, and Syrian immigrants. The area of a settlement house's activities typically extended about ten blocks and reached approximately three hundred people. According to this criterion, the South End had seven neighborhoods. Among the three tenement neighborhoods to the east of Washington Street, one was covered by Denison House, a second by Lincoln House and St. Stephen's House, and the third by South End House (Woods 1898, 270–72).

   This map of the South End is a thorough accounting of the district's major institutions. Woods identified public health, amusements, churches, schools, and "social recovery"—the category most similar to redemptive places. He perceived a hierarchy of social recovery needs among immigrants similar to those a sick patient would experience. During the acute stage of the disease, an immediate remedy was necessary. The second stage of illness required a recuperative change of scene. The final stage required a radical reorganization of habits to promote better health in the future. Woods thought charity served the remedial function, philanthropy served the recuperative function, and settlement houses had the most important reconstructive mission. This was one of the reasons children's well-being was so important in settlement work. Boys and girls' clubs would educate, assimilate, and morally enlighten chil-

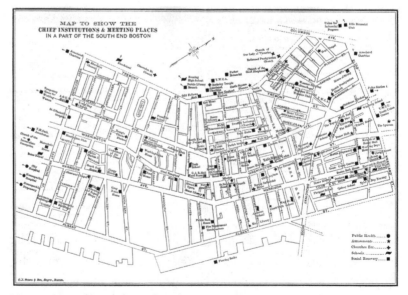

Map 6.2. Map of Boston's South End, c. 1898. (From Woods 1898.)

dren while their souls were both "wax to receive and marble to retain" (Woods 1898, 248, 259).

The YWCA had been engaged in social recovery work in the South End long before Robert Woods arrived. Mrs. Lucretia Boyd proposed a YWCA to the Boston City Missionary Society in 1859, but local ministers decided it would be "hazardous for the ladies to undertake such a scheme" and kindly prevented them from trying and failing (although the clergy had endorsed a Young Men's Christian Association in 1851). Several years later, however, pastors realized that the provision of "effective religious appeal with a humanitarian social-service emphasis" for the "tempted young man" was even more important for women "who from their position and sex are more unprotected and more helpless." Thirty women formed the YWCA, patterned after the YMCA, in the home of Mrs. Henry F. Durant in 1866; soon they had established a reading room and office at 23 Chauncy Street and boarding houses for eighty women at 25 and 27 Beach Street—all supported by donations from the clergy and supporters (one of whom was Prof. Henry W. Longfellow) (Wilson [1916] 1987, 29–34).

Figure 6.8. The Beach Street YWCA on the outskirts of Boston's South End, c. 1900. (Courtesy of the Boston Public Library, Print Department.)

Mrs. Boyd was a city missionary when she organized Boston's YWCA after observing first-hand the attic rooms occupied by working girls. The YWCA soon opened a Training School for Domestics with a two-year curriculum reviewed by Ellen Swallow Richards. Classes were offered in cooking, general household management, sanitation, dressmaking, millinery, and light industrial arts. An experimental kitchen was equipped as a laboratory with charts, a food museum, and appliances (Wilson [1916] 1987, 46).

The Beach Street quarters soon became too small. The Boston Association raised $120,000 to create "a structure so appropriate to the needs of girls that they should find in it a typical Christian home after the New England pattern." Funds were contributed from donations at a ten-day fair and through subscriptions. In 1874 the new Warrenton Street Home, designed by architect George Ropes, opened its doors for two hundred residents. There they could secure meals, room, light, heat, and personal laundry for $3.00 to $5.50 per week (Geary 1913; Wilson [1916] 1987, 34–38).[11]

The same year the Warrenton Street Home opened, the YWCA acquired an adjoining house on Carver Street for the employment bureau. When the Boston YWCA moved into new accommodations at 40 Berkeley Street in 1884, it included a training school, employment bureau, assembly hall, administrative offices, parlors, readings rooms, dining room, sleeping rooms for 156 residents, and the Pauline Durant gymnasium, the first gym to be incorporated into a YWCA building (Wilson [1916] 1987, 38, 43).[12]

To insure that newcomers to the city found their way to the YWCA, the Travelers' Aid Committee sent matrons to intercept young women when and where they arrived. The YWCA hired Miss M. E. Blodgett in 1887 to greet boats arriving from Atlantic coast states and from Europe. The YWCA combined forces with the Young Travelers' Aid Association, which had been meeting young women at the railroad station. The YWCA and Travelers' Aid divided the territory, and the YWCA took responsibility for the docks. In case they missed girls at the docks, YWCA volunteers copied the ships' manifest lists of names and addresses for all incoming immigrants and paid them a "friendly visit" later (YWCA of the USA n.d.). During her first three months on the job, Miss Blodgett served 508 girls "who were helpless because they could not speak

Figure 6.9. Postcard of YWCA residence at 40 Berkeley Street on the outskirts of Boston's South End, c. 1900. (Courtesy Archives of the National Board of the YWCA of the USA.)

English, [and taught them] how to talk and act and think like Americans" (Wilson [1916] 1987, 44, 45).

The YWCA's 1919 multicity study of accommodations for working women reported that almost one-half of all employed women in Boston lived away from home. Two settlements (South End House and the Frances E. Willard Settlement House) provided rooms for women; the Catholic diocese had two homes; and the Volunteers of America opened another at $1 per week. In addition, private associations ran four homes, and unions or societies another two. The YWCA also identified "a very good home for [twelve] colored girls" in the Harriet Tubman House (Geary 1919).

The Harriet Tubman House was created in 1904 by a black branch of the WCTU, the Harriet Tubman Crusaders.[13] The Crusaders rented a brownstone as a residence for black women who were excluded from Boston's college dormitories and respectable rooming houses. In 1909 Mrs. Julia O. Henson, a member of the NACW, donated her own townhouse as permanent headquarters. The Tubman House provided fewer services than comparable homes for white women. It offered only rooms, a kitchen, and some recreational activities. Although black churches provided meeting places for numerous women's organizations, the Tubman House was Boston's "only autonomous space created and run for and by black women until after World War I" (Deutsch 1994, 213).

The 1919 YWCA survey also identified two Salvation Army homes in the South End. The home at 20 Common Street rented rooms to forty women at rates ranging from $1.25 per week for three persons per room to $1.75 and $2.25 per week for private rooms. This building was old and lacked bathing facilities, although women could do their own washing and they could cook on a gas stove on the enclosed fire escape of each floor landing. No children were allowed in this facility — "only respectable women." The other Salvation Army home, at 1 Fayette Street, had rooms for twenty-eight women at $1.05 per week. The home was described as "made up of dormitories where people of all kinds and conditions are put together in a rather dingy place. The fact that the lower classes are taken in makes it impossible, I suppose, to give them better accommodations and these are probably much better than they are accustomed to. Some working women use it as their temporary home" (Geary 1919).

The Salvation Army catered to the most transient of the South End's population, what Robert Woods called the "roving class." Woods noted that thousands of men drifted into the Salvation Army and Volunteers of America rescue missions each year. The Salvation Army Working-men's Hotel at 888 Washington Street offered rooms for five to fifteen cents a night. Lodgers without the means to pay could work at the adjacent lumberyard. Woods credited The Salvation Army with having more direct contact with "the casual and semi-criminal classes than any other religious organization." He also acknowledged the work of The Salvation Army Slum Sisters, six of whom lived "in some of the meanest streets, in order to help fallen women" (Woods 1898, 217, 278).

Emily Balch, one of the first residents of Denison House, apparently spent New Year's Eve of 1892 at a Salvation Army service. Her diary for January 1, 1893, begins with an underlined entry for "Salvation Army, evening since, Washington Street over Public Market." She and a friend contributed fifteen cents to the "silver collection" at the door and were admitted to a "good sized, well-filled hall" of lower-middle-class men and women. Miss Balch proceeded to describe her experience:

> The army members who faced the congregation from the platform were most of them of much the same class. Some were lower — almost all seemed English or from a British dependency. Only one . . . or two were of an American type, one of these an old man perhaps a shopkeeper or

clerk. The service was very earnest and a tambourine and a guitar gave less grotesque effects than would seem possible. The leader was a woman Captain Stevenson and very attractive. I had some talk with one woman who is [in] charge of a Rescue Home in Dorchester (15?) (55)? Everett St (or Ave). She was formerly in a state reformatory institution for girls in N.Y. State but left because convinced that moral persuasion without conversion was futile. I promised to visit and let her have my name and address. (Denison House Papers, n.d.)[14]

The presence of settlement houses assured that the South End was well supplied with public baths and playgrounds. Denison House offered play space, and South End House cooperated with the city to provide space for organized recreation. Residents of South End House also maintained several vacant-lot playgrounds and lobbied the mayor vigorously for public baths; head resident Robert Woods was a member of Mayor Quincy's Municipal Bath Commission for ten years (Woods and Kennedy [1911] 1970, 126, 127).

South End House was one of the few American settlement houses managed predominantly by men. It was established in 1891 by Prof. William J. Tucker and originally named Andover House after Tucker's affiliation with Andover Theological Seminary. Robert Woods became head resident after his visit to London's Toynbee Hall. South End House included a number of properties at several different locations: the Men's Residence on Union Park, the Women's Residence on East Canton Street, a Boarding Club on West Brookline, a music school on Pembroke Street, a children's center on A Street, and an industrial school on Bartlett Street in Roxbury. The boarding club for stenographers and teachers housed seven women in 1919 who committed one night a week to settlement work in addition to paying $6.00 to $9.00 per week for their rooms (Geary 1919).

The goals of South End House were educational rather than evangelical. Residents mapped conditions in the neighborhood and established the South End Improvement Association to carry out their recommendations. South End House was founded to "bring about a better and more beautiful life in its neighborhood and district and to develop new ways (through study and action in this locality) of meeting some of the serious problems of society." It also worked to create the "healthy corporate vitality [of] a well-ordered village"; to investigate local labor conditions; to "furnish a neutral ground where separated classes, rich and poor, professional and industrial, capitalist and wage-earner, may meet each other on the basis of common humanity"; and to take part in municipal affairs. These goals were carried out by twelve female and twelve male residents in cooperation with fifty-two female and thirteen male volunteers (Woods and Kennedy [1911] 1970, 125–31). Even South End House, typically identified as a predominantly male endeavor, had more women than men among its volunteers.

Denison House, on the other hand, was a decidedly female institution. Sixteen women and one man were in residence, aided by eighty-three female and thirteen male volunteers. Denison House was founded in 1892 by CSA president Vida Scudder and named after Alfred Toynbee's friend Edward Denison. Denison House cofounder Helena Dudley was the head resident for many years. Denison House literature boasted that "a women's Settlement knows women especially well" when it came to balancing housekeeping, childrearing, and waged labor (Settlements File n.d.).

Residents of Denison House were charged $5.50 to $6.50 per week for their room and board. They were expected to devote an average of four hours per day to settlement work, one hour daily to sociological reading, and half an hour a day to light housework in addition to one half-day a week helping the headworker. Their spare time could be spent in "friendly visiting, in helpfulness in household activities, and in any special branch of work, teaching, or investigation where [they proved] most effective" (Settlements File 1897).

The Denison House Neighborhood

Denison House consisted originally of two connected rowhouses on Tyler Street. A city-sponsored kindergarten met on the first floor in the mornings, followed by study clubs for older children in the afternoon and evening groups of adults discussing labor issues or city problems. The basement had rooms for boys' clubs, cooking classes, and a kitchen garden, while College Extension classes in Italian art and Shakespearian plays were offered to working women upstairs. When a benefactor purchased a third adjacent rowhouse, the staff added a first-floor reading room and basement classrooms, and they rented out rooms upstairs. The reading room and library were eventually given over to city management, as were Denison House's gymnasium and public bath in the Old

Figure 6.10. Photo of Denison House from *Denison House College Settlement Report for 1900*. (Courtesy Sophia Smith Collection, Smith College, Northampton, Mass.)

Figure 6.11. Denison House kindergarten from *Denison House College Settlement Report for 1900*. (Courtesy Sophia Smith Collection, Smith College, Northampton, Mass.)

Figure 6.12. Children's activities in the backyard of Denison House, 1915. (Courtesy of the Schlesinger Library, Radcliffe Institute, Harvard University.)

Colony chapel building on the same block (Settlements File n.d.; Woods and Kennedy [1911] 1970, 110).

By 1910 Denison House residents were veterans of the settlement movement. Helena Dudley had lived at the house for seventeen years; others had been there for ten to twelve years. A "faithful band of outside workers" composed of one hundred men and women supplemented the residents' efforts. One Denison House priority was the provision of recreational space to compete with the forty-six saloons and ten movie theaters in the neighborhood. Residents raised $10,000 of the $60,000 needed to build a small hall that could be used for dances, lectures, and plays staged by neighbors. Dudley hoped the building would be beautiful "inside and out," for "such a building standing on our dingy street would speak aloud for the higher things of life and for the spirit of adventure which placed it there" (Dudley 1910, 6).

Denison House boasted twenty-seven clubs for girls and boys and six large clubs for adults by 1910. Four of the adult clubs were for groups of Italian men and women (the Circolo Italo-Americano) and Syrians. A resident nurse operated a Wednesday evening dispensary for men who could not take off work and mothers who had no one to care for their

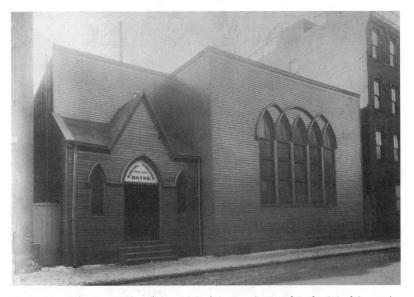

Figure 6.13. Tyler Street Church, Municipal Gymnasium and Baths, Ward Seven, in Denison House neighborhood. (Courtesy of the Boston Public Library, Print Department.)

children during the day. In 1910 alone, 534 patients were treated at the dispensary and 50 were taken to hospitals. The nurse made more than four thousand visits to the sick in their homes. Denison House sponsored summer retreats to the country for children and mothers. They also cosponsored a vacation summer school with Boston's Associated Charities. In 1910 the summer school ran for six weeks and served approximately two hundred children per day (Dudley 1910).

The Sanborn map shows that Denison House occupied three of the units in a three-story rowhouse stretching from 89 to 101 Tyler Street. A storage warehouse, stable, and Chinese laundry were at one end of the block. At the other end were another Chinese laundry, the public bathhouse, and the Harvard Street Baptist Church. Across the street were the Tyler Street nursery, a Syrian church, the Quincy School, another stable, and a bakery. A tailor's shop, ice cream factory, and lying-in hospital were on Harrison Street in the block immediately behind Denison House.

Interspersed among the shops, and sometimes in the same building, were two- to four-story flats of frame and brick construction. The 1911 list of registered (male) voters for Precinct Five of Ward Seven reveals

Figure 6.14. Drawing of Denison House with proposed additions. (From "Denison House, The Boston College Settlement, Annual Report for the Year Ending October 1st 1914." Courtesy Sophia Smith Collection, Smith College, Northampton, Mass.)

that it was a transient neighborhood where only one-half of the residents were living in the same place as the year before. It was a neighborhood of occupational and ethnic extremes. At 87 Tyler Street, right next door to Denison House, lived five men (some undoubtedly with families) ranging in age from twenty-three to fifty-four. The youngest, Charles Abdalah, worked as a silk salesman and the oldest, John Noonan, was employed as a freight clerk. The others listed their occupations as machinist, waiter, and barber. Next door to them, at 85 Tyler Street, seven men listed occupations as bartender, actor, storekeeper, leather shipper, waiter, and stage carpenter (one was unemployed) (Boston 1911).

Clergyman Gabriel Korkeman lived in a dwelling in front of the Syrian Church at 66 Tyler Street. One of his neighbors was a stableman who probably worked down the street. Assad and Habib Tradd, a peddler and a barber both in their twenties, lived upstairs over the Chinese laundry at 77 Tyler Street and shared quarters with Naif Tamer, a middle-aged merchant. Sam Lee lived in the same building as the Chinese laundry at 115 Tyler Street. A firemen named Michael O'Connor lived

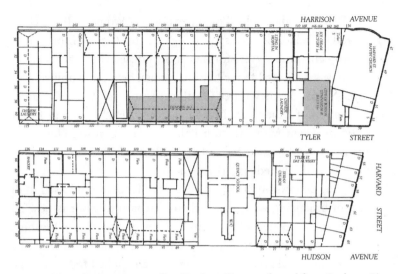

Map 6.3. Map of streets surrounding Denison House, adapted from Sanborn Fire Insurance map of 1909.

two doors down from Kachadour and Nasareb Shirvanian, who worked as a butcher and laborer, respectively. Napali Francesco, a barber, lived on the same block as Spyros Papas, the fruit dealer.

The most crowded flat was the three-story (plus basement) dwelling at 104 Tyler Street. It was also one of the most ethnically diverse. Ten men lived there, only two of whom shared the same surname (O'Leary). George Spaniapolis, William Seekoohoos, and James Warrenitiss were some of the other voters at the same address. Assuming some of these men were married and had children, the number of people living in the flat could have been twenty or more. Eight of the men were laborers, suggesting that their unpredictable wages contributed to the necessity to save on housing costs. They used Denison House as a "neighborhood living room" for respite from the inevitable commotion of so many bodies. Children from 104 Tyler Street might also have visited Denison House to learn English (Boston 1911).

Like many other settlement houses, Denison House supported laborers in word and deed. Information for potential volunteers included reference to connections with Labor for candidates who wanted to study the "social and industrial situation." Denison House literature extolled the virtues of "sharing with those to whom has fallen the task of providing for the material wants of society, those higher social experiences which alone make society worthwhile" (Settlements File 1897). Head resident Helena Dudley helped organize Boston's Women's Trade Union League and served for two years as a delegate to the Central Labor Union. Several women's unions were formed at the house, where its Social Science Club was dedicated to facilitating contact between employers and employees. Mary Kenney (later O'Sullivan), an Irish-Catholic American Federation of Labor organizer invited from Hull House to Boston by WEIU president Mary Morton Kehew, called Denison House "the first open door in the workers' district in Boston" (Blair 1980; Deutsch 1994; Woods and Kennedy [1911] 1970, 110).

During the depression of 1893–94, Denison House found itself in the business of practicing what it preached in regard to labor issues. The settlement house opened Wells Memorial Sewing Rooms on Washington Street to provide temporary needlework for women thrown out of work by the financial crisis. Nearly 700 women applied for jobs, 324 of whom were investigated (for need and abilities) and accepted. Applicants who were turned away were referred to the Women's Educational and Industrial Union or relief rooms elsewhere in the district. Workers received seventy-five cents a day for sewing garments. Women were divided into three categories, depending on their skills, and each grade worked in a separate room under the supervision of a forewoman. Their products were dispensed to charities, The Salvation Army, Travelers' Aid, and the city hospital. The intent was to avoid competition with the private market while providing women with a decent wage. Orders filled for the hospital, for example, were for clothes usually made by nurses in their spare time. Women worked seven hours a day and were fined for tardiness. During their one-hour lunch break, women could buy a hot lunch delivered by the New England Kitchen for eight cents each, but this was too expensive for most (Dudley 1894).

Helena Dudley analyzed the strengths and weaknesses of the experiment in an article describing the Wells Memorial work project. She concluded that the employment of housewives rather than the usual male breadwinners was a mistake because it took women away from their families, but acknowledged that it was often necessary. Dudley also saw competition with regular business a serious danger, as was the possibility of depressing wages with work-relief. She thought the Denison House project was successful precisely because it avoided competing with private enterprise and because it paid its employees in cash that could be cycled back into the local economy. Dudley waxed evangelical in her summary, stating that "these women were saved from the demoralizing results of complete idleness and from that degradation of character which comes from receiving aid without giving a return. In some cases this work alone saved them from utter discouragement" (Dudley 1894, 77).

Boston's Ties to Chicago

Boston's South End was connected to one of Chicago's most significant events through the work of Ellen Swallow Richards and her New England Kitchen. During the same period that Caroline Bartlett Crane was consulting around the country as a municipal housekeeper, Ellen Swallow Richards was conducting research on water quality that would establish her reputation as a noted sanitary specialist. In 1873 Richards became the first female graduate of MIT and in 1884 she was appointed to the MIT faculty as an instructor of sanitary chemistry (Hoy 1980).

Richards soon applied her interest in sanitation to women's sphere in the home. In 1882 she published *The Chemistry of Cooking and Cleaning: A Manual for Housekeepers,* and in 1887 she coauthored (with former student Marion Talbot, dean of women at the University of Chicago) *Home Sanitation: A Manual for Housekeepers.* These were followed by six more books on sanitation and conservation between 1904 and 1911. In *Sanitation in Daily Life* (1904), she proposed that concerns about the environment should run along "two chief lines—first, what is often called municipal housekeeping... second, family housekeeping" (Hoy 1980, 180). Richards was elected the first president of the American Home Economics Association in 1909.

Richards was one of many "material feminists" influenced by utopian visions of cooperative housekeeping at the turn of the century. She and Mary Hinman Abel had read Edward Bellamy's *Looking Backward* (1887) when they opened their New England Kitchen in 1890. The kitchen was a laboratory designed to produce nutritious food at low cost through experiments with newly invented equipment such as the Aladdin cooker. Richards thought the "mission of the [Aladdin] Oven and Cooker is in the ideal life of the twentieth century, as shown by Bellamy.... I believe the idea is destined to give a much-needed relief to multitudes of overworked women" (Hayden 1981, 148).

Richards took her ideas for scientific domesticity to the World's Columbian Exposition, where she set up the Rumford Kitchen. The

Rumford Kitchen was designed to be a small, white clapboard public building that would fit into any neighborhood of modest single-family homes. Inside was all the modern equipment of a laboratory demonstrating how to extract maximum nutrition at minimum cost and effort (Hayden 1981, 151; Weimann 1981, 258, 462). The Rumford Kitchen was so successful that it spawned the National Household Economics Association, founded by women interested in introducing public kitchens into poor urban neighborhoods. Marion Talbot acquired the exhibit's equipment for her students when the fair was over, and Jane Addams adopted the model for Hull House (Hayden 1981, 151).

Richards published the *New England Kitchen Magazine* throughout the 1890s. One of the first departments of home economics was established at the University of Chicago by Marion Talbot. Municipal housekeeping links between Boston and Chicago thus were firmly established through Ellen Swallow Richards's influence (Hayden 1981, 177; Hoy 1980; Solomon 1985, 85).

CHAPTER SEVEN

Men Build Chicago's Skyline, Women Redeem the City

> Striding, like some modern Colossus, the southwestern shore of Lake Michigan, Chicago, the capital, the metropolis of the wealth-producing West, rears her stately head, the most remarkable city in the world. Within the past nine decades a swamp, the story of her subsequent rise and progress has no parallel in the whole history of the country. Men and women still live among us who remember when Chicago was, so to speak, in her swaddling clothes; when there were no mansions and no villas, no huge factories and no mamouth stores; when a ride of half a mile from the site of the Palmer House block was a trip to the country. (*Chicago of Today* 1892, 33)

These were the first sentences in a 248-page magazine advertising the World's Columbian Exposition. *Chicago of Today* was sponsored by the business community to flaunt the city's accomplishments and promote their own products. The back cover of the magazine was a full-page advertisement for the Wisconsin Central Lines Railroad that boasted Pullman sleepers for comfortable travel to the fair.

Chicago at the turn of the century had reasons to brag. When the Census Bureau officially recorded its population in 1840 there were fewer than 5,000 residents; by 1870 the city had exploded to 300,000 people. The 1871 fire conveniently erased much of the original landscape just before radical changes in building technology allowed construction of the world's first skyscrapers. The zeal with which distinguished firms raced to rebuild the city contributed to the architectural genre known as Chicago's "commercial style." The city hosted an internationally rec-

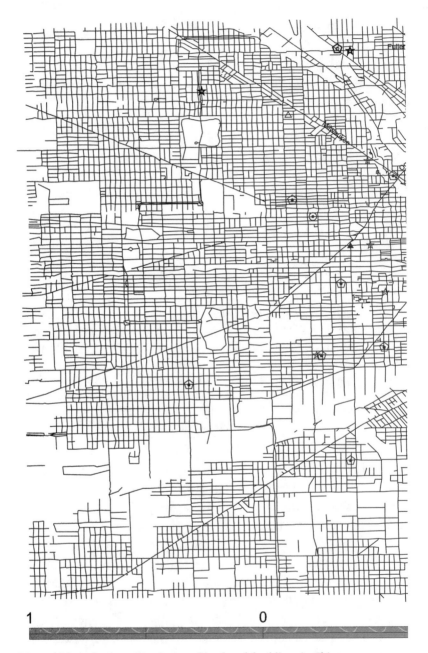

Map 7.1. Map of redemptive places and landmark buildings in Chicago, c. 1915.

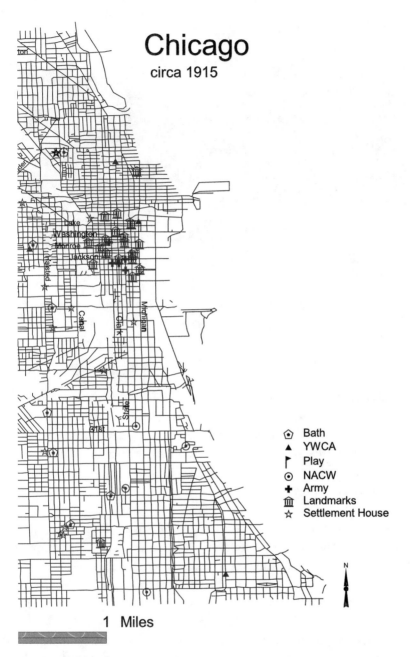

Chicago

circa 1915

ton

der

Lake
Washington
Monroe
Jackson

Halsted

Canal

Clark

Michigan

State

51st

⬠ Bath
▲ YWCA
⌐ Play
⊙ NACW
✚ Army
🏛 Landmarks
☆ Settlement House

N

1 Miles

Map 7.1. *Continued.*

CHICAGO
CENTRAL BUSINESS SECTION

Figure 7.1. Aerial view of Chicago, 1915. (Arno B. Reincke, photographer. Courtesy Library of Congress, 701585, G & M 1336.)

ognized exposition in 1893 associated with the City Beautiful movement, and the Chicago Commercial Club commissioned its own City Beautiful plan by Daniel Burnham in 1909. Between the Civil War and World War I Chicago almost completely reinvented itself.

The spatial changes, of course, were intertwined with social and political changes. All sorts of strangers were streaming into Chicago as its skyline rose. Immigrants, blacks, and single women arrived in droves, some to labor in the slaughterhouses and others destined for offices downtown. Poet Carl Sandburg immortalized both types of workers, most notably when he called Chicago the "Hog Butcher for the World," and in lesser-known poems titled "Skyscraper" and "Working Girls" (Sandburg 1992).

Women volunteers were also highly visible in Chicago. The white Woman's Club of Chicago, counterpart to the elite white all-male Commercial Club, pursued a mission to clean up the city. From the World's Columbian Exposition to Burnham's City Beautiful plan, the Woman's Club was involved in most of the significant architectural and planning events in Chicago. The club's municipal housekeeping agenda encouraged members to participate in settlement work, public bath campaigns, and the playground movement. Jane Addams relied on the Woman's Club to maintain her connections with wealthy patrons of Hull House. The Woman's Club also was implicated in the formation of the National Association of Colored Women through the role Bertha Potter Palmer

Figure 7.2. Chicago of Today, The Metropolis of the West. Inside front cover of a magazine, 1892. (Artist unknown. Courtesy Chicago Historical Society, F38H/32488/A18.)

occupied as president of the Board of Lady Managers at the Columbian Exposition.

The World's Columbian Exposition played a pivotal part in Chicago's success story. By displaying a wealth of material goods in the midst of a serious economic depression, the fair symbolized the nation's increasingly polarized income distribution. While the fair advertised what money could buy, however, Hull House and other settlements dealt with the dispossessed. There is no need to repeat here all the excellent studies of Hull House (Bryan and Davis 1990; Horowitz 1983; Lissak 1989; Sklar 1985, 1990; Stebner 1997). Rather, I focus on its history in the year following the closing of the World's Fair. Hull House, Northwestern University Settlement, and the University of Chicago Settlement all strained to provide adequate services to newcomers during the grim winter of 1893/94.

As in other cities, women were at the forefront of voluntary efforts to deal with the city's problems. Some women volunteers benefited from their association with men at the top of the social ladder, some renounced their privileges to live among the poor, other volunteers started and stayed at the bottom, and still others were left out of the system entirely. This last group deserves special attention. Separated from slavery by only a few decades, African American women led a sustained assault on the system that supported lynchings, suffrage only for men, and extreme economic inequalities by race. Blacks' exclusion from the Columbian Exposition fueled their attack.

The Emerging Skyline

Chicago is the undisputed birthplace of the skyscraper. The 1891 *Maitland's American Standard Dictionary*, the first to include the word "skyscraper," defined it as "a very tall building such as now are being built in Chicago" (Girouard 1985, 319). Architect William Jenney created the prototype of the skyscraper in 1884 when he designed a steel skeleton to support the roof and walls of the Home Insurance Company. Traditional masonry construction methods previously had limited building heights to five or six stories. New technologies, however, including the steel frame, telephones, and improved Otis electric elevators, made skyscrapers practical and economical. The building's weight could be reduced and its interior space expanded vertically. Jenney's ten-story Home Insurance Company became the model for skyscrapers constructed nationwide between 1890 and 1920 (Condit 1964, 83; Girouard 1985).

The Home Insurance building was just the beginning. Chicago quickly converted its four- to six-story facade line constructed after the fire of 1871 into taller and more profitable buildings (Bluestone 1991, 109). New York was close behind. Until the 1880s the skylines of Chicago and New York consisted of church spires interspersed with the domes or towers of public buildings. By 1920, however, traditional buildings "had been submerged by the rising tide of skyscrapers in both cities: the down-town silhouette which was ultimately to be exported all over the world had arrived" (Girouard 1985, 319).

Skyscrapers came to represent Chicago's commercial style of architecture, and Jenney's student Louis H. Sullivan became the style's most recognized champion. Sullivan arrived in Chicago in 1873 after being laid off from the Philadelphia firm of Furness and Hewitt during the depression. He then joined Jenney's office, where he met Daniel Burnham and other influential architects. In writing about this era, social critic Lewis Mumford called Sullivan "the father of the modern skyscraper" and "the Whitman of American architecture" (Mumford 1955, 142, 143). Among Sullivan's buildings, many built with his partner Dankmar Adler, were the Carson, Pirie, Scott department store, the Schiller Building, the Stock Exchange, the Auditorium Building, and the Transportation Building at the World's Columbian Exposition. The Auditorium Building was ten stories high when completed in 1889; its 63,350 square feet took up the entire block on Congress Parkway from Michigan to Wabash Avenue. The massive complex included a theater with

Figure 7.3. Aerial view of Chicago's Federal Building and Post Office, c. 1889. A church spire is the tallest building. (Photographer unknown. Courtesy Chicago Historical Society, ICHi-21795.)

Figure 7.4. View of Chicago's skyline post-1900. (Burke and Koretke, photographers. Courtesy Chicago Historical Society, ICHi-21722.)

seating capacity for over four thousand people, a hotel, and offices, at a cost of $3.5 million (Condit 1964, 69, 70; Kaufmann 1956, 29).[1]

Smaller projects also altered Chicago's streetscape at the end of the nineteenth century. While William Jenney and Louis Sullivan were constructing skyscrapers, Drs. Gertrude Wellington, Sarah Stevenson, and Julia Lowe were conducting a vigorous campaign for public hygiene. A federal Bureau of Labor investigation in 1893 revealed that fewer than 5 percent of Chicago's tenement families had plumbing. In response, the Municipal Order League appointed the three female physicians to a committee to investigate the need for public baths. After observing successes in New York City, Dr. Wellington argued that a "free public bath will help prevent typhoid, cholera, and crime" and "will inspire sweeter manners and a better observance of the law." Hull House donated the land and the city appropriated $12,000 for its first bathhouse, named in honor of Mayor Carter H. Harrison (Williams 1991, 82–93).

When the Carter H. Harrison Bath opened one block north of Hull House in 1893, it was a more modest enterprise than Sullivan's Auditorium Building. The public bathhouse was 25 by 110 feet, two stories high, with a front of Milwaukee pressed brick and brownstone trim. It contained a waiting room, seventeen showers and dressing rooms, one tub bath, and a small swimming pool (Williams 1991, 87, 88, 125). The Carter H. Harrison Bath was one of the first in the country to provide showers on a year-round basis. It made little impact on the public imagination, however. Compared with the Columbian Exposition that opened the same year, the Carter Harrison Bath House was an obscure event in Chicago's history, much less the history of urban development. (This particular bathhouse was so ordinary, in fact, that no photographs of the building could be found at either the Chicago Historical Society or the University of Illinois archives.) Serving just its neighborhood and the immigrants who lived there, it fell outside the boundaries of civic boosterism. Yet its importance as a model for redemptive places easily matched the World's Fair's influence on the City Beautiful movement.

The World's Columbian Exposition of 1893

The idea for the World's Columbian Exposition arose from public enthusiasm during the 1880s for an event commemorating Columbus's discovery of America. Planning began too late to open the fair by the four-hundredth anniversary date of 1892, but dedication ceremonies held in 1892 met the spirit, if not the letter, of the intent (opening day followed on May 1, 1893). More than one million people jammed the streets of Chicago for the two-day dedication. A grand civic parade of 100,000 people marched down Michigan Avenue to the rousing sounds of John Philip Sousa's Marine Band, and 1,800 little girls formed an American flag at the Government Building. Although Pres. Benjamin Harrison was absent due to the First Lady's illness, Vice President Levi Morton led the procession consisting of hundreds of carriages filled with Supreme Court justices, senators, congressional representatives, governors, and ambassadors. Between 100,000 and 500,000 people attended the ceremonies at the fairgrounds (Bolotin and Laing 1992; Cameron 1893).

The World's Columbian Exposition was symbolically as important to the rest of the country as it was for the city of Chicago. It was meant to display all of America's momentous achievements in the fine arts, industry, technology, and agriculture to Americans and to visitors from around the world. The exposition was "a celebration of America's coming of age a grand rite of passage" that demonstrated what a well-designed city could be (Burg 1976, xiii).

One of the fair's best examples of American technological genius was George Ferris's huge revolving ride that trumped the Eiffel Tower as an engineering marvel. The steel Ferris Wheel, 264 feet high and weighing forty-six tons, was only part of the show. The fair also gave Americans an entirely new way of experiencing their surroundings. At the fair they were spectators of a city they visited rather than participants in a city they helped create. Women were granted the privileges of a *flaneur* for the first time, so they could safely stroll through the fairgrounds and observe others without raising suspicions about their own virtue (Bolotin and Laing 1992, 23; Rabinovitz 1998).

Credit for design of the World's Fair generally goes to Daniel Burnham and Frederick Law Olmsted. They, along with a team of professional architects and artists, juxtaposed a large naturalistic lagoon with neoclassical buildings to form a Court of Honor (Bolotin and Laing 1992; R. Wilson 1979). The 686-acre exposition was built by men who already enjoyed considerable reputations in architecture and landscape architecture. Daniel Burnham, Louis Sullivan, and Frederick Law Olmsted had careers that both enhanced, and were enhanced by, the fair's success.

By contrast, women's participation in the World's Columbian Exposition depended almost entirely on their husbands' reputations. Suffragist Susan B. Anthony's efforts to have women appointed to the World's Columbian Commission were thwarted when Congress established a separate "Board of Lady Managers." Bertha Palmer, wife of the real estate tycoon Potter Palmer who built the elaborate Palmer House Hotel mentioned in *Chicago Today,* was elected president of that board.[2] The other 116 Lady Managers (two from every state, territory, and the District of Columbia and eight members at large) were nominated by politicians or prominent businessmen. Thus Lady Managers tended to be active in elite clubs and philanthropies that made them highly visible. Mrs. Palmer, for example, was a member of Chicago's prestigious Woman's Club. Nominees for the board were also economically comfortable enough to dedicate time to the fair. No black women, and no factory workers, were appointed to the Board of Lady Managers. Neither was Susan B. Anthony (Weimann 1981, 1–43).

Suffragists and professional women were not completly excluded from the board, however. Phoebe Couzins of Missouri, who had a law degree and was the first woman appointed to be a U.S. marshal, was elected secretary of the Board of Lady Managers. Miss Couzins had delivered the Declaration of Women's Rights in Philadelphia with Susan B. Anthony and represented the feminist faction on the Board called the Isabellas. The Isabella Association, named for members' belief that Queen Isabella should have shared Columbus's glory for sponsoring his mission, was adamantly opposed to a segregated women's exhibit at the fair. The Woman's Department (represented by Mrs. Palmer), on the other hand, insisted on a women's pavilion as one of their original goals. The composition of the Board of Lady Managers epitomized the national rift that existed between women who wanted to work for general reform and those who were dedicated primarily to women's rights. Mrs. Palmer's faction prevailed and the Woman's Building became one of the fourteen "Great Buildings" circling the Court of Honor (Weimann 1981, 43).

The Great Buildings were surrounded by two hundred smaller buildings and a midway featuring the Ferris Wheel. The Great Buildings included exhibits on manufacturing, transportation, mining, agriculture, and electricity. The Woman's Building was located at the northern end of the lagoon near the Horticulture Building. Frances Willard described it as a "charming structure in the purest style of the Italian Renaissance" whose graceful lines were appropriate to the "temple of womanhood." Corner pavilions were connected to the raised center pavilion by a shaded promenade in a structure that was four hundred feet long, two hundred feet deep, and two stories high. The interior of the building was decorated with murals and sculptures by women artists, most notably Mary Cassatt (Willard 1893).

The Woman's Building contained an international display of women's accomplishments in science, the arts, and industry. A library of volumes written by women authors included Grace Dodge's *A Bundle of Letters to Busy Girls*. Dodge, future president of the national YWCA, was at the fair representing her Working Girls' Association (Weimann 1981, 370, 512). Exhibits of fabric design, dressmaking, weaving, pottery, practical housekeeping, nursing, and dozens of other types of work performed by American women filled the first floor. One wall was dedicated to Women's Exchanges from cities across the country, where they sold articles "too familiar to require specific mention." Women's work from Spain, France, Italy, and Japan, among other countries, was also represented. The second-floor Assembly Room could seat seventeen hundred people and was used daily for lectures by "the great thinkers of the day." The model kitchen was also on the second floor. It had seats for a small audience and a demonstration platform equipped with a gas stove and appliances. The Woman's Building also housed representatives from more than sixty voluntary organizations, including the YWCA, WCTU, WEIU, and the Chicago Woman's Club (Willard 1893).

Near the Woman's Building was the free-standing Rumford Kitchen created by Ellen Swallow Richards. The kitchen was named after Benjamin Thompson, Count Rumford of Germany, who experimented with nutritious, affordable food cooked efficiently to save fuel. The Rumford Kitchen was patterned on the New England Kitchen in Boston's South End that Richards had opened in 1890 with Mary Hinman Abel (Hayden 1981, 151–59; Weimann 1981, 258, 462).

Ellen Swallow Richards was only one of MIT's female graduates to establish a reputation at the fair. Sophia Hayden, designer of the Woman's Building, earned her architecture degree from MIT in 1890. Hayden won the national competition from among twelve entries by women architects. Her design for a three-story Italian Renaissance building was modeled on her thesis project for a fine arts museum. Professional ar-

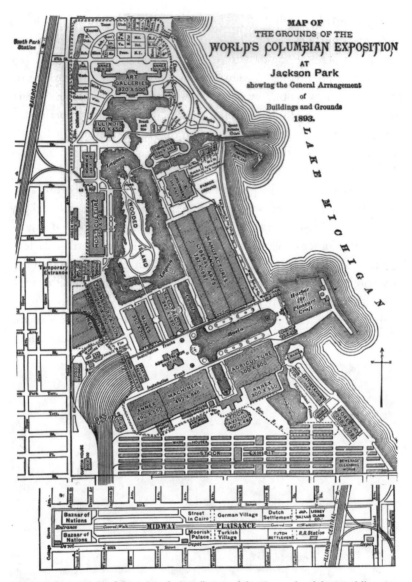

Map 7.2. Engraving of the printed piece "Map of the Grounds of the World's Columbian Exposition at Jackson Park Showing the General Arrangement of Buildings and Grounds, 1893." (From World's Columbian Exposition, unknown source. Courtesy Chicago Historical Society, ICHi-02552.)

chitects initially feared that a woman lacked the practical knowledge to supervise construction of a building, but Hayden assuaged those concerns with her working drawings. A formal pictorial history of the fair assured the public that Hayden "had no help whatever in working up the designs. It was done by herself in her own home" (Cameron 1893, 167). The Woman's Building won the fair's Artists' Medal for Design because "its balconies, loggias, and vases for flowers, [made it] the lightest and gayest in its general aspect, and consequently best adapted for a joyous and festive occasion" (Weimann 1981, 148).[3]

The fair was especially popular with women, perhaps because it included daycare. Mothers who arrived at the fair early enough could pay for supervised daycare in the Children's Building, which provided a nursery, gymnasium, roof garden, play rooms, and a kitchen garden. African Americans, who were excluded from participating in the fair's exhibits, were nonetheless expected to work there. Black women staffed the nursery, although it is unclear whether they were hired by the Board of Lady Managers or if they accompanied their white employers to the fair. For older children, the kitchen garden was "devoted to teaching little

Figure 7.5. Woman's Building at the World's Columbian Exposition of 1893 in Chicago. (Photographer unknown. Courtesy Chicago Historical Society, ICHi-13662.)

girls in a practical way how to make good housewives when they grow up." In the middle of the room were low tables with tiny beds on them, and around the edges were little chairs, dishes, washtubs, and brooms for forty girls to polish their domestic skills. The Children's Building was so popular that hundreds of children were turned away daily (Bolotin and Laing 1992, 105; Cameron 1893, 729).

The World's Columbian Exposition became known as the "White City," partly because the major buildings were painted white. The fair was also referred to as white because it contrasted so sharply with the dirt and grime of real cities. Its streets were swept and cleaned nightly, for example, whereas in the rest of Chicago whole weeks might pass between sweepings. Powered by the novel alternating current electricity (provided by George Westinghouse, who beat out Thomas Edison for the contract), the White City was free of the coal soot of industry. The entire fair projected cleanliness, beauty, and visual order. The latest sanitary facilities helped promote that image. More than 3,000 water closets were installed, compared with only 250 at the 1889 Paris Ex-

Figure 7.6. Interior of Woman's Building at the World's Columbian Exposition of 1893 in Chicago. (William H. Jackson, photographer. Courtesy Chicago Historical Society, ICHi-25047.)

Figure 7.7. Interior of Children's Building at the World's Columbian Exposition of 1893 in Chicago. (C. D. Arnold, photographer. Courtesy Chicago Historical Society, ICHi-23823.)

position and 900 at the Philadelphia Centennial in 1876 (Brands 1995, 49; Goldfield and Brownell 1979, 214; Hoy 1995, 78; Schuyler 1986, 189).

Another reason the fair seemed white was that African Americans were almost completely absent. Antislavery activist Frederick Douglass was invited to participate, but only as a representative of black culture in Haiti. Neither the men's Columbian Commission nor the Board of Lady Managers included black members. Their exclusion galled the militant antilynching crusader and journalist Ida B. Wells. She translated her fury into an eighty-one-page pamphlet titled *The Reason Why the Colored American Is Not in the World's Columbian Exposition*. The tract consisted of six chapters written by Wells and by Frederick Douglass, the journalist I. Garland Penn, and Wells's future husband, Frederick L. Barnett. It was an impassioned account of discrimination against blacks in the post-Reconstruction years. Wells planned to publish the pamphlet in English, French, German, and Spanish for foreign visitors to the fair, but she ran out of money before it could be printed in any

Figure 7.8. Lantern slide of creche for babies in the Children's Building at the World's Columbian Exposition of 1893 in Chicago. (Photographer unknown. Courtesy Chicago Historical Society, ICHi-21087.)

language except English. Wells credited African Americans with performing one-half of the labor in the United States, allowing "the white people of this country the leisure essential to their great progress in education, art, science, industry and invention" (Wells 1893). Wells's radical stance was so controversial that some black newspaper editors condemned it out of fear it would harm the race.

The exclusion of blacks from the Columbian Exposition figured prominently in the formation of the NACW. An organizational meeting of the Board of Lady Managers in 1890 resulted in the appointment of a white woman to represent black women's interests in the fair. After much protest, Mrs. Fannie Barrier Williams, the light-skinned wife of a black lawyer and central member of Chicago's black elite, was appointed as secretary to the Art Department. Since Mrs. Williams had not been involved in the original struggles to gain black women's representation in the fair, however, her appointment was politically unpopular among more militant black women (Shaughnessy 1997).

Hallie Q. Brown was the next African American woman appointed to a clerical position in the fair's Department of Publicity and Promotion. At the time Brown was principal of women at Tuskegee Institute and she would eventually become a colleague of Victoria Earle Matthews at the White Rose Mission. In her capacity as secretary for the fair, Brown wrote to black women's organizations and black newspapers to see whether they had been solicited for contributions to the fair. When she concluded that exhibits by blacks had been ignored, she wrote to the Board of Lady Managers complaining that "it seems to be a settled conviction among colored people that no adequate opportunity is to be offered them for representation in the World's Fair." Mrs. Palmer informed Miss Brown that membership on the Board of Lady Managers was by organization and not by individuals, so Brown decided to organize. She was a founding member and secretary to the Washington, D.C., Colored Woman's League established in 1892, which eventually merged with Josephine St. Pierre Ruffin's National Federation of Afro-American Women to form the National Association of Colored Women in 1896 (Brown [1926] 1988, 215; Shaughnessy 1997; Wesley 1984, chapter 3).

Blacks may have been invisible at the fair, but they were a significant presence in Chicago. Thousands of black men, women, and children arrived annually from the South. Chicago's black population was less than 7,000 in 1870, but by 1920 it had increased to more than 100,000 (Spear 1967, 12; Waring 1886). All these newcomers vastly outnumbered the small black aristocracy, whom Fannie Barrier Williams described in 1905 as "better dressed, better housed, and better mannered than almost anywhere else in the wide west ... real gentle folks in the highest and best sense of the term" (Gatewood 1990, 121–22).

Black newcomers were in particular need of redemptive places and black women volunteers in more than 150 clubs provided them. Two of the earliest women's clubs were the Ida B. Wells Club formed in 1893 (in conjunction with Wells's fair activities) and the Phyllis Wheatley Club formed by Elizabeth Lindsay Davis in 1896, both of which were affiliates of the NACW. Members of the Phyllis Wheatley Club discussed literature and drama, worried about how to protect young girls from urban temptations, and encouraged municipal reform. In 1900 Dr. Carrie Golden presented a paper at the Phyllis Wheatley Club titled "The

Sanitary Condition of the City and Its Relation to the Homes." Her study of six hundred tenements on the South Side found that African Americans' homes were decidedly "less sanitary" than those of whites (Knupfer 1996, 49).

The Phyllis Wheatley Club established the Phyllis Wheatley Home in 1907 to "befriend ... the Colored girls and women who [came] into this great city seeking work, often without relatives, friends, or money." Like the YWCA, the Phyllis Wheatley Home tried to provide a "Christian influence," taught domestic skills, and tried to find respectable jobs for their boarders—all for the relatively modest fee of $1.25 per week. The home's advisory board included prominent African American men, but clubwomen were in charge of all the fundraising, cleaning, and home improvements. Their motto reflected their determination: "If you can't push, pull, and if you can't pull, please get out of the way." Between 1907 and 1914 the home provided lodging for more than three hundred girls and found jobs for five hundred. In 1915 a new home was bought at 3256 Rhodes Avenue that could accommodate forty-four girls (Knupfer 1996, 81–83).

Another member of the NACW through her affiliation with the West Side Woman's Club, Elizabeth McDonald, began her rescue work in Chicago as a volunteer probation officer. The 1900 annual report of the Cook County Juvenile Court noted that six probation officers were paid from private sources, one of which was the Chicago Woman's Club. The report singled out McDonald as "one colored woman who devotes her entire time to the work, free of charge, and whose services are invaluable to the court as she takes charge of all colored children." McDonald opened the Louise Juvenile Home at 630 Ada Street in 1907. There, with another woman volunteer named Elizabeth Scott, McDonald provided care for fifty-six white and African American children. The children attended a neighborhood school during the day and after school learned industrial education with classes in washing, ironing, cooking, sewing, and needlework. Within a year McDonald bought an eleven-room house, large enough to care for eighty-nine children, and by 1913 she had incorporated as the Louise Juvenile Industrial School for Colored Boys (Knupfer 1996, 71–74).

Amanda Smith, a former slave and member of the Ideal Woman's Club, founded the Amanda Smith Home for Colored and Dependent Children in 1899. The home was outside Chicago in Harvey, a temperance town founded in 1891 by Turlington Harvey, lumber magnate and benefactor of evangelist preacher George Moody (Gilbert 1991, 192–98). The Amanda Smith Home opened with five children and was accommodating thirty children by 1903. Like the Louise Juvenile Home, the Amanda Smith Home took in children referred by the Cook County Juvenile Court. The home relied on community contributions until 1911, when NACW member Hallie Q. Brown arranged for an English benefactor to secure its financial future (Knupfer 1996, 76–81).

The NACW emerged partially in response to black women's exclusion from YWCA facilities. Members of the YWCA were well represented at the fair in contrast to the absence of black women. Mrs. Leander Stone, president of the Chicago YWCA, was an alternate member of the Board of Lady Managers and wound up resolving a dispute about exhibit space. Mrs. Springer of St. Louis, president of the International Board of the YWCA (i.e., the urban associations), complained about the space they had been allocated and threatened to move to the Liberal Arts Building. Mrs. Stone thought that would be ill-advised and negotiated a compromise between Mrs. Springer and the Board of Lady Managers. The YWCA stayed in the Woman's Building, but when Mrs. Springer furnished the space with carved mahogany settees the extravagance caused such an uproar that Mrs. Springer declined her travel reimbursement to the fair to restore the peace. A less controversial part of the exhibit was the display of boarding houses built by the YWCA after a survey found hundreds of girls living in attic rooms (Weimann 1981, 490).

In addition to its strong presence in the Woman's Building, the YWCA played an important role in Chicago outside the fair's gates. The YWCA built the Hotel Endeavor on the Chicago waterfront to accommodate the thousands of women who flocked to the fair in search of work. The Hotel Endeavor offered rooms with three beds at the rate of $1.00 per day; its capacity was soon exceeded and an annex added. The fair created something of a crisis, as Mrs. Stone reported:

> Young women from all parts of the world rushed to this city, determined to see the Fair, believing that work with large salaries and unlimited leisure was easily obtained. They came only to discover that thousands of others had entertained the same opinions, and instead of their Eldorado, found themselves, in many instances, stranded, and in others with positions hardly affording them a living. (Weimann 1981, 491)

The YWCA soon opened an employment office, leased five more board-ing houses, and set up its own administrative office at 5930 Rosalie Court near the Fifth-ninth Street entrance to the fair. YWCA Travelers' Aid ladies, wearing bright blue badges, waited at railway stations and steamship docks to get "hold of a large number of girls before sinfully disposed persons could do so." With luck, some of those girls would have read the brochure the YWCA sent to its 20,000 members in 1893. They were advised to carry as little money as possible, to buy a map of Chicago and try to remember where they were, to carry the names of local friends, to memorize landmarks, and to keep identification on them at all times (Sims 1936, 42; Weimann 1981, 491).

A 1919 YWCA investigation of living conditions among working women reported thirteen boarding houses in Chicago, one of which was the Jane Club affiliated with Hull House. The Jane Club accommo-dated thirty women at a cost of $3.25 per week. The YWCA noted that the club had housed fifty women during the Columbian Exposition, but that had been too many; thirty seemed to be the right number to make the club self-supporting and prevent overcrowding. The Ruth Club and the Miriam Club for Jewish women housed sixteen and twenty-nine women, respectively, at costs ranging from $2.50 a week for a shared room to $4.50 for single rooms. Roman Catholics had two homes accom-modating 150 women; nonsectarian Christian denominations accounted

Figure 7.9. Postcard of the Carrie McGill Memorial Residence of the YWCA at 4938 Drexel Boulevard in Chicago, c. 1900. (Courtesy Archives of the National Board of the YWCA of the USA.)

for another three homes for nearly 400 women; and the Volunteers of America sponsored the Women's Christian Home for twenty-four women who paid $3.00 to $4.00 per week for lodging. Another five secular homes sheltered about 370 women, one of which had fairly low expectations and would accept "any applicant who appears respectable and not intoxicated, or a fit subject for the police" (Geary 1919).

Hull House

Hull House was to the settlement movement what the World's Fair was to international expositions. It was so successful at its work, and at promoting its work, that it grew in actual and mythic stature after other settlement houses had faded from the scene. Jane Addams's inspiration for Hull House, like Vida Scudder's for the CSA, came from a visit to Toynbee Hall. Yet Jane Addams was such a powerful force in the settlement movement that she eclipsed Scudder. In 1908 the *Ladies Home Journal* named Addams the "First American Woman"; and her ranking matched Theodore Roosevelt's and Thomas Edison's among "the most socially useful Americans" in a 1913 national poll (Davis 1973, 200). Addams's towering reputation was built on her vision of the settlement movement, and Hull House was the incarnation of that vision. (Addams was never a member of the CSA. It is interesting to speculate that she might have been a CSA cofounder with Scudder, however, if her father had allowed her to attend Smith as she had wished instead of sending her to the Rockford Institute in Illinois.)

Addams and Ellen Gates Starr visited London to tour Toynbee Hall and the People's Palace, a large philanthropic institute containing meeting rooms, workshops, and clubrooms for the working class (Davis 1973, 49). Addams and Starr also were influenced by the Reverend Mearns's *The Bitter Cry of Outcast London* (1883) and John Ruskin's *Unto This Last* (1890), books that William and Catherine Booth read. For Addams, Hull House represented "essentially a religious commitment, but the kind of Christianity she witnessed at Toynbee Hall and the People's Palace was a religion of social action, a version of religion that . . . demanded only a desire to serve" (Davis 1973, 51).

Like many redemptive places, Hull House began in rented quarters. Addams described seeing it for the first time as a "fine old house standing well back from the street, surrounded on three sides by a broad piazza which was supported by wooden pillars of exceptionally pure Corinthian design and proportion." The ground floor was rented to offices and storerooms for a factory out back. The house had been a second-hand furniture store and a home for the elderly, reputedly with a haunted attic, since being built in 1856 by Charles Hull. Addams and Starr leased the second floor of the house on Halsted Street in 1889 from Helen Culver, the niece and beneficiary of Charles Hull (Addams [1910] 1960, 77–78).

An ambitious construction program began in 1891. One of the first projects was the public kitchen. Because immigrant women sewing all day in sweatshops had little time to feed their families, Addams and Starr tried to provide nutritional, inexpensive food for the neighborhood. They sent a Hull House resident to Boston to visit Ellen Swallow Richards's New England Kitchen to learn the principles of scientific food production. The beef stew made from inexpensive cuts of meat, the boiled corn mush, and rice pudding that made up the public kitchen's menu, however, held little appeal for immigrants. Addams soon closed the kitchen and replaced it with a coffeehouse (Addams [1910] 1960, 101–2).

The need for Hull House was particularly acute in 1893, "that terrible winter after the World's Fair, when the general financial depression throughout the country was much intensified in Chicago by the numbers of unemployed stranded at the close of the exposition." In *Twenty Years at Hull House* Jane Addams recalled how desperate people had been for food and shelter, and that Hull House had taken in homeless women with nowhere else to go. Addams was appointed to a city-wide committee to study the unemployment problem. In that capacity she helped organize relief stations, employment opportunities, and temporary lodging throughout the city. Addams soon resigned from the committee after a disagreement about the proper way to reimburse men for sweeping streets. That same winter the Bureau of Organized Charities was established by a resident of Hull House (Addams [1910] 1960, 121, 122).

Addams had a strong ally in the British journalist William Stead. Stead visited Hull House often during the winter of 1894 while he was writing his indictment of the city titled *If Christ Came to Chicago!* He believed that by moving to Halsted Street Addams was one of the few who practiced Christ's teachings to live among the poor and redeem the "least of these." Stead identified Hull House as "one of the best institutions in Chicago" that should have been duplicated all over the city to meet the needs of the poor. "What the original Brotherhood of St. Francis was to the Franciscan order, so Hull House will be to the brotherhoods and sisterhoods of helpers and neighbors, who in increasing numbers will take up their residence in the midst of the crowded and desolate quarters of our over-crowded cities" (Stead [1894] 1978, 410).

Stead placed particular emphasis on the neighboring aspect of settlement work. He was impressed that Addams "began by living among the people, visiting them and asking her neighbors to call as friends and guests. They responded to her invitation so willingly that Hull House has 2,000 visitors a week." Stead continued his praise with a recital of all the classes, clubs, and services Hull House provided. His favorite image of Addams was "pale and weary, but indomitable to the last," answering the ringing doorbell over and over again as she met the needs of "every appeal from without" (Stead [1894] 1978, 419). Addams's memory of Stead was of him sitting in front of the fireplace drinking hot chocolate at midnight after he had stood freezing in an unemployment line to experience the labor crisis he chronicled (Addams [1910] 1960, 122).

Hull House prospered despite the depression. Another floor was added to the original house in 1894 to provide space for a kindergarten, nursery, and music school. In 1896 the Butler Art Gallery was enlarged to include a men's residence, and in 1898 an entire building was added for the Jane Club, a women's cooperative apartment. A coffeehouse with an upstairs theater was built in 1899 by architects Allen and Irving Pond. The physical plant at Hull House continued to expand, helped in part by Helen Culver's donation in 1906 of the house and land surrounding it; Mary Rozet Smith and Louise deKoven Bowen also made major contributions. An apartment building with a Men's Club was completed in 1902, Bowen Hall for the Women's Club in 1904, a dining hall in 1905, Boys' Club in 1906, and the Mary Crane Nursery in 1907. The thirteen-building complex, covering a large city block, was completed in 1907 (Deegan 1988, 41; Sklar 1990, 106).[4]

Three baths were located in the basement of Hull House before the city board of health built the Carter H. Harrison Bath on a neighboring street. City officials were skeptical that the baths would be used, citing

Figure 7.10. Exterior of Hull House complex on Halsted Street in Chicago, c. 1905–10. (Barnes-Crosby, photographers. Courtesy Chicago Historical Society, ICHi-19288.)

stories of tenement bathtubs being converted to coal bins. But Addams argued that their basement baths were in great demand and neighbors soon confirmed her judgment with "immediate and overflowing use of the public baths" (Addams [1910] 1960, 221).

The first model playground was started at Hull House in 1894 on a lot approximately 300 by 100 feet. It contained a sand pile, swings, building blocks, and gymnasium equipment for children and youths supervised by "an experienced kindergartner and a policeman" (Rainwater 1922, 56). Construction of this playground represents one of the more significant ways in which settlements could affect the design of their neighborhoods. After being given a free lease on property occupied by slum housing, Jane Addams had the worst of the buildings demolished, sold three more, and moved them across the street with the understanding that they would not be used for junkshops or saloons. Then she built the public playground. The benefactor paid all taxes for fifteen years, but "the dispossessed tenants, a group of whom had to be evicted by legal process before their houses could be torn down, . . . never ceased to mourn their former estates" (Addams [1910] 1960, 206).

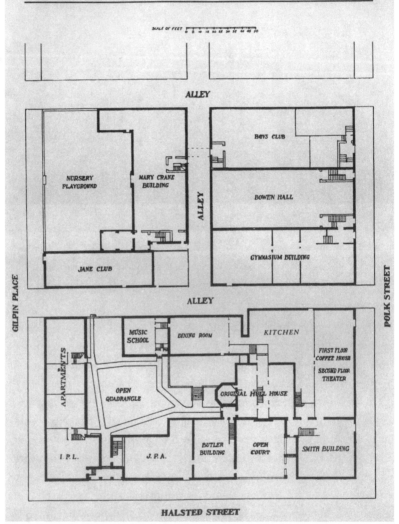

Figure 7.11. Plan of Hull House buildings, c. 1963. (Courtesy Jane Addams
Memorial Collection [JAMC negative 511], Special Collections, University Library,
University of Illinois at Chicago.)

Other Settlement Houses

The Northwestern University Settlement created the city's second model playground. This settlement house was established by Prof. Charles Zueblin in 1891. It opened at 143 West Division Street and moved to 1400 Augusta Street in 1901. Both these addresses were on the northwest side, where Poles, Bohemians, Russians, Italians, and Germans had settled. Zueblin identified the settlement's mission as facilitating American citizenship: "All about us the problem of the Americanization of foreign peoples is being slowly worked out, and 'Americans in process' is the order of the day." The Northwestern University Settlement provided a dispensary, day nursery, food station, and coffeehouse in addition to the playground. In the summer it sponsored a Fresh Air station and clinic for babies in cooperation with the Relief Aid and Visiting Nurse Association. The settlement had a large staff. Twelve women and two men were in residence, and they were aided by the volunteer work of 140 women and 10 men (Woods and Kennedy [1911] 1970, 66–67).

The University of Chicago Settlement created the city's third model playground in 1898. Open from June through September and supervised by a kindergarten teacher and policeman, this playground was about the size of the one at Hull House and contained $50 worth of equipment. Patrons also had access to an indoor gymnasium and a public bath across the street (Rainwater 1922, 57). Ten other settlement houses in Chicago included playgrounds and seven included vacant lots and window boxes.

The University of Chicago Settlement was located at 4630 Gross Avenue behind the stockyards. Begun in 1894 by the Philanthropic Committee of the Christian Union of the University of Chicago, it was meant to "provide a center for educational, religious, and philanthropic work." Mary McDowell, lifelong crusader for public sanitation, was head resident for many years. Among its facilities were a kindergarten, classrooms, library, public bath, and playground. Twenty-one women and five men lived in residence at the house (Woods and Kennedy [1911] 1970, 71). McDowell lobbied the city tirelessly for a public bath to be located near the stockyards on the South Side. McDowell and the Women's Club of the settlement circulated a petition throughout their Packingtown neighborhood, and their successful efforts resulted in the construction of the William Mavor Bath in 1900 (Williams 1991, 90).

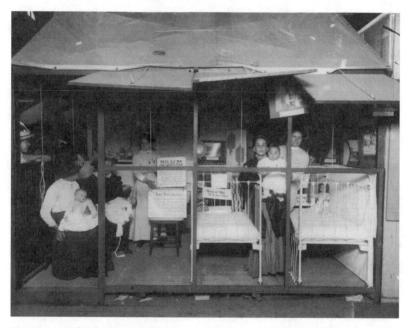

Figure 7.12. Babies' tent started by the Visiting Nurse Association of Northwestern University Settlement and Association House, for the treatment of sick babies. Chicago, c. 1905. (Photographer unknown. Courtesy Chicago Historical Society, ICHi-30673.)

McDowell also campaigned for proper waste removal most of her life, earning the nickname "The Garbage Lady." After her death she was remembered because

> Miss McDowell said that garbage disposal was a symbol of the community's life; and that that life should not be carried on for the benefit of a political party, but for the welfare of human beings. She repeatedly said that women must come to regard their city as their home, and must apply to it the standards of the home, dismissing incompetent public servants by their votes as they would discharge incompetent domestic help. The home must not end with the front doorstep. . . . How long will it be before the scientific method so characteristic of modern life in other respects will be applied to the problems of Municipal Housekeeping — with the intelligence, the energy, and the democratic spirit which were Mary McDowell's gifts to her city? (Hill 1938, vi, vii)

This chapter of Chicago's history ended in tragedy. The World's Columbian Exposition was scheduled to close on October 30, 1893, with

Figure 7.13. Exterior of Baby Tent Fresh Air Station sponsored by the Visiting Nurse Association, Chicago, c. 1906. (Courtesy Chicago Historical Society, ICHi-21466.)

elaborate formal ceremonies. On the night of October 28, however, Mayor Harrison was shot at the threshold of his home by a disgruntled political-office seeker. The planned festivities turned into a funeral. The White City was darkened, and the public bathhouse named in honor of the mayor's support now stood as his memorial (Badger 1979; Burg 1976).

We know more about Chicago's skyscrapers and the World's Columbian Exposition than about its redemptive places for several reasons. Famous buildings and the fair were designed by corporate firms, while redemptive places were created by volunteers. Any single celebratory event attracting millions of visitors is more noteworthy than street-corner facilities, like public baths, used by people in their weekly routines. Expenses and relative size are also issues, of course. The World's Fair covered 686 acres and cost more than $30 million, compared with the Carter H. Harrison Bath, which occupied less than one city block and was built for just $12,000.

Another part of the explanation for differential attention to places created by men and by women is the process by which they came into existence. Chicago was chosen as the site of the Columbian Exposition

Figure 7.14. Across the street from 4630 Gross Avenue, playlot seen from the roof of University of Chicago Settlement House, c. 1910. (Photographer unknown. Courtesy Chicago Historical Society, ICHi-15015.)

through a national competition sponsored by Congress. Civic boosters were anxious to substitute a positive image of the city for that of the Great Fire and the Haymarket Riot. Their aggressive lobbying was so effective in the national arena that "finally Congress said yes to the pushy men from the shores of Lake Michigan who had wrested the quadri-centennial celebration away from New York City" (Brands 1995, 42; Gilbert 1991, 1). In contrast, a Chicago city council member described the persistent character of lobbying for the Carter Harrison Bath:

> I have been importuned both night and day for I don't know how long
> to lend my aid toward the construction of public bath houses. The
> persuasive manner in which these ladies came upon council at all times
> and hours is what led that body to finally conclude that there was plenty
> of money in the treasury to be used for the purpose they desired.
> (Williams 1991, 86)

Chicago was especially important to the history of redemptive places because Hull House was the quintessential settlement house and it stood in such stark contrast to the World's Columbian Exposition. Extreme ends of the architectural continuum were represented in Chicago at the turn of the twentieth century: the practical Hull House covering one

Figure 7.15. Free public bathhouse #3 (William Mavor Bathhouse) for men and boys. Located on the 4600 block of McDowell Avenue, Chicago, 1950. (Mildred Mead, photographer. Courtesy Chicago Historical Society, ICHi-21723.)

city block and the fabricated White City spread over more than six hundred acres. As unusual as Chicago was because of these two success stories, its redemptive places shared similar characteristics with those in Boston, New York, and dozens of other cities. They were all stages on which the drama surrounding debates about immigration, race relations, and women's status unfolded.

CHAPTER EIGHT

How Women Saved the City

> Make big plans; aim high in hope and work, remembering that a
> noble, logical diagram once recorded will never die, but long after
> we are gone will be a living thing asserting itself with ever-growing
> insistency. Remember that our sons and grandsons are going to do
> things that would stagger us. (Hines 1974, xxiii)

Compare this sentiment attributed to the noted architect Daniel Burnham in 1910 with the following statement by one of his contemporaries,
civic reformer and president of the General Federation of Women's Clubs,
Sarah S. Platt Decker. Decker expressed hope in 1906 that "[t]he Federation may become a mighty factor in the civilization of the century —
an army of builders, ready, alert, systematic, and scientific, not only a
potent force in this generation, but transmitting to the next a vigor and
strength which have never been given by any race of women to their
inheritors" (Decker 1906, 204).

Most planners and architects associate Burnham with the mandate
to "make no little plans," but few have heard of Decker's equally stirring
"army of builders" decree. Burnham's big plans included the World's
Columbian Exposition of 1893 and City Beautiful designs for Chicago,
Cleveland, and Washington, D.C. Decker's army of builders created boarding houses, vocational schools, settlements, playgrounds, and public
baths in these same cities. Burnham and his professional colleagues built
the foreground, while volunteers like Decker redeemed the city with
necessary projects in the background. Regrettably, the legacy Burnham

left to his sons and grandsons has had greater visibility than the one Decker left to her daughters and granddaughters.

Women volunteers saved the American city at the turn of the twentieth century by converting religious doctrine and domestic ideology into redemptive places that produced social order at a critical moment in the nation's development. Urbanization in the United States was accompanied by a flood of newcomers. Only one out of four Americans was urban at the end of the Civil War, but by the end of World War I more than one out of two Americans lived in a city. Participants in constructing this new culture included native-born whites, European immigrants, black migrants, and independent women. Almost everyone seemed "out of place" as these different groups collided daily, putting the city at risk of literal and symbolic pollution. Without redemptive places the city could never have absorbed the millions of people seeking new identities as urban Americans. Neither could women volunteers have paved their own way out of the home so successfully.

This book has highlighted redemptive places in order to learn something we might otherwise have missed. Redemptive places make the invisible more visible by clarifying the roles women and religion played in materially shaping the industrial city. Knowledge of redemptive places also adds a spatial and spiritual dimension to the history of women and of voluntary organizations. By locating black and working-class women in the same Progressive Era as white middle-class and elite women, it becomes possible to identify points of conflict (race and class) and convergence (the Social Gospel and municipal housekeeping). Most important, perhaps, redemptive places emerge as sites where significant issues of the day were actively negotiated. Were the actual buildings and playgrounds so important? Jane Addams thought so. She believed that "Hull House clothed in brick and mortar and made visible to the world that which we were trying to do; [the first buildings] stated to Chicago that education and recreation ought to be extended to immigrants" (Addams [1910] 1960, 114).

Redemption connotes salvation, deliverance, and rescue, all of which characterized the Social Gospel and municipal housekeeping. Both ideologies were fundamental to Protestant voluntary organizations that established a physical presence in the city. The Young Women's Christian Association (YWCA) and the National Association of Colored Women (NACW) were organized primarily by women and for women, as their names indicate, although they occasionally included facilities for children. The College Settlements Association (CSA), on the other hand, was organized by women for the benefit of women, men, and children, and many men were active in the larger settlement movement. Only The Salvation Army was gender-neutral in the composition of both its providers and clientele. William and Catherine Booth established The Salvation Army together, and together their sons and daughters carried its evangelical mission into the twentieth century.

Names of the people associated with these four voluntary associations are less familiar than famous architects or city planners. Grace Dodge, Josephine St. Pierre Ruffin, Vida Scudder, and William and Catherine Booth lacked the reputations that put Daniel Burnham, Frederick Law Olmsted, and Charles Mulford Robinson in the history books. Women volunteers provided an orderly system by which to assimilate newcomers and in the process they cleaned up literal and symbolic dirt. This was unglamorous work compared with building grand monuments. In the end, however, more cities were influenced by the creation of redemptive places than by skyscrapers or City Beautiful plans.

Newcomers to the city prompted women volunteers to establish places that cleansed bodies, saved souls, and created American citizens. European immigrants, 27 million of whom arrived in the United States between 1870 and 1920, had the greatest numerical impact on cities. Some of the largest cities had more residents of foreign birth and parentage than native-born Americans. Alien languages, customs, and religious practices identified immigrants as strangers demanding special attention. Black migrants from the rural South had the next greatest effect on the demography of northeastern and midwestern cities. Blacks were native-born Americans who spoke the same language and subscribed to the same Protestant religion as whites, yet their recent status as slaves and their skin color created a greater degree of "otherness" than it did for European immigrants.

The third group of strangers, women adrift, were objects of suspicion for their economic independence and absence of family connections. They may even have provoked envy due to their very lack of domestic responsibilities. Women volunteers themselves were also urban newcomers. Most were part of a growing middle class in which men relied increasingly on educational and occupational credentials to establish professional identities. The fact that most women volunteers entered public life without those advantages speaks to their zeal. Rather than feeling daunted, they were positively inspired by the challenges. Jane Edna Hunter established the Phillis Wheatley Association because "here was my work, my salvation; here was the supreme task for which God had designed me" (Hunter 1940, 83). Vida Scudder declared that settlement houses allowed women to "share in the strange increase of power that comes from a collective work" (Scudder 1890, 11). Mary Kingsbury Simkhovitch referred to settlement workers as "passionate democrats" (Wirka 1996, 62).

Women assimilated newcomers through voluntary organizations by using domestic metaphors to describe their actions. Salvation Army Slum Sisters ministered to "somebody's brother" while YWCA and NACW boardinghouse "matrons" took care of "poor motherless daughters." Settlement workers relied on cooking, kitchens, and baths to promote American middle-class values; homelike environments legitimated their contact with strangers. Even after the YWCA outgrew its small boarding houses, it tried to make its hotels as cozy as possible. NACW facilities often remained in actual domestic quarters (such as Josephine St. Pierre Ruffin's or Janie Porter Barrett's home) due to a lack of financial resources. Settlement houses typically began on a small scale, although they sometimes expanded as their support grew. Even The Salvation Army, which managed some of the largest hotels, used the voluntary vernacular for its rescue homes.

Women's concern for newcomers translated into concern for the city. It, too, needed to be saved and sanitized. Unpaved streets littered with horse manure and dead animals were common, as were skies blackened with soot from coal-powered factories. Garbage and human sewage flowed unrestricted into municipal water supplies. Ramshackle tenements leaned into the street with the weight of too many occupants. The lack of indoor plumbing in tenements made cleanliness difficult for even the most diligent. Poor families could visit public baths, but the rooms they lived in were harder to keep scrubbed. Under such conditions illnesses soon became epidemics: high infant mortality reigned and life expectancy was short.

To say that poverty was rampant in the city at the turn of the century is an understatement. Depressions in 1873 and again in 1893 crippled the economy. People moved to American cities because of the absence of opportunities elsewhere, so they brought few resources with them. They lacked either material wealth or the appropriate human capital, having been trained primarily for agricultural or craft jobs that were rapidly being eliminated by industrialization. People may have been poor before they arrived, but the city spatially concentrated poverty in ways that made its effects especially severe. Starving children, parents out of work due to injuries, lack of clothing, contaminated drinking water, and filthy tenements were routine concerns for women volunteers.

Redemptive places filled a gap while poverty was being transformed from a private trouble into a public issue. The urban poor became highly visible long before municipal agencies were formed to deliver services. Voluntary organizations took on the responsibility for medical, nutritional, shelter, and child-care facilities. Now, of course, the state provides many of these services. In fact, much of the growth in government welfare over the past century was introduced with the specific intention of replacing voluntary efforts that were inadequate to the task (Skocpol 1992; Wuthnow 1991a).

Contemporary welfare reform, however, raises the possibility that many of these same services will be returned to the voluntary sector. Can volunteers close the gap between the demands of the poor and what the government once supplied? Probably not. Current estimates are that nonprofit social service organizations would have to raise over seven times more in private donations than they do now to replace the government's safety net (Blank 1997). The poor already depend heavily on voluntary organizations for supplements to federal welfare. Because they lack medical benefits, wage-earning mothers often need *more* outside assistance than mothers receiving welfare. The problem with welfare reform, then, is that demands on the voluntary sector may *increase* as more poor mothers enter the labor force. This creates a dilemma for organizations dependent on volunteer labor. The pessimistic view is that social service agencies trying to take on the mantle the federal government has abandoned might have to ration their services to the point where they are useless to the individuals they are trying to serve (Edin and Lein 1998, 569).

A tremendous amount of the nation's work occurred in redemptive places. Women's status, immigration, and race relations were all topics of public debate at the end of the nineteenth century. Redemptive places translated these abstract issues into daily routines. Boarding houses and hotels challenged prevailing ideas about proper living arrangements for unmarried women. By providing rooms where young women could live cheaply on their own, the YWCA and NACW endorsed women's independence. These organizations also sponsored schools where women learned new technologies like typewriting, where they could improve their English or sewing sufficiently to earn a livelihood, or where they were taught the proper skills for domestic employment. The YWCA and NACW did more than encourage women to live away from their families; they made it economically possible for them to do so by training them for the jobs that existed at the time.

Public opinion about immigration was actively negotiated in settlement houses. Many Americans discouraged new immigrants but settlement houses welcomed them. Settlement volunteers taught immigrants English, provided baths, instructed them in middle-class manners, and built playgrounds to supervise their children, all of which made immigrants better workers. At the same time they were producing an efficient labor force, however, women volunteers were sponsoring labor unions and encouraging workers to organize. Denison House was the headquarters for Mary Kenney O'Sullivan's Boston Woman's Union Label League; College Settlement on Rivington Street in New York City held meetings of the Consumers' League, which lobbied for shorter hours for working girls; and the Women's Trade Union League met at Hull House (Addams [1910] 1960; Settlements File n.d.). These contradictions were worked out within settlement-house walls. Residents prided themselves on "settling" inherent tensions between capital and labor by the sheer force of their presence in the neighborhood.

The important work involving race relations proceeded along parallel lines, with the NACW filling many of the needs for blacks that the YWCA, CSA, and The Salvation Army met for whites. The YWCA endorsed prevailing customs of racial segregation when it turned away African American women from its boarding houses and schools. Members of the NACW created homes and schools for black women, but they were never comparable to the ones sponsored by the YWCA. Black organizations simply lacked the resources to create "separate but equal" facilities. Cleveland's Phillis Wheatley Association capitulated to economic realities when Jane Edna Hunter accepted a governing board of white members of the local YWCA as a condition for funding. As a consequence, Cleveland's Phillis Wheatley Home and YWCA were locked in a dance of mutual dependency that mirrored the uncertainties of the larger society.

The Fate of Redemptive Places

Redemptive places shared several characteristics. The first was their relatively small size — they tended to be modest rather than monumental. On a continuum from completely private to totally public space, redemptive places more closely resembled the private home than the public plaza. The fact that redemptive places had features of both private and public space, however, made them *liminal* institutions. Some redemptive places required an invitation to enter and others did not. Redemptive places were temporary solutions to various problems of transition: how to assimilate immigrants and blacks; how to protect working women living away from their families; how to hold college-educated women in abeyance until professions opened to them; where to provide services for the poor while poverty was being redefined as a public responsibility. Although redemptive places seldom had an overt political agenda, they became theaters of political drama.

Redemptive places operated at multiple levels. At the individual level women volunteers performed good deeds and established public identities for themselves, while working-class clients found respite from daily hardships. At the neighborhood level, redemptive places provided local facilities for children and adults who needed services close to home. Vernacular and parochial spaces were an integral part of every poor neighborhood. At the city level, they maintained social order and promoted American middle-class values (like the importance of personal hygiene and the Protestant work ethic). At the largest scale, that of the national economy, redemptive places dampened some of the labor conflict that could have paralyzed industrialization if left unchecked. Not only did redemptive places provide training for the new economy, but women volunteers performed work for which the state would eventually pay salaried employees.

Redemptive places were significant because they emerged as the nation evolved from an agricultural to an industrial economy. Once that transformation was complete, and with it the rise of more proactive government agencies, redemptive places virtually disappeared. European immigration dwindled after World War I, African Americans born in the rural South gave birth to generations born in northern and midwestern cities, and women adrift, once suspect for their lack of family affiliation, became a valuable source of cheap labor precisely *because* they had no dependents to support.

Perhaps most important, new opportunities began to open for women. In 1870 less than 1 percent of women aged eighteen to twenty-one were enrolled in college and they were a distinct minority of all students. By 1920 almost 8 percent of young women were enrolled in college and nearly one-half of all college students were women (Solomon 1985, 63, 64). Although men were more likely than women to attend college at both these dates, women had begun a trajectory of significant educational progress that would continue unabated. As educational levels rose, women became more likely to work for pay outside the home. Between 1870 and 1920 the proportion of all women in the labor force increased from 13 to 21 percent (U.S. Bureau of the Census 1975, 128).

By the time women were granted the vote in 1920 they were more likely to have spent time outside the home — in schools and in the workplace — than in 1870. As women became more highly educated, they could individually perform the types of work they could only have accomplished collectively at the end of the nineteenth century. They soon began to move directly into political and professional engagement with the city. Florence Kelley and Mary Kingsbury Simkhovitch are striking examples of "transitional" women whose civic careers emerged out of voluntarism. Kelley's lobbying for fair labor legislation and Simkhovitch's crusade for affordable housing were both fueled by their settlement work.

What has happened to redemptive places? Some, like public baths, became obsolete when housing ordinances demanded the installation of indoor plumbing. Others, like playgrounds and kindergartens, were eventually absorbed by the public sector. Still others, like the three hundred settlement houses that now exist nationwide, created new structures to survive (Husock 1992). Boston's North End Union and North Bennet Street School, for example, merged during the 1980s. The North End Union provides social services and the North Bennet Street School is an accredited postsecondary school for craftsmen. The North End Union is an affiliate of the United Way and the Unitarian-Universalist Urban Ministry whose students are eligible for federal financial aid (Henry and Williams n.d.).

The YWCA has shifted its emphasis from lodging and occupational training for women to leadership and racial equality. The CSA became the Intercollegiate Community Services Association in 1918 and now operates loosely through three city-based settlements federations (Husock 1992). The NACW still has headquarters in Washington, D.C., but it no longer offers lodging or occupational training. Only The Salvation Army provides the same redemptive places today that it did a century ago.

Community Development Corporations (CDCs) approximate some functions of the old-fashioned settlement house. CDCs are nonprofit (501[C]3) neighborhood organizations that have governing boards representative of the community. They typically focus on affordable housing and economic development; some are actively engaged in neighborhood planning. Many CDCs started with federal funding during the War on Poverty while others emerged from active ministries involved with civil rights. CDCs are public/private partnerships whose main purpose is to leverage resources and remove barriers to private market reinvestment (Keating, Krumholz, and Star 1996).

A large part of the voluntary sector still depends on the church, and women are more likely than men to give time and contribute money to charitable activities associated with their church (Regnerus, Smith, and Sikkink 1998; Verba, Schlozman, and Brady 1995, 259). "Faith-based community development" is particularly effective in central city neighborhoods that other institutions have deserted. For African Americans, religious institutions provide the value system and leadership opportunities often denied in other arenas. One of the most successful faith-based efforts is the Nehemiah project in East Brooklyn, which built twenty-three hundred single-family rowhouses. Focus: HOPE in Detroit, under the sponsorship of the Catholic Church, began in the 1960s in response to urban riots. Focus: HOPE administers a machinist training institute with a job placement service, a Montessori school, and remedial classes in reading and math. The complex covers twenty-five acres. Other biracial church initiatives in Detroit have developed shopping centers, franchise food outlets, and auto repair shops (Thomas and Blake 1996).

What other forms do redemptive places take now? The Salvation Army's soup kitchens and homeless shelters are the clearest descendants of nineteenth-century redemptive places. Halfway houses for re-

covering drug addicts or victims of domestic violence are usually sponsored by nonprofit groups. Most nonprofit women's centers provide
interview skills for "displaced homemakers" entering the job market.
Empowerment and enterprise zones that bring federal funding to entire distressed minority neighborhoods might also be considered redemptive; they are certainly meant to save the city (Lehman 1994). Habi-
tat for Humanity volunteers provide affordable housing to the poor.
These are all actual places in which issues of poverty, race relations, and
women's status become materially manifest.

Many of the services once available only through redemptive places
are now performed by the public sector for all citizens, not just for the
poor. Largely as a result of Progressive reforms, the federal government
regulates food quality, working conditions, and wage rates. State and
local governments pay for kindergartens, playgrounds, and libraries. State
and local funds also cover city trash removal and street maintenance.
Yet efforts to streamline and "downsize" big government have created a
retreat from public responsibility. Private contractors now perform work
"outsourced" by the government. Americans have grown accustomed
to "Adopt-a-Street" signs that announce which volunteer group is cur-
rently responsible for keeping the road clean. Literacy Volunteers of
America tries to reach adults who never learned to read in school.

Campaigns on behalf of children's welfare are as important today as
they were one hundred years ago. In 1997 President Clinton appointed
Gen. Colin Powell to chair a special committee on the needs of children
at risk. Powell defined his mission as helping "young people who are dis-
engaged from American life, who don't believe in the American Dream."
The April 28, 1997, edition of *Newsweek* featured the impending conference at Philadelphia's Independence Hall with a cover photograph
of General Powell pointing his finger at the reader, in the style of old
Army recruitment posters, with the caption "I WANT YOU: Why Colin
Powell Is Asking America to Volunteer."

The story began with a list of the dignitaries attending the conference,
including President and Mrs. Clinton, and the following observation:

> If the era of big government is over, the era of big citizen is just getting
> underway. The nonpartisan Presidents' Summit for America's Future
> aims to mobilize corporate America and a vast volunteer army to rescue
> "at-risk" youths with tutoring, mentoring, and other citizen service that

brings caring adults directly into their lives. The battle plan is to get the public, the private and the nonprofit sectors all marching in the same direction at the same time on the same fundamental needs of young people. The troops are you. (Alter 1997)

Who Are the New Volunteers?

Who are the "you" to which the *Newsweek* article referred? Women are no longer the reserve army of volunteers they were at the end of the nineteenth century. Once women were granted the vote, began to earn college degrees, and gained control of their own fertility through the use of legalized contraception and abortion, they entered the labor force in unprecedented numbers. Many people who are employed outside the home still volunteer time or money to a worthy cause, of course, but the days when a woman's entire public identity depended on her voluntary activities are largely over. Women are now architects, city planners, landscape architects, social workers, and elected officials who are directly engaged with saving the city.

The aging baby boom generation is the logical group to become the next army of volunteers. Living longer and retiring earlier, millions of the "young elderly" may choose to work for the benefit of the community once they leave employment. Both women and men of this generation will have the educational and occupational experiences — and the time — to create a productive volunteer force. Public schools are also requiring students to volunteer as part of a "citizenship curriculum," although receiving academic credit for mandatory community work strains the definition of voluntarism. The courts have created another source of volunteers. Community service has become such a popular form of punishment for minor crimes that court-ordered "volunteers" are now a primary source of unpaid labor for many charities in the Washington, D.C., area (Loose 1999, A-1). It may take a combination of all three — retirees, students, and petty thieves — to produce the same results that women did one hundred years ago.

A remaining question is whether a significant demographic group that challenges the city's ability to cope, whose needs are not yet being met by the state or the private sector, and whose presence becomes a public concern exists in cities today. That group could well be the growing population of the elderly: men and women aged sixty-five and over, many of whom now live alone. Recent debates over Social Security and Medicare illustrate that the aging population is clearly central to the public agenda. While some retirement and nursing homes are run by the private sector, many others are nonprofits sponsored by religious organizations. The government does not yet provide facilities for the elderly in proportion to their rising numbers. Will the voluntary sector fill this niche, or will these redemptive places eventually be transformed into a state responsibility?

Does the City Still Need Saving?

Historian Thomas Bender has observed that "it is embarrassing how rapidly life in our cities is coming to resemble the circumstances of a century ago, when Jane Addams founded Hull House" (Bender 1996, 132). Most Americans would agree that the city still needs saving. Cities continue to be the sites of the nation's work, although the economy is finishing the transition from an industrial to an informational base rather than from agricultural to industrial (Clarke and Gaile 1998). The country is once again admitting almost one million immigrants per year, and major cities like New York and Chicago are still their destinations (U.S. Department of Justice 1997). Sporadic riots remind us that cities remain stages for racial and ethnic conflict. Women now have voting and reproductive rights, but their access to abortion clinics is being violently challenged. Thus the century is ending as it began, with the city the crucible for racial, ethnic, and gender issues.

This brief history holds lessons for contemporary urban planning. It reminds us of the ability of volunteers, especially those motivated by religious faith, to save the city. Planners often negotiate relationships of unequal power between the public and private individuals (Forester 1989). Ideally they accomplish this ethically and as advocates for those with less power (Davidoff 1965; Friedmann 1987). Yet planners tend to underestimate the power of religious conviction to shape the world. This research suggests that planners who acknowledge the possibility of faith-based solutions to urban problems have a more complete understanding of the political realities affecting their work than professionals who ignore its potential.

Redemptive places are as important for the questions they raise about the future as for those they answer about the past. For example, are assimilation and integration still goals for newcomers to the city, or have pluralism and diversity become the prevailing models? To the extent that multiculturalism has displaced assimilation, redemptive places organized from the top down by volunteers will be less effective than they were one hundred years ago. Redemptive places also raise more questions than they answer. Will women play an important role in the future? Will a voluntary sector consisting of retirees fill the gap created by women's participation in the labor force? Will nonprofits be able to meet the demands created by federal welfare reform?

Redemptive places were the sites at which the assimilation of newcomers was accomplished one hundred years ago. They provided theaters where the impact of immigrants, free blacks, and independent women on American society were debated. Women volunteers collectively created a safety net of places in which millions of newcomers learned how to become urban Americans. At the same time, redemptive places contributed to social order as the nation constructed its urban identity. It is now possible to answer questions about where women fit into urban history by pointing to the places they built. Although most redemptive places have faded from collective memory, *How Women Saved the City* resurrects their spirit.

APPENDIX A

Literature Review

Redemptive places are absent from standard architectural and planning histories that focus on public monuments, commercial skyscrapers, and national movements associated with recognized architects (Bluestone 1991; Condit 1964; Girouard 1985; Hall 1988; Reps 1965; Scott 1969; Siegel 1965; Wilson 1989). If the inquiry into women in architecture and planning is confined to questions about professional designers or wealthy patrons, there is little to write about. If we expand the meaning to include the ways in which women have claimed and used space, however, the ways in which they have defined and revised it through the channels historically open to them, then the story of women and cities is a rich one (Wells 1995).

Municipal housekeeping is conspicuously absent from conventional histories of the Progressive Era. Robert Wiebe's *The Search for Order* (1967), Richard Hofstadter's *The Age of Reform* (1955), Samuel Hays's *The Response to Industrialism* (1995), Paul Boyer's *Urban Masses and Moral Order in America* (1978), and Thomas Bender's *Toward an Urban Vision* (1975) all seem to overlook municipal housekeepers' contributions to sanitary reform. Since traditional histories focus on the transformation of the formal economy and the polity, both of which were largely closed to nineteenth-century women, it is not surprising that the unpaid, informal work of women failed to enter the written record (Scott 1991, 158).

Less understandable is why municipal housekeeping, so clearly related to the City Beautiful movement, has been omitted from architectural and planning histories. Charles Mulford Robinson made no formal reference to municipal housekeeping in *The Improvement of Towns and Cities* (1913 edition) or *Modern Civic Art* (1918 edition), nor did Werner Hegemann and Elbert Peets in *The American Vitruvius* (1922). Accounts from thirty years ago, such as John Reps's *The Making of Urban America* (1965) or Mel Scott's *American City Planning since 1890* (1969), fail to mention the topic. More recent histories, like Richard Foglesong's *Planning the Capitalist City* (1986), Peter Hall's *Cities of Tomorrow* (1988), William Wilson's *The City Beautiful Movement* (1989), Robert Stern, Gregory Gilmartin, and John Massengale's *New York, 1900* (1983), and Daniel Bluestone's *Constructing Chicago* (1991) all seem to ignore municipal housekeeping. The oversight is especially puzzling in the case of Chicago, where Jane Addams and the Woman's City Club had such high profiles. Peter Hall (1988, 7, 41) found "alas, almost no founding mothers" in his intellectual history of urban planning and referred to Jane Addams as a "do-gooder."

Feminist research about urban architectural and planning issues has a shorter history, dating mainly from *Women and the American City,* by Catharine Stimpson, Elsa Dixler, Martha J. Nelson, and Kathryn B. Yatrakis, published in 1980. Eugenie Birch's *The Unsheltered Woman* (1985), Galen Cranz's *The Politics of Park Design* (1982), Dolores Hayden's *Grand Domestic Revolution* (1981), Helen Lefkowitz Horowitz's *Alma Mater* (1984), and Suzanne Keller's *Building for Women* (1981) are further examples of groundbreaking scholarship in this field. Elizabeth Wilson's *The Sphinx in the City* (1991), my earlier work in *Gendered Spaces* (1992), and Lois Kanes Weisman's *Discrimination by Design* (1992) continued the legacy.

Historians Maureen Flanagan (1997), Suellen Hoy (1995), Anne Firor Scott (1991), Christine Stansell (1982), and Louise Tilly (1989) have raised questions about where women and social class fit in urban history, while historian Mary Ryan (1997) and political scientist Susan Clarke (Clarke, Staeheli, and Brunell 1995) have examined the gendered nature of urban political participation. Sociologist Theda Skocpol (1992) applied a compelling (although aspatial) gendered account of the origins of the American welfare state that has relevance for this work. The range of civic activities sponsored by women's voluntary associations at the turn of the century has been well documented (Berg 1978; Birch 1994; Daniels 1988; Gelb and Gittell 1986; McCarthy 1990a; Sklar 1995a). The relevant geography literature includes Doreen Massey and John Allen's *Geography Matters!* (1984) and Mona Domosh's *Invented Cities* (1996).

How Women Saved the City incorporates women's history into urban, architectural, and planning histories in an attempt to make the invisible more visible (Birch 1994; Hayden 1981, 1995; Higginbotham 1993; Lofland 1975; Sandercock 1998; Scott 1991; Spain 1992). To paraphrase historian Paul Boyer (1978, vii), it is less a presentation of new material than an attempt to understand the connections among well-known trends that typically are analyzed separately. For example, traditional architectural historians like Thomas Hines (1974) and Robert Stern, Gregory Gilmartin, and John Massengale (1983) refer frequently to the commentaries of turn-of-the-century architectural critic Herbert Croly, while feminist architectural historian Dolores Hayden (1981) identifies Jane Cunningham Croly as a suffragist and early advocate of municipal housekeeping. Herbert is as absent from Hayden's historical narrative as is Jane from Hines's and Sterns's. Yet Herbert was Jane's son, and it enriches our understanding of urbanism at the turn of the century to know that Herbert was influenced by a mother who actively promoted women's involvement in cities by forming New York City's Sorosis, one of the first women's clubs (*Encyclopedia Americana* 1996, 235; Hayden 1981, 93).

Scholarship in historic preservation has recently begun to acknowledge the importance of the voluntary vernacular. Readers are referred to the excellent work of Gail Dubrow ("Women and Community" [1992]) and Dolores Hayden (*The Power of Place* [1995]). Comprehensive edited volumes on preserving the built environment associated with women's history include Ellen Perry Berkeley and Matilda McQuaid's *Architecture: A Place for Women* (1989) and Page Putnam Miller's *Reclaiming the Past* (1992) (also a good source for the names of the first female architects). The U.S. Department of the Interior published a special issue of the National Park Service journal, *Cultural Resource Management* (1997), titled "Placing Women in the Past" that enlarges the field considerably.

These researchers have pointed out that one of the limitations of formal historic preservation guidelines is that they privilege not just men's activities, but artifacts associated with nationally famous women and their domestic surroundings. Places associated with locally known women or with an organization's community-building activities are seldom deemed important enough to save (Dubrow 1992). The YWCA national headquarters built in 1912 at 600 Lexington Avenue is an example of this bias. It was sold in 1982 and later demolished for construction of a 200,000-square-foot office tower because it did not meet the criteria for designation as a national historic landmark (Norris 1996). According to the National Trust for Historic Preservation, criteria for inclusion in the National Register of Historic Places are that the building be associated with (1) events that have made a significant contribution to the broad patterns of our history, (2) lives of persons significant in our past, (3) embody the distinctive characteristics of a type, period, or method of construction, or (4) have yielded, or may be likely to yield, information important in prehistory or history (U.S. Department of the Interior 1992).

The "600" was the first building in the United States erected solely for use by a women's organization and national movement. It incorporated innovations like a central mail chute, built-in bookcases, fireproof stairwells, large windowpanes for easy cleaning, and lightning rods. It attracted 1,002 visitors from twenty-seven states and eleven countries during March and April of 1913. It also provided meeting facilities for labor organizations, drama and music clubs, the State Charities Organization, and the Smith College Club (no doubt strengthening Dodge's affiliation with Vida Scudder's College Settlements Association) (Norris 1981; YWCA of the USA 1982). Yet these claims to historic significance were insufficient to save the "600" from demolition. (YWCA national headquarters is now at the Empire State Building, constructed in 1931.)

Municipal housekeeping and its accompanying voluntary vernacular deserve a chapter in architectural and planning histories. The Laurel Hill Village Improvement Association first espoused municipal housekeeping principles in 1853, material feminist Jane Cunningham Croly embraced them in 1869, Boston's Women's Educational and Industrial Union endorsed them in 1877, Chicago's Free Bath and Sanitary League used them in 1895, and numerous representatives of the General Federation of Women's Clubs wrote about Municipal Housekeeping between 1906 and 1912. Yet historians date the City Beautiful movement from 1900 to 1910 and give little attention to municipal housekeeping. Daniel Burnham, Charles Mulford Robinson, and Frederick Law Olmsted, identified as founders of the City Beautiful movement, are credited with having "planted the seed and cultivated the growth of city planning in the relatively infertile ground of urban America at the beginning of the present century" (Reps 1965, 497). Far from barren, the soil of the city had already been prepared for the City Beautiful movement, and for city planning, by women volunteers.

A Note on Research Methods

Several places that might ordinarily be considered redemptive are omitted from this book. Ina Law Robertson's Eleanor Clubs, for example, provided safe, affordable lodging for clerical workers in Chicago. Residences included libraries, parlors with pianos, dining rooms, and rooms with sewing machines and typewriters. Eleanor Clubs were, in fact, a secular alternative to the YWCA. At its peak the Eleanor Association operated six residence clubs, a lunchroom and social center, a junior club, a lodge, and a summer camp in Chicago (Fine 1990).

Visiting Nurse Associations in various cities also participated in the creation of redemptive places. Many settlement houses retained nurses who saw patients at the settlement or went out into tenements and alleys to treat the sick. The Henry Street Settlement in New York City, for example, was also known as the "Nurses' Settlement" because of its founders' occupations. The Visiting Nurse Association in Cleveland, formed in 1902, was an outgrowth of organized charitable efforts to provide for the public health (Gerstner 1998). The Visiting Nurse Association in Chicago at the turn of the century provided fresh-air tents on the sidewalk where mothers could bring their babies for medical care. Nursing, however, was an occupation that required professional training, unlike voluntary activities. For that reason the Visiting Nurse Association falls outside the type of organizations covered here.

Still another group of redemptive places omitted from this research is the type created formally by non-Protestant organizations. The Catholic Sisters of the Good Shepherd, for example, opened the Magdalen Asylum for abandoned women in Chicago in 1859 and the Chicago Industrial School for Girls in 1889 (Hoy 1997). While Catholic homes, Eleanor Clubs, and Visiting Nurse Associations all deserve recognition, they are different from redemptive places created by national voluntary organizations. Eleanor Clubs were associated with one individual in a single city rather than with a nationwide collective effort. Catholic homes were created by semicloistered nuns who chose the church as a lifelong commitment rather than by women who typically balanced domestic and family responsibilities with voluntarism. Members of the Visiting Nurse Associations, like teachers, were professionals whose identities included an occupation for which they had been trained. I have also emphasized Protestant-based organizations because the vast majority of African Americans at the end of the nineteenth century were Protestant. The greatest potential for similarities between redemptive places for blacks and whites, therefore, existed within the Protestant faith.

The maps printed here, depicting the location of redemptive places in Boston, Chicago, and New York, were produced using ArcView GIS. ArcView is a software package that automates the process of pinpointing addresses on a map of road networks. Data from the U.S. Census Bureau 1997 TIGER/Line Database were combined with the historical addresses listed in Appendix III to produce maps dated circa 1915. Although it appears that all these places existed simultaneously, individual facilities often opened and closed in rapid succession. These maps are a snapshot of the cumulative impact of redemptive places between 1870 and 1920.

The mixing of historical data with contemporary street grids introduces imprecision into the accuracy of locations. Addresses from the beginning of the twentieth century have been matched, where possible, with maps from the end of the century. Street systems and the numbers within them have changed over time depending on the effects of urban renewal and development in each city. The sites of places with some longevity were verified with Sanborn Fire Insurance Company maps. Overall, however, the maps are meant to give the reader a sense of the number and density of redemptive places rather than their exact location.

APPENDIX B

Organizational Charters

Constitution of the
Ladies' Christian Association of New York City, 1858

We, the undersigned, believing that increase of social virtues, elevation of character, intellectual excellence and the spread of Evangelical Religion can be best accomplished by associated effort, do hereby adopt for our mutual government the following:

Constitution

Any lady who is in a good standing of an Evangelical church, may become an active member by paying one dollar annually in advance.

Any lady not a communicant may become an associate member — except voting and holding office.

Duties of Members

They shall seek out especially young women of the operative class, aid them in procuring employment and in obtaining suitable boarding places, furnish them with proper reading matter, establish Bible classes and meetings for religious exercises at such times and places as shall be most convenient for them during the week, secure their attendance at places of public worship on the Sabbath, surround them with Christian influences and use all practicable means for the increase of true piety in themselves and others.

Source: Wilson [1916] 1987, 23.

The Doctrines of The Salvation Army
(as set forth in the Deed Poll of 1878)

1. We believe that the Scriptures of the Old and New Testaments were given by inspiration of God; and that they only constitute the divine rule of Christian faith and practice.

2. We believe there is only one God, who is infinitely perfect — the Creator, Preserver, and Governor of all things — and who is the only proper object of religious worship.

3. We believe that there are three persons in the Godhead — the Father, the Son, and the Holy Ghost — undivided in essence and co-equal in power and glory.

4. We believe that in the person of Jesus Christ the divine and human natures are united; so that He is truly and properly God, and truly and properly man.

5. We believe that our first parents were created in a state of innocency but, by their disobedience, they lost their purity and happiness; and that in consequence of their fall all men have become sinners, totally depraved, and as such are justly exposed to the wrath of God.

6. We believe that the Lord Jesus Christ has, by his suffering and death, made an atonement for the whole world, so that whosoever will may be saved.

7. We believe that repentance toward God, faith in our Lord Jesus Christ, and regeneration by the Holy Spirit are necessary to salvation.

8. We believe that we are justified by grace, through faith in our Lord Jesus Christ; and that he that believeth hath the witness in himself.

9. We believe that continuance in a state of salvation depends upon continued obedient faith in Christ.

10. We believe that it is the privilege of all believers to be "wholly sanctified" and that their "whole spirit and soul and body" may "be preserved blameless unto the coming of our Lord Jesus Christ" (1 Thessalonians 5:23).

11. We believe in the immortality of the soul; in the resurrection of the body; in the general judgment at the end of the world; in the eternal happiness of the righteous; and in the endless punishment of the wicked.

Source: McKinley 1995, 351.

Constitution of the College Settlements Association, 1890

   I. The name of this organization shall be the College Settlements Association.

  II. The object of this Association shall be the support and control of College Settlements for Women.

 III. Any person may become a member by paying an annual fee of five dollars, and will thereby be entitled to all the reports and publications issued.

 IV. Every College which has at least twenty representatives in the membership of the Association shall be entitled to two representatives on its Electoral Board, one to be elected by members of the Association who are graduates and former students of said college, the other by members who are undergraduates. The Electoral Board thus formed shall add to its number two women to represent the noncollegiate members of the Association.

  V. The term of office on the Electoral Board shall be two years, half the members of the Board being elected each year.

 VI. The Electoral Board shall hold an annual meeting before May 1, for the discussion of the interests of the Association and the election of the Executive Committees. The further duties of the Electoral Board shall be to maintain and extend interest in the Settlements among the Colleges represented, and elsewhere, and to collect the annual fees, handing them to a Treasurer appointed by the Electoral Board.

 VII. Special meetings of the Electoral Board may be held at the request of three members of the Board or of any Executive Committee.

VIII. Five members of the Electoral Board shall constitute a quorum for all purposes except the election of the Executive Committees. For this purpose, absent members must send in their votes, and a majority vote of the entire Board is necessary to election.

 IX. The Executive Committee for each Settlement shall consist of three elective members, and, ex-officio, the Head-Worker of the Settlement. The Committee shall add to its number one member. The majority of the Committee must be chosen from members of the Association resident in the neighborhood of the Settlement.

  X. The officers of each Committee shall be a Chairman, a General Secretary on Residents, a Secretary and a Treasurer.

XI. The Executive Committees shall be responsible for the entire management of the Settlements, and shall control in whatsoever way seems to them best, the admission of residents and the administration of funds. They shall, when necessary, elect Head-Workers. They shall, through their General Secretary, draw up every year a Report of the work, and submit this Report at the annual meeting of the Electoral Board. The Report, if accepted, shall be printed and sent to all members of the Association.

XII. The majority of the residents in a Settlement at any one time shall always be College women.

XIII. This Constitution may be amended or enlarged by a majority of the Electoral Board an any annual meeting.

Source: College Settlements Association, 1890.

National Association of Colored Women

Josephine St. Pierre Ruffin's Call to Meeting of 1895

The coming together of our women from all over the country for consultation, for conference, for the personal exchange of greetings, which means so much in the way of encouragement and inspiration, has been a burning desire in the breasts of colored women in every section of the United States.

The matter has been discussed and re-discussed. Of some things all are convinced — the need of such a conference is great, the benefit to be derived inevitable and inestimable. In view of this, we, the women of the Woman's Era Club of Boston, send forth a call to our sisters all over the country, members of all clubs, societies, associations, and circles to take immediate action, looking toward the sending of delegates to this convention.

Boston has been selected as a meeting place because it has seemed to be the general opinion that here, and here only, can be found the atmosphere which would best interpret and represent us, our position, our needs, and our aims. One of the pressing needs of our cause is the education of the public to a just appreciation of us, and only here can we gain the attention upon which so much depends.

It is designed to hold the convention three days, the first of which will be given up to business, the second and third to the consideration of vital questions concerning our moral, mental, physical and financial growth and well-being, these to be presented through addresses by representative women.

Although this matter of a convention has been talked over for some time, the subject has been precipitated by a letter to England, written by a southern editor, and reflecting upon the moral character of all colored women; this letter is too indecent for publication, but a copy of it is sent with this call to all the women's bodies throughout the country. Read this document carefully and use discriminately and decide if it be not time for us to stand before the world and declare ourselves and our principles.

The time is short, but everything is ripe and remember, earnest women can do anything.

Source: Davis 1935 (1981), 14.

APPENDIX C

Addresses of Redemptive Places for Boston, New York City, and Chicago

Boston

Type	Name and Street Address
NACW	Harriet Tubman House NACW, 37 Holyoke Street
Play	Harriet Tubman House NACW, 12 Carver Street
Settlement	Boston Music School Settlement, 110 Salem Street
	Cambridge Club Neighborhood House, 79 Moore Street
	Cottage Place Neighborhood House, 1049 Columbus Avenue
	Denison House, 91–95 Tyler Street
	Dorchester House, 7 Gordon Place
	East End Christian Union, 7 Burleigh Street
	Elizabeth Peabody House, 357 Charles Street
	Ellis Memorial and Eldredge House, 12 Carver Street
	Frances E. Willard Settlement, 38–44 Chambers Street
	Frederick Ozanam House, 35 Linden Street
	Guild of St. Elizabeth, 59 East Springfield Street
	Hale House, 6–8 Garland Street
	Hawthorne Club, 3–4 Garland Street
	Homemaking Center, 11 Armstrong Street
	Hull Street Settlement, 36 Hull Street
	The Italian Mission, 177 Webster Street
	Jamaica Plain Neighborhood House, 23 Carolina Avenue
	Library Club House, 18 Hull Street

Lincoln House, 68 Emerald Street
The "Little" House, 73 A Street
Louisa Alcott Club, 15 Oswego Street
Margaret Fuller House (YWCA), 71 Cherry Street
North Bennet Street Industrial School, 39 North Bennet
   Street
North End Union, 20 Parmenter Street
The Prospect Union, 744 Massachusetts Avenue
Robert Gould Shaw House, 6 Hammond Street
Roxbury Neighborhood House, 858 Albany Street
Ruggles Street Neighborhood House, 155 Ruggles Street
St. Stephen's House, 2 Decatur Street
Settlement of Ladies' Catholic, 1472 Washington Street
South End House, 611 Harrison Avenue
South End Industrial School, 45 Bartlett Street
South End Music School, 19 Pembroke Street

Bath
Cabot Street Bath and Gym, 203 Cabot Street
D Street Bath and Gym, D Street, South Boston
Dover Street Bath, 249 Dover Street
East Boston Bath and Gym, 116 Paris Street
L Street Bath and Gym, 1663 Columbia Road
Ward 3 Bath and Gym, Bunker Hill and Lexington Streets
Ward 7 Bath and Gym, 75 Tyler Street
Ward 9 Bath and Gym, Harrison Avenue and Plympton
   Street
Ward 15 Bath and Gym, Broadway between G and H
   Streets
Ward 16 Bath and Gym, Columbia Road and Bird Street
Ward 17 Bath and Gym, Vine and Dudley Streets

YWCA
Elizabeth Peabody House, 357 Charles Street
25 Beach Street
23 Chauncey Street
68 Warrenton Street
40 Berkeley Street

New York

Type	*Name and Street Address*
NACW	White Rose Mission, 217 East 86th Street
	Stillman Branch (of Henry Street Settlement), 205 West 60th Street
Play	Hamilton Fish Park, Houston, Stanton, and Sheriff Streets
	Clinton Park, 52nd-54th Streets, 11th Avenue, and Hudson
	Thomas Jefferson Park, 111th-114th Streets, First Avenue and East River
	Seward Park, Division and Canal Streets
	84–86 First Street
	265–301 Henry Street
	205 West 60th Street
YWCA	Central Club for Nurses, 132 East 45th Street
	Laura Spelman Residence Club, 840 8th Avenue
	Main Building, 7 East 15th Street
	135 East 52nd Street
	Margaret Louisa Home, 14 East 16th Street
	National Training School Headquarters, 600 Lexington Avenue
	Tatham House, 138 East 38th Street
	Training School, 3 Gramercy Park
	Upper Manhattan, 361 West 125th Street
Bath	Upper Manhattan, 23rd Street and Avenue A
	52nd Street and 11th Avenue
	111th Street and 1st Avenue
	138th Street and 5th Avenue
	Milbank Memorial Bath, 325–327 East 38th Street
	5 Rutgers Place
	133 Allen Street
	83 Carmine Street
	407 West 28th Street
	327 West 41st Street
	342 East 54th Street
	232 West 60th Street
	243 East 109th Street

Army   Ardmore Hotel, 83 Bowery
        The Braveman, 18 Chatham Square
        Dry Dock Hotel, 118 Avenue D
        The Glyndon, 243 Bowery
        Industrial Home, 528 West 30th Street
        Rescue Home, 316 East 15th Street
        Workingmen's Hotel, 21 Bowery

Settlement Alfred Corning Clark Neighborhood House, 283
            Rivington Street
        Amity Baptist Church and Settlement House, 313 West
            53rd Street
        The Barat Settlement, 296 Elizabeth Street
        Calvary House, 102–106 East 22nd Street
        Children's Home Settlement, 319 East 125th Street
        Chinatown Rescue Settlement, 10 Mott Street
        Christ Church Memorial House, 334–344 West 36th Street
        Christadora House (for men), 603 East 9th Street
        Christadora House (for women), 147 Avenue B
        The College Settlement, 95 Rivington Street
        Doe Ye Nexte Thynge Society, 18 Leroy Street
        Down Town Ethical Society, 216 Madison Street
        East Side House, 540 East 76th Street
        East Side Parish Church, 9 2nd Avenue
        Emanu-El Brotherhood Social House, 309–311 East 6th
            Street
        God's Providence House, 330 Broome Street
        The Gospel Settlement, 211 Clinton Street
        Grace Church Neighborhood House, 94–96 Fourth
            Avenue
        Grace Church Settlement, 413 East 13th Street
        Greenwich House, 26–30 Jones Street
        Hamilton House, 15 Hamilton Street
        The Harlem Club, 84 East 111th Street
        Harlem Federation for Jewish Communal Work, 238–240
            East 105th Street
        Hartley House, 414 West 47th Street
        Henry Street Settlement, 299–301 Henry Street

Homemaking Settlement, 518 East 16th Street
House of Aquila, 130 Stanton Street
Hudson Guild, 436–438 West 27th Street
Jacob A. Riis Neighborhood Settlement, 48–50 Henry
    Street
Kennedy House, 423 West 43rd Street
Lenox Hill Settlement, 444–446 East 72nd Street
Margaret Bottome Memorial, 216 East 128th Street
Memorial House of St. George's Church, 203 East 16th
    Street
Music School Settlement, 51 Third Street
Neighborhood House of the Church of the Holy
    Apostles, 365 West 27th Street
Parish House, 432–436 Third Avenue
People's Home Church, 543 East 11th Street
People's Three Art School, 240 Houston Street
Phelps Memorial House, 314–316 East 35th Street
Recreation Center and Neighborhood Rooms, 316 East
    5th Street
Riverside House, 259 West 69th Street
St. Bartolomew's, 209 East 42nd Street
St. Christopher's House, 316 East 88th Street
St. John's Italian Settlement, 308 Pleasant Avenue
St. Rose's, 257 East 72nd Street
Spring Street Neighborhood House, 244 Spring Street
Union Settlement, 248 East 105th Street
The University Settlement, 184 Eldridge Street
Warren Goddard House, 325 East 35th Street
Welcome House Settlement, 223 East 13th Street
Wesley House, 212 East 58th Street

Chicago

Type	Name and Street Address
Bath	Fernand Henrotin, 2415 North Marshfield Street
	DeWitt Cregler, 1153 Cambridge Street
	Theodore T. Gurney, 1141 West Chicago Street
	Joseph M. Medill, 2140 West Grand Street
	Robert A. Waller, 19 South Peoria Street
	Frank Lawler, 806 South Paulina Street
	William Loeffler, 1217 South Union Street
	Pilsen, 1849 South Throop Street
	Simon Baruch, 1911 West Cullerton Street
	Kedzie Avenue Bath, 2401 South Kedzie Street
	John Wentworth, 2838 South Halsted Street
	William B. Ogden, 3346 Emerald Street
	Graeme Stewart, 1642 West 35th Street
	Thomas Gahan, 4226 Wallace Street
YWCA	Carrie McGill Memorial Residence, 4938 Drexel Boulevard
	Main Building, 1001 North Dearborn Street
	Secretaries' Training Institute, 923 West Monroe Street
	YWCA Settlement, 2150 West North Avenue
	288 Michigan Avenue
Play	Neighborhood House, 6710 May Street
	South End Center, 3212 91st Street
NACW	Charles Sumner Settlement, 1951 Fulton Street
	Frederick Douglas Settlement, 3032 Wabash Avenue
	Institutional Church and Social Settlement, 3825 Dearborn Street
	Phillis Wheatley Home, 3256 Rhodes Avenue
	Phillis Wheatley Home, 5128 Michigan Avenue
Army	Beacon Hotel, 515 State Street
	Evangeline Hotel, 387 South Clark Street
	Harbor Lights Hotel, 118 West Madison Street
	The Mina Women's Hotel, 394 Dearborn Street
	New Century Hotel, 306 State Street
	Rescue Home, 6201 Wabash Avenue
	Scandinavian Sailor, 155 Hamilton Street

Landmark   Auditorium Building, Michigan at Congress
            Cable Building, 57 East Jackson
            Chapin and Gore Building, 63 East Adams
            Dwight Building, 626 South Clark
            Edison Shop, 229 South Wabash
            Fisher Building, 343 South Dearborn
            Fourth Presbyterian Church, 126 East Chestnut
            Gage Building, 18 South Michigan
            Getty Tomb, 4001 North Clark
            Hunter Building, 337 West Madison
            Leiter Building, 208 West Monroe
            McClurg Building, 218 South Wabash
            Meyer Building, 307 West Van Buren
            Monadnock Building, 53 West Jackson
            Old Chicago Stock Exchange, 30 North LaSalle
            Park Buildings, 45th Street and Princeton
            Reid, Murdoch, and Co., 325 North LaSalle
            Reliance Building, 32 North State
            Rookery Building, 209 LaSalle
            Schiller Building, 64 West Randolph
            Schlesinger and Mayer Store, State at Madison
            Wirt Dexter Building, 630 South Wabash

Settlement Archer Road Settlement 250 West 22nd Street
            Central Settlement, 1409 Wabash Avenue
            Chase House, 637 West 43rd Street
            Chicago Commons, 955 Grand Avenue and Morgan
            Chicago Hebrew Institute, 1258 West Taylor Street
            Christopher House, 1528 East Fullerton Avenue
            Eli Bates House, 621 Elm Street
            Emerson House, 1802 Emerson Avenue
            Esther Falkenstein Settlement, 1917 North Humboldt
                Street
            Fellowship House, 831 West 33rd Place
            The Forward Movement, Monroe and Loomis Streets
            Gads Hill Center, 1959 West 20th Street
            Henry Booth House, 701 West 14th Place
            Hull House, 800 South Halsted Street
            Maxwell Street Settlement, 1214 South Clinton Street

Neighborhood Guild, 2512 Wentworth Avenue
Neighborhood House, 6710 May Street
Northwestern University Settlement, 1400 Augusta
    Avenue and Noble Street
St. Elizabeth Settlement, 317 Orleans Street
St. Mary's Settlement, 656 West 44th Street
South Deering Neighborhood Center, 10441 Hoxie
    Avenue
South End Center, 3212 91st Street
Union Avenue Parish House, 4356 Union Avenue
University of Chicago Settlement, 4630 Gross Avenue

Sources: Rainwater 1922; Siegel 1965; Williams 1991; Woods and Kennedy 1911 (1970); The Salvation Army Disposition of Forces; Wilson 1916 (1987).

Notes

1. Voluntary Vernacular

1. Edna St. Vincent Millay was taking classes at Barnard during the spring of 1913 prior to enrolling at Vassar. She was in New York City under the auspices of Caroline Drew, head of the YWCA National Training School. Drew heard Millay recite her poetry and offered YWCA accommodations while she prepared for college (Gould 1969, 36–44).

2. The most famous of these was the Chicago Fire of 1871 that killed 300 people and burned down 18,000 buildings across more than 2,000 acres (Smith 1995, 22).

3. Diane Winston's recent work on The Salvation Army points out that some officers were middle-class women, and that leaders of The Salvation Army made frequent overtures to the middle class and to the elite for funds. Class differences between volunteers and their clientele, however, were less pronounced in The Salvation Army than in the other three organizations considered here (Winston 1999).

4. There were few formal ties among these four organizations, but informally they knew of one another's work. Grace Dodge, president of the YWCA, was a member of the College Settlements Association. Frances Willard, president of the Woman's Christian Temperance Union, was an advisor to Evangeline Booth of The Salvation Army; Willard was, in turn, connected with the NACW (McKinley 1995; Settlements File n.d.).

5. The WCTU's campaign to abolish liquor verged on the xenophobic. One of the reasons for their crusades was that "thousands of immigrants made their drinking customs popular here" (Tyler 1949, 17).

6. In 1869 the National Woman Suffrage Association was formed by Susan B. Anthony and Elizabeth Cady Stanton, and the American Women's Suffrage Association was begun by Lucy Stone and Henry Blackwell; in 1890 they merged into the National American Woman Suffrage Association.

7. The WCTU Temple has since been demolished.

8. Readers familiar with the range of temporary accommodations for women at the turn of the century may wonder why some of them do not appear here. They are acknowledged in appendix A with an explanation for their exclusion.

2. Why Cities Needed Saving

1. See Spencer-Wood (1987) for a discussion of privies and wells as resources for urban archeologists.

2. The "Kansas Exodus" of 1877 was the first time many blacks moved out of the South after the Civil War, but significant outmigration did not occur until 1917. The Kansas Exodus was organized by Benjamin "Pap" Singleton, the self-styled "Moses of the Colored Exodus." Comparing the movement with the Hebrew exodus from Egypt, Singleton advertised opportunities for free land in Kansas. One poster announced, "All Colored People that want to GO TO KANSAS on September 5th, 1877 can do so for $5.00." Estimates of the actual number of people who moved vary from 6,000 to 82,000. "Kansas Fever" eventually waned as Kansas officials and Southern plantation owners discouraged it. Between the 1860 and 1880 censuses, however, the black population of Kansas increased from only 627 persons to 43,100 (Johnson and Campbell 1981, 49–56).

3. William Stead was a frequent visitor at Hull House. He died in 1912 on the *Titanic*.

4. YWCA president Grace Dodge worked for Emily Huntington as a volunteer before organizing New York City's Working Girls Club. Dodge also established the New York Kitchen Garden Association (Weimann 1981, 339).

5. The United States hosted one previous World's Fair, the 1876 Exposition in Philadelphia, in honor of the country's centennial.

6. Architects may consider Werner Hegemann and Elbert Peets's *The American Vitruvius: An Architect's Handbook of Civic Art* (1922) as the authoritative City Beautiful publication. It includes chapters on street design, city plans, parks, and public gardens.

7. Ironically, the National Conference on City Planning was organized by Mary Kingsbury Simkhovitch and Florence Kelley as an extension of work they had done with the New York City Committee on Congestion of Population (Wirka 1996).

3. Sacred and Secular Organizational Ideologies

1. The Moody Church is still standing at Clark Street and North Avenue in Chicago, across the street from the Chicago Historical Society.

2. The two sides were temporarily reconciled when the National Conference on Charities and Corrections elected Addams its president in 1904, two years after she published a detailed critique of the Charity Organization movement in *Democracy and Social Ethics* (Boyer 1978, 155–61).

3. Historian Elizabeth Lasch-Quinn argues that the National Federation of Settlements unintentionally reinforced the irrelevance of blacks to the settlement movement when it made a rigid distinction between religious work and settlement work. (She also acknowledged that more than twenty-five hundred Catholic settlements were excluded by this definition.) Lasch-Quinn is only partially correct in her assessment of the fate of black settlements. The African Methodist Episcopal Institutional Church on South Dearborn Avenue in Chicago opened by Rev. Reverdy Ransom in 1900, for example, was included in *The Handbook,* but the black Olivet Baptist Church in Chicago was not. Other black settlements included in *The Hand-*

book were Flanner Guild in Indianapolis, Locust Street Settlement in Hampton, Virginia, and Eighth Ward House in Philadelphia. Neighborhood Union in Atlanta and Phillis Wheatley Houses in Chicago, Cleveland, and Minneapolis were omitted (Crocker 1992; Lasch-Quinn 1993, 27–52; Wood and Kennedy [1911] 1970).

4. The university maintained the building for many years, but eventually demolished it. The Buffalo Public Library system has no record of the Mary C. Ripley Memorial Library (*Buffalo Express,* January 24, 1915; Van Ness 1996).

5. See Sander (1998) for a discussion of the Women's Exchange movement between 1832 and 1900.

4. Voluntary Associations with an Urban Presence

1. The YWCA, like the Young Men's Christian Association, originated in England. Two Christian groups for women were started in London in 1855: Miss Emma Robarts's Prayer Union and Mrs. Arthur Kinnaird's General Female Training Institute for nurses returning from the Crimean War. Mrs. Kinnaird's group sponsored a home in which thirty-nine women lived, including governesses, schoolteachers, nurses, "2 foreigners" and "1 Lady in Distress." Among those for whom Miss Robarts's group prayed were "our princesses and all who are in the glitter of fashionable life," young wives, mothers, and daughters of the middle class, governesses, seamstresses, domestic servants, factory girls, young women in hospitals and jails, and "those who are enchained by Judaism, Popery, and Heathenism." When Miss Robarts and Mrs. Kinnaird met in 1857 they agreed to combine forces under the name of the Young Women's Christian Association, "the feminine of Young Men's, which had already become known to many of the same friends" (Sims 1936, 2, 3; Wilson [1916] 1987, 7–21).

2. The national headquarters of the YWCA is now in the Empire State Building.

3. Secondary sources refer to Ruffin's club by two names, the Woman's Era Club and the New Era Club. I refer to it as the Woman's Era Club throughout the book.

4. The NACW built an impressive range of facilities. Davis's 1935 history of the organization included photographs of a girl's home in Peaks Turnout, Virginia; a home for the blind and a Negro Woman's Club Home in Denver; Phillis Wheatley Homes in Chicago (one at 3256 Rhodes Avenue and another at 5128 Michigan Avenue), Cleveland, Ohio, and Evansville and Terre Haute, Indiana; the Ida M. Grayson Home for Girls in York, Pennsylvania; the Ruth L. Bennett Club Home and the Wilson Memorial Day Nursery in Chester, Pennsylvania; and the Excelsior Library in Guthrie, Oklahoma. Reports on the activities of local chapters included descriptions of a Colored Orphan and Industrial Home in Henderson, Kentucky; the Crispus Attucks Home for aged colored people in Minneapolis; and the Women's Christian Union Old Folks Home in Vicksburg, Mississippi (Davis 1934). Susan Dart Butler operated a library for blacks in Charleston, South Carolina (Shaw 1991). Ida Harris raised money for a Boys' Gymnasium in Indianapolis in 1909; Mary McLeod Bethune founded the Daytona Literary and Industrial School for Training Negro Girls in Florida in 1904 (now Bethune Cookman College); Charlotte Hawkins Brown of Henderson, North Carolina, founded Palmer Memorial Institute in Sedalia, the Efland Home for Wayward Girls in Orange County, and the Colored Orphanage at Oxford.

5. William harnessed the militaristic imagery that captured the Victorian imagination after the Crimean War and Indian Mutiny of the 1850s. The Salvation Army was patterned after Britain's citizen army of over 600,000 "Volunteers." Just as Maj. Gen. Garnet Wolesley turned "urban idlers, waifs, and strays" into disciplined soldiers in three years at a national training school, General Booth in 1880 opened training homes for male and female cadets. He manufactured officers from the working class in three months, although the cadets' illiteracy meant the three months were spent as much on basic education as on evangelistic, theological, or administrative training (Murdoch 1994, 88, 89, 102, 118).

6. Booth thought part of the solution to urban poverty was to remove the "submerged tenth" from cities, and to this end he devised a "farm colonies" scheme that would take "the landless man to the manless land." Booth's son Ballington and his son-in-law Frederick Booth-Tucker opened farm colonies in Ohio, Colorado, and California that received recognition from the U.S. Bureau of Labor in 1903, but these were short-lived experiments (Booth-Tucker [1899] 1972).

7. William Stead was the author of *If Christ Came to Chicago!* (1894) and a frequent visitor to Hull House.

8. These Slum Sisters were the target of George Bernard Shaw's satire in *Major Barbara* ([1907] 1957). Act II depicts two derelicts talking in London's West Ham Salvation Army shelter.

9. The programs and facilities at the Rivington Street Settlement are described in chapter 5.

10. CSA membership was open to noncollegiate members in recognition of the small number of college-educated women.

11. When the NACW national convention met in Chicago in 1899, Jane Addams invited some of the delegates to lunch at Hull House. The event was considered a significant break in the color barrier. The *Chicago Times Herald* reported that "[t]his is the first time that colored women have been given the decided recognition in a social way by a woman of lighter skin" (Wesley 1984, 48).

5. New York City Headquarters, Smaller City Branches

1. Hamilton Fish was the U.S. Secretary of State from 1869 to 1877.

2. This bath now houses an outdoor pool in addition to the original indoor pool. Renamed the Asser Levy Bath and designated a historic landmark by the Landmarks Preservation Commission, it underwent an $8-million restoration before reopening in 1990 (Williams 1991, chapter 3).

3. The feminist Victoria Woodhull scandalized the nation with her accusations that Henry Ward Beecher had an affair with the wife of a church member. Woodhull, a spiritualist and free-love advocate, resented Beecher's hypocrisy in publicly refusing to endorse free love. See Goldsmith 1998.

4. Kalsomine, or calcimine, was a form of whitewash.

5. The New York City YWCA that sponsored the Margaret Louisa was an independent organization until financial difficulties forced it to merge with the Harlem Association in 1911 (Bittar 1979).

6. Jane Edna Hunter passed the Ohio state bar in 1925 after graduating from the Cleveland Law School (Hunter 1940).

7. Hunter allied herself with the Ohio Federation of Colored Women's Clubs in 1925 and proceeded to develop a network among other black women leaders. She was soon corresponding with Mary McLeod Bethune, Nannie Helen Burroughs, and Charlotte Hawkins Brown. By 1928 Hunter headed the NACW's Big Sister Department and by 1934 she headed a Phillis Wheatley Department that used her institution as a model for similar homes in cities without a black branch of the YWCA. Numerous Phillis Wheatley Clubs were started across the country, and houses were opened in Atlanta, Boston, Denver, Detroit, Greenville, S.C., Minneapolis, Seattle, Winston-Salem, N.C., Toledo, Canton, Oberlin, and Steubenville, Ohio, and New Haven, Connecticut (Hine 1990, 81; A. Jones 1990, 96, 97, 122).

8. Phillis Wheatley, an eighteenth-century slave, was "the first colored poetess in America." Numerous clubs were named in her honor. Her first name is sometimes spelled as "Phillis" and sometimes as "Phyllis" (Davis 1935, 138–265; A. Jones 1990, 44–62).

9. The Phillis Wheatley Association still exists in Cleveland, at 4450 Cedar Avenue, although it no longer provides lodging.

10. The Cleveland YWCA was designed by the architectural firm of Scofield and Scofield (YWCA Archives n.d.)

11. The National Association was short-lived; it disbanded by 1926 (Higginbotham 1993, 219).

12. The National Training School for Women and Girls was renamed the Nannie Helen Burroughs School in 1964 and is now a private, predominantly black Christian elementary school. The school is located close to the Maryland border at 601 Fiftieth Street Northeast in the District. Although none of the original buildings remain, Principal Shirley G. Hayes has preserved many artifacts from the school's rich history. Among her collection are photographs of the original buildings, furnishings from their rooms, copies of the curriculum (listing liberal arts courses as well as those in domestic science), and correspondence from Booker T. Washington.

6. Boston, the Cradle of Redemptive Places

1. The Swedish word *sloyd*, like the Middle English word *sleight*, means dexterity or skill (Henry and Williams n.d., 18).

2. The original North Bennet Street School still operates as a crafts school in the North End to train artisans in furniture-making, carpentry, bookbinding, jewelry design, and musical instrument construction.

3. Elizabeth Palmer Peabody, who never married, was *not* the wife of the architect Robert Peabody of Boston's Peabody and Stearns architectural firm.

4. The YWCA report was missing diagrams for the first and fourth floors of Elizabeth Peabody House (YWCA National Archives).

5. The North End Union still serves as a neighborhood resource center with a mission to "provide educational, vocational, socio-cultural, and psychological services to people who live, work, or visit the North End" (North End Union n.d.).

6. Much of the credit for spreading the sand-garden innovation goes to CSA member Ellen M. Tower, who delivered addresses on sand gardens around the country in her capacity as chair of the Playground Committee of the Massachusetts Emergency and Hygiene Association (Rainwater 1922, 42).

7. Boston's municipal bath program was discontinued in 1959. Bath houses were gradually phased out and ceased operating in the early 1970s (Williams 1991, 82).

8. The WEIU now operates a nonprofit "Shop at the Union" at 356 Boylston Street that carries hundreds of unique items made by women and distributed by women-owned companies. It also sponsors a special program to offer technical assistance and market access to minority and low-income women with handmade products to sell (WEIU brochure). The shop's logo is a swan (standing for the swan boats in the Public Garden established in the same year as the WEIU) and its motto is "An extraordinary Shop with a past and a purpose."

9. Ruffin's home was on the same street as the Elizabeth Peabody House.

10. Boston had a black population of 10,000 in 1900. About one-third of those residents had been born in the state of Massachusetts and another one-third were migrants from Virginia (Pleck 1979, 46).

11. Rothman (1978, 90) points out that these rates were affordable only for women earning a steady income.

12. The building and corner lot combined cost $132,500; the architect was G. F. Meacham (YWCA Archives).

13. Harriet Tubman, a significant figure in the Underground Railroad, helped slaves from the South escape to freedom in the North.

14. The Salvation Army rescue home for "fallen women" in Dorchester to which Miss Balch referred may have been the Little Wanderers' Home established in 1888. The service she attended was at (or near) the Workingmen's Hotel on Washington Street several blocks away from Denison House.

7. Men Build Chicago's Skyline, Women Redeem the City

1. Sullivan's Auditorium Building has been renovated and is now the home of Roosevelt University.

2. Neither Bertha nor her husband, Potter, was related to Thomas Palmer, president of the Columbian Commission (Weimann 1981, 39). The Palmer House is now a Hilton Hotel.

3. Architect Sophia Hayden and architectural historian Dolores Hayden are *not* related (Hayden 1980).

4. The Hull House complex stood until 1963, when all but the original house was demolished in an urban renewal campaign to create a site for the University of Illinois's Chicago Circle campus (Deegan 1988, 41; Sklar 1990, 106). Historic preservationist Gail Dubrow (1992) cites the incomplete preservation of the entire complex as an example of the tendency to identify women with private dwellings rather than major building projects.

References

Abell, Aaron Ignatius. 1962. *The Urban Impact on American Protestantism, 1865–1900*. London: Archon.

Abelson, Elaine S. 1989. *When Ladies Go A-Thieving: Middle-Class Shoplifters in the Victorian Department Store*. New York: Oxford University Press.

Addams, Jane. [1910] 1960. *Twenty Years at Hull House with Autobiographical Notes*. Reprint, New York: Signet.

Alland, Alexander. 1993. *Jacob A. Riis: Photographer and Citizen*. New York: Aperture Foundation.

Alter, Jonathan. 1997. "Powell's New War." *Newsweek* 28, April, 28–34.

Arnold, Judith R., and Olivia Martin. 1976. "The Friendly Inn Social Settlement: A Register of Its Records." Cleveland, Ohio: Western Reserve Historical Society.

Badger, Reid. 1979. *The Great American Fair: The World's Columbian Exposition and American Culture*. Chicago: Nelson Hall.

Barrows, Esther G. 1929. *Neighbors All: A Settlement Notebook*. Boston: Houghton Mifflin.

Barth, Gunther. 1980. *City People: The Rise of the Modern City Culture in Nineteenth-Century America*. New York: Oxford University Press.

Beard, Mary Ritter. 1915. *Woman's Work in Municipalities*. New York: D. Appleton.

Beauregard, Robert A. 1993. *Voices of Decline: The Postwar Fate of U.S. Cities*. Oxford: Blackwell.

Bellamy, Edward. 1887. *Looking Backward, 2000–1887*. Boston: Houghton Mifflin.

Bender, Thomas. 1975. *Toward an Urban Vision: Ideas and Institutions in Nineteenth Century America*. Lexington: University Press of Kentucky.

———. 1996. "Clients or Citizens?" *Critical Review* 10:123–34.

Berg, Barbara J. 1978. *The Remembered Gate: Origins of American Feminism (The Woman and the City, 1800–1860)*. New York: Oxford University Press.

Bergmann, Hans. 1995. *God in the Street: New York Writing from the Penny Press to Melville*. Philadelphia: Temple University Press.

Berkeley, Ellen Perry, and Matilda McQuaid, eds. 1989. *Architecture: A Place for Women*. Washington, D.C.: Smithsonian Institution Press.

Best, Lassalle. N.d. "History of the White Rose Mission and Industrial Association." WPA Writers' Program Research Paper. Microfilm 974.7-W, Reel 3. New York: Schomburg Center for Research of Black Culture, New York Public Library.

Birch, Eugenie Ladner, ed. 1985. *The Unsheltered Woman: Women and Housing in the '80s.* New Brunswick, N.J.: Rutgers University Center for Urban Policy and Research.

————. 1989. "An Urban View: Catherine Bauer's Five Questions." *Journal of Planning Literature* 4 (Summer): 239–58.

————. 1994. "From Civic Worker to City Planner: Women and Planning, 1890–1980." Pp. 396–427 in *The American Planner,* edited by Donald Krueckeberg. 2d ed. New Brunswick, N.J.: Center for Urban Policy Research.

Bittar, Helen. 1979. "The Y.W.C.A. of the City of New York, 1870 to 1920." Ph.D. dissertation, Department of History, New York University.

Blair, Karen J. 1980. *The Clubwoman as Feminist: True Womanhood Redefined, 1868–1914.* New York: Holmes and Meier.

Blank, Rebecca. 1997. *It Takes a Nation: A New Agenda for Fighting Poverty.* Princeton, N.J.: Princeton University Press.

Bledstein, Burton J. 1976. *The Culture of Professionalism: The Middle Class and the Development of Higher Education in America.* New York: W. W. Norton.

Bluestone, Daniel. 1991. *Constructing Chicago.* New Haven: Yale University Press.

Bolotin, Norman, and Christine Laing. 1992. *The Chicago World's Fair of 1893: The World's Columbian Exposition.* Washington, D.C. The Preservation Press.

Booth-Tucker, Frederick. [1899] 1972. *The Salvation Army in America: Selected Reports, 1899–1903.* Reprint, New York: Arno Press.

Bordin, Ruth. 1990. *Woman and Temperance: The Quest for Power and Liberty, 1873–1900.* New Brunswick, N.J.: Rutgers University Press.

Boston, City of. 1900. City Directory. Boston: Boston Public Library.

Boston, City of. 1911. List of Registered Male Voters, Ward Seven, Precinct 5. Boston: Boston Public Library.

Boston Society of Architects. 1976. *Architecture Boston.* Barre, Mass.: Barre Publishing.

Bowlker. 1912. "Woman's Homemaking Function Applied to the Municipality." *The American City* 6 (June) 863–69.

Boyer, M. Christine. 1988. *Dreaming the Rational City: The Myth of American City Planning.* Cambridge: MIT Press.

Boyer, Paul. 1978. *Urban Masses and Moral Order in America, 1820–1920.* Cambridge: Harvard University Press.

Brands, H. W. 1995. *The Restless Decade: America in the 1890s.* New York: St. Martin's Press.

Breckinridge, Sophonisba P. 1933. *Women in the Twentieth Century: A Study of Their Political, Social, and Economic Activities.* New York: McGraw-Hill.

"Brief: Re The Shelters." 1904. March 2. Alexandria, Va.: The Salvation Army National Archives and Research Center.

Brown, Hallie Q. [1926] 1988. *Homespun Heroines and Other Women of Distinction.* Reprint, New York: Oxford University Press.

Bryan, Mary Lynn McCree, and Allen F. Davis, eds. 1990. *100 Years at Hull House.* Bloomington: Indiana University Press.

Buder, Stanley. 1967. *Pullman: An Experiment in Industrial Order and Community Planning, 1880–1930.* New York: Oxford University Press.

Buechler, Steven M. 1990. *Women's Movements in the United States*. New Brunswick, N.J.: Rutgers University Press.

Burg, David F. 1976. *Chicago's White City of 1893*. Lexington: University Press of Kentucky.

Calhoun, Craig. 1993. "Civil Society and the Public Sphere." *Public Culture* 5:267–80.

Callow, Alexander B. 1966. *The Tweed Ring*. New York: Oxford University Press.

Cameron, William E., ed. 1893. *The World's Fair, Being a Pictorial History of The Columbian Exposition*. Syracuse, N.Y.: H. C. Leavenworth.

Caron's Directory of the City of Louisville. 1901. Louisville, Ky.: University of Louisville Archives and Record Center.

Cash, Floris Barnett. 1992a. "Josephine St. Pierre Ruffin." Pp. 961–66 in *Notable Black American Women*, edited by Jessie Carney Smith. Detroit: Gale Research.

———. 1992b. "Victoria Earle Matthews." Pp. 736–39 in *Notable Black American Women*, edited by Jessie Carney Smith. Detroit: Gale Research.

Cavallo, Dominick. 1981. *Muscles and Morals: Organized Playgrounds and Urban Reform, 1880–1920*. Philadelphia: University of Pennsylvania Press.

Chesham, Sallie. 1965. *Born to Battle: The Salvation Army in America*. Chicago: Rand McNally.

Chicago of Today. 1892. Chicago: Chicago Historical Society.

Clarke, Susan E., and Gary Gaile. 1998. *The Work of Cities*. Minneapolis: University of Minnesota Press.

Clarke, Susan E., Lynn Staeheli, and Laura Brunell. 1995. "Women Redefining Local Politics." Pp. 205–27 in *Theories of Urban Politics*, edited by David Judge, Gerry Stoker, and Harold Wolman. Thousand Oaks, Calif.: Sage.

Condit, Carl W. 1964. *The Chicago School of Architecture: A History of Commercial and Public Building in the Chicago Area, 1875–1925*. Chicago: University of Chicago Press.

Converse, Florence. N.d. "95 Rivington Street, 1889–1914." Settlements File, Sophia Smith Collection. Smith College, Northampton, Mass.

Conway, Jill. 1972. "Women Reformers and American Culture, 1870–1930." *Journal of Social History* 5 (Winter): 164–77.

Cott, Nancy F. 1990. "Across the Great Divide: Women in Politics before and after 1920." Pp. 98–120 in *Women, Politics, and Change*, edited by Louise A. Tilly and Patricia Gurin. New York: Russell Sage Foundation.

Crane, Mrs. Caroline Bartlett. 1912. "Some Factors of the Street Cleaning Problem." *The American City* 6 (June): 895–97.

Cranz, Galen. 1982. *The Politics of Park Design: A History of Urban Parks in America*. Cambridge: MIT Press.

Crocker, Ruth Hutchinson. 1992. *Social Work and Social Order: The Settlement Movement in Two Industrial Cities, 1889–1930*. Urbana: University of Illinois Press.

Cromley, Elizabeth Collins, and Carter L. Hudgins, eds. 1995. *Gender, Class, and Shelter: Perspectives in Vernacular Architecture 5*. Knoxville: University of Tennessee Press.

Daniels, Arlene Kaplan. 1988. *"Invisible Careers" Women Civic Leaders from the Volunteer World*. Chicago: University of Chicago Press.

Davidoff, Paul. 1965. "Advocacy and Pluralism in Planning." *Journal of the American Institute of Planners* 31 (November): 12–25.

Davis, Allen F. 1967. *Spearheads for Reform: The Social Settlements and the Progressive Movement.* New York: Oxford University Press.

———. 1973. *American Heroine: The Life and Legend of Jane Addams.* New York: Oxford University Press.

Davis, Elizabeth Lindsay. [1935] 1981. *Lifting As They Climb: The National Association of Colored Women.* Reprint, Ann Arbor, Mich.: University Microfilms International.

Decker, Sarah S. Platt. 1906. "The Meaning of the Woman's Club Movement." *Annals of the American Academy of Political and Social Science,* no. 513 (September): 200–204.

Deegan, Mary Jo. 1988. *Jane Addams and the Men of the Chicago School, 1892–1918.* New Brunswick, N.J.: Transaction Books.

Degler, Carl. 1980. *At Odds: Women and the Family in America from the Revolution to the Present.* New York: Oxford University Press.

Denison House Papers. N.d. Boston: Radcliffe College of Harvard University Schlesinger Library.

"Department of the Metropolis." 1905. *Disposition of Forces* (January): 5–13. Alexandria, Va.: The Salvation Army National Archives and Research Center.

Deutsch, Sarah. 1992. "Learning to Talk More Like a Man: Boston Women's Class-Bridging Organizations, 1870–1940." *American Historical Review* 97:379–404.

———. 1994. "Reconceiving the City: Women, Space, and Power in Boston, 1870–1910." *Gender and History* 6 (August): 202–23.

Dodge, Grace H. 1887. *A Bundle of Letters to Busy Girls on Practical Matters.* New York: Funk and Wagnalls.

Domosh, Mona. 1996. *Invented Cities: The Creation of Landscape in Nineteenth-Century New York and Boston.* New Haven: Yale University Press.

Dorr, Rheta Childe. [1910] 1971. *What Eight Million Women Want.* Reprint, New York: Kraus Reprint Company.

Dorsett, Lyle W., ed. 1968. *The Challenge of the City, 1860–1910.* Lexington, Mass.: D. C. Heath.

Douglas, Mary. 1966. *Purity and Danger: An Analysis of the Concepts of Pollution and Taboo.* London: Routledge and Kegan Paul.

Downing, Andrew Jackson. [1853] 1974. *Rural Essays.* Reprint, New York: DaCapo Press.

Drake, St. Clair, and Horace R. Cayton. 1962. *Black Metropolis: A Study of Negro Life in a Northern City.* New York: Harper and Row.

DuBois, W. E. Burghardt. [1903] 1961. *The Souls of Black Folk.* Reprint, Greenwich, Conn.: Fawcett Publications.

Dubrow, Gail. 1989. "Restoring a Female Presence: New Goals in Historic Preservation." Pp. 159–70 in *Architecture: A Place for Women,* edited by Ellen Perry Berkeley. Washington, D.C.: Smithsonian Institution Press.

———. 1992. "Women and Community." Pp. 83–118 in *Reclaiming the Past,* ed. Miller.

Dudley, Helena S. 1894. "Relief Work Carried On in the Wells Memorial Institute." *American Academy of Political and Social Science* (November): 61–81.

———. 1910. "The Boston College Settlement: Report of the Headworker." Boston: Denison House.

Edin, Kathryn, and Laura Lein. 1998. "The Private Safety Net: The Role of Charitable Organizations in the Lives of the Poor." *Housing Policy Debate* 9:541–73.

Egleston, Nathaniel Hilyer. 1878. *Villages and Village Life with Hints for Their Improvement.* New York: Harper and Brothers.

Encyclopedia Americana. 1996. Vol. 8. Danbury, Conn.: Grolier.

Enstam, Elizabeth York. 1998. *Women and the Creation of Urban Life: Dallas, Texas, 1843–1920.* College Station: Texas A&M University Press.

Farley, Reynolds, and Walter R. Allen. 1987. *The Color Line and the Quality of Life in America.* New York: Russell Sage Foundation.

Farrington, Julia B. 1898. "Philadelphia Settlement." Settlements File, Sophia Smith Collection. Smith College, Northampton, Mass.

Fenske, Gail, and Deryck Holdsworth. 1992. "Corporate Identity and the New York Office Building: 1895–1915." Pp. 129–59 in *The Landscape of Modernity,* edited by David Ward and Olivier Zunz. New York: Russell Sage Foundation.

Fine, Lisa M. 1990. *The Souls of the Skyscraper: Female Clerical Workers in Chicago, 1870–1930.* Philadelphia: Temple University Press.

"Fire Insurance Maps in the Library of Congress." 1981. Washington, D.C.: Library of Congress.

Fisher, Robert. 1996. "Neighborhood Organizing: The Importance of Historical Context." Pp. 39–49 in *Revitalizing Urban Neighborhoods,* edited by W. Dennis Keating, Norman Krumholz, and Philip Star. Lawrence: University of Kansas Press.

Fitzpatrick, Ellen. 1990. *Endless Crusade: Women Social Scientists and Progressive Reform.* New York: Oxford University Press.

Flanagan, Maureen A. 1990. "Gender and Urban Political Reform: The City Club and the Woman's City Club of Chicago in the Progressive Era." *American Historical Review* 95 (October): 1032–50.

———. 1996. "The City Profitable, the City Livable: Environmental Policy, Gender, and Power in Chicago in the 1910s." *Journal of Urban History* 22 (January): 163–90.

——— 1997. "Women in the City, Women of the City: Where Do Women Fit in Urban History?" *Journal of Urban History* 23, no. 3 (March): 251–59.

Flexner, Eleanor. 1975. *Century of Struggle.* Cambridge: Harvard University Press.

Foglesong, Richard. 1986. *Planning the Capitalist City: The Colonial Era to the 1920s.* Princeton, N.J.: Princeton University Press.

Forester, John. 1989. *Planning in the Face of Power.* Berkeley: University of California Press.

Friedmann, John. 1987. *Planning in the Public Domain: From Knowledge to Action.* Princeton, N.J.: Princeton University Press.

Fuller, Mary V., ed. 1909. "Gleanings: The Unnecessary Fly." *The American City* 1 (November): 139.

Gale, Zona. 1914. "How Women's Clubs Can Co-operate with the City Officials." *The American City* 6 (June): 537.

Gamm, G., and R. Putnam. 1998. "The Growth of Voluntary Associations in America, 1840–1940." *Journal of Interdisciplinary History* 29:15–24.

Gatewood, Willard B. 1990. *Aristocrats of Color: The Black Elite, 1880–1920.* Bloomington: Indiana University Press.

Geary, Blanche. 1913. Survey of YWCA Properties. Unpublished data, YWCA Archives. New York, N.Y.

———. 1919. Survey of Homes for Working Women for the Sociological Investigation Committee of the YWCA. Unpublished data, YWCA archives. New York, N.Y.

Gelb, Joyce, and Marilyn Gittell. 1986. "Seeking Equality: The Role of Activist Women in Cities." Pp. 93–109 in *The Egalitarian City*, edited by Janet K. Boles. New York: Praeger.

Gerhard, William Paul. 1908. *Modern Baths and Bath Houses*. New York: John Wiley and Sons.

Gerstner, Patsy. 1998. "Looking for a Healthy Cleveland, 1810–1960." Cleveland, Ohio: Western Reserve Historical Society.

Gilbert, James. 1991. *Perfect Cities: Chicago's Utopias of 1893*. Chicago: University of Chicago Press.

Gilmartin, Gregory F. 1995. *Shaping the City: New York and the Municipal Art Society*. New York: Clarkson Potter.

Ginzberg, Lori D. 1990. *Women and the Work of Benevolence: Morality, Politics, and Class in the Nineteenth-Century United States*. New Haven: Yale University Press.

Girouard, Mark. 1985. *Cities and People: A Social and Architectural History*. New Haven: Yale University Press.

Gittell, Marilyn, and Teresa Shtob. 1980. "Changing Women's Roles in Political Volunteerism and Reform of the City." Pp. 64–75 in *Women and the American City*, edited by Catharine R. Stimpson et al. Chicago: University of Chicago Press.

Glaab, Charles N., and A. Theodore Brown. 1976. *A History of Urban America*. 2d ed. New York: Macmillan.

Goldfield, David R., and Blaine A. Brownell. 1979. *Urban America: From Downtown to No Town*. Boston: Houghton Mifflin.

Goldsmith, Barbara. 1998. *Other Powers: The Age of Suffrage, Spiritualism, and the Scandalous Victoria Woodhull*. New York: Knopf.

Goodrich, Henrietta I. N.d. "Possible Alleviation of Present Difficulties in Domestic Service." Papers of the Women's Educational and Industrial Union, Box 1, Folder 5. Cambridge, Mass.: Schlesinger Library of Radcliffe College.

Gould, Jean. 1969. *The Poet and Her Book: A Biography of Edna St. Vincent Millay*. New York: Dodd, Mead.

Green, Roger J. 1989. *War on Two Fronts: The Redemptive Theology of William Booth*. Atlanta: Georgia State University Press.

Gusfield, Joseph R. 1986. *Symbolic Crusade: Status Politics and the American Temperance Movement*. Urbana: University of Illinois Press.

Gutheim, Frederick. 1977. *Worthy of the Nation: The History of Planning for the National Capital*. Washington, D.C.: Smithsonian Institution Press.

Habermas, Jurgen. 1989. *The Structural Transformation of the Public Sphere*. Cambridge: MIT Press.

Hall, Peter. 1988. *Cities of Tomorrow: An Intellectual History of Urban Planning and Design in the Twentieth Century*. Oxford: Blackwell.

Hardy, Stephen. 1982. *How Boston Played: Sport, Recreation, and Community, 1865–1915*. Boston: Northeastern University Press.

Hartman, Edward T. 1909. "Town and Village." *The American City* 1 (November): 131–34.

Hayden, Dolores. 1980. "Sophia Hayden." In *Notable American Women*, edited by Barbara Sicherman and Carol Green. Cambridge: Harvard University Press.

———. 1981. *The Grand Domestic Revolution: A History of Feminist Designs for American Homes, Neighborhoods, and Cities*. Cambridge: MIT Press.

————. 1995. *The Power of Place: Urban Landscapes as Public History.* Cambridge: MIT Press.

Hayes, Shirley. 1997. Interview with author at Nannie Helen Burroughs School, Washington, D.C. August 19.

Hays, Samuel P. 1995. *The Response to Industrialism, 1885–1914.* 2d ed. Chicago: University of Chicago Press.

Hegemann, Werner, and Elbert Peets. [1922] 1988. *The American Vitruvius: An Architect's Handbook of Civic Art.* Reprint, New York: Princeton Architectural Press.

Henri, Florette. 1975. *Black Migration: Movement North, 1900–1920.* Garden City, N.Y.: Anchor Press.

Henry, Sarah, and Mary A. Williams. N.d. "North Bennet Street School: A Short History, 1885–1985." Boston: Chadis Printing.

Hersey, Heloise E. 1903. "History of the Domestic Reform League." *The Federation Bulletin* (November). Papers of the Women's Educational and Industrial Union, Box 1, Folder 5. Cambridge, Mass.: Schlesinger Library of Radcliffe College.

Hewitt, Nancy A. 1984. *Women's Activism and Social Change: Rochester, New York, 1822–1872.* Ithaca, N.Y.: Cornell University Press.

Higginbotham, Evelyn Brooks. 1993. *Righteous Discontent: The Women's Movement in the Black Baptist Church, 1880–1920.* Cambridge: Harvard University Press.

Hill, Caroline M. 1938. *Mary McDowell and Municipal Housekeeping.* Chicago: Chicago Council of Social Agencies.

Hill, Joseph A. 1929. *Women in Gainful Occupations, 1870 to 1920.* Washington, D.C.: U.S. Bureau of the Census.

Hine, Darlene Clark. 1981. *When the Truth Is Told: A History of Black Women's Culture and Community in Indiana, 1875–1950.* Indianapolis: National Council of Negro Women.

————. 1990a. "We Specialize in the Wholly Impossible: The Philanthropic Work of Black Women." Pp. 70–93 in *Lady Bountiful Revisited,* ed. McCarthy.

————, ed. 1990b. *Black Women in United States History.* Brooklyn, N.Y.: Carlson.

————, ed. 1993. *Black Women in America: An Historical Encyclopedia.* Brooklyn, N.Y.: Carlson.

Hines, Thomas S. 1974. *Burnham of Chicago: Architect and Planner.* New York: Oxford University Press.

Hirsch, Arnold R. 1983. *Making the Second Ghetto: Race and Housing in Chicago, 1940–1960.* New York: Cambridge University Press.

Hofstadter, Richard. 1955. *The Age of Reform: From Bryan to FDR.* New York: Knopf.

Hopkins, Charles Howard. 1967. *The Rise of the Social Gospel in American Protestantism, 1865–1915.* New Haven: Yale University Press.

Horowitz, Helen Lefkowitz. 1983. "Hull House as Women's Space." *Chicago History: The Magazine of the Chicago Historical Society* 12:40–55.

————. 1984. *Alma Mater: Design and Experience in the Women's Colleges from Their Nineteenth-Century Beginnings to the 1930s.* Boston: Beacon Press.

Howe, Barbara J. 1992. "Women and Architecture." Pp. 27–62 in *Reclaiming the Past,* ed. Miller.

Hoy, Suellen M. 1980. "Municipal Housekeeping": The Role of Women in Improving Urban Sanitation Practices, 1880–1917." Pp. 173–98 in *Pollution and Reform in American Cities, 1870–1930,* edited by Martin V. Melosi. Austin: University of Texas Press.

————. 1995. *Chasing Dirt: The American Pursuit of Cleanliness.* New York: Oxford University Press.

————. 1997. "Caring for Chicago's Women and Girls: The Sisters of the Good Shepherd, 1859–1911." *Journal of Urban History* 23:260–94.

Humphreys, Mary Gay. 1896. "Women Bachelors in New York." *Scribners Magazine* 20:626–36.

Hunter, Albert. 1985. "Private, Parochial, and Public Social Orders: The Problem of Crime and Incivility in Urban Communties." Pp. 230–42 in *The Challenge of Social Control: Citizenship and Institution Building in Modern Society,* edited by Gerald Suttles and Mayer Zald. Norwood, N.J.: Ablex.

Hunter, Jane Edna. 1940. *A Nickel and a Prayer.* Cleveland, Ohio: Elli Kani Publishing.

Husock, Howard. 1992. "Bringing Back the Settlement House." *The Public Interest* 109 (Fall): 53–72.

"The Improvement of Villages." 1889. *Garden and Forest* (March 27): 145–46.

Irwin, Elizabeth, and Mary Alden Hopkins. 1927. "College Settlement." Settlements File, Sophia Smith Collection. Smith College, Northampton, Mass.

Jackson, John Brinckerhoff. 1994. *A Sense of Place, a Sense of Time.* New Haven: Yale University Press.

Jacobs, Jane. 1961. *The Death and Life of Great American Cities.* New York: Vintage.

Jasso, Guillermina, and Mark R. Rosenzweig. 1990. *The New Chosen People: Immigrants in the United States.* New York: Russell Sage Foundation.

Jerome, Mrs. Amalie Hofer. 1911. "The Playground as a Social Center." *The American City* 5 (July): 33–35.

Johnson, Daniel M., and Rex R. Campbell. 1981. *Black Migration in America: A Social Demographic History.* Durham, N.C.: Duke University Press.

Jones, Adrienne Lash. 1990. *Jane Edna Hunter: A Case Study of Black Leadership, 1910–1950.* Brooklyn, N.Y.: Carlson.

————. 1997. "Struggle among Saints: African American Women and the YWCA, 1870–1920." Pp. 160–87 in *Men and Women Adrift,* ed. Mjagkij and Spratt.

Jones, Beverly Washington. 1990. *Quest for Equality: The Life and Writings of Mary Eliza Church Terrell, 1863–1954.* Brooklyn, N.Y.: Carlson.

Kaminer, Wendy. 1984. *Women Volunteering: The Pleasure, Pain, and Politics of Unpaid Work from 1830 to the Present.* Garden City, N.Y.: Anchor Press.

Kaufmann, Edgar, Jr. 1956. *Louis Sullivan and the Architecture of Free Enterprise.* Chicago: Art Institute of Chicago.

Keating, W. Dennis, Norman Krumholz, and Philip Star, eds. 1996. *Revitalizing Urban Neighborhoods.* Lawrence: University of Kansas Press.

Keller, Suzanne, ed. 1981. *Building for Women.* Lexington, Mass.: D. C. Heath.

Kerber, Linda K. 1980. *Women of the Republic: Intellect and Ideology in Revolutionary America.* Chapel Hill: University of North Carolina Press.

Kessler-Harris, Alice. 1982. *Out to Work: A History of Wage-Earning Women in the United States.* Oxford: Oxford University Press.

Knowles, Jane S. 1991. "Boston Young Women's Christian Association: Records, 1858–1988." Unpublished Finding Aid. Cambridge, Mass: Arthur and Elizabeth Schlesinger Library, Radcliffe College.

Knupfer, Anne Meis. 1996. *Toward a Tenderer Humanity and a Nobler Womanhood: African American Women's Clubs in Turn-of-the-Century Chicago.* New York: New York University Press.

Landau, Sarah Bradford, and Carl W. Condit. 1996. *Rise of the New York Skyscraper,* 1865–1913. New Haven: Yale University Press.

Lasch-Quinn, Elisabeth. 1993. *Black Neighbors: Race and the Limits of Reform in the American Settlement Movement,* 1890–1945. Chapel Hill: University of North Carolina Press.

Lattimore, Florence. 1915. "A Palace of Delight: The Locust Street Social Settlement for Negroes at Hampton, Virginia." Hampton, Va.: The Press of the Hampton Normal and Agricultural Institute.

Lee, Antoinette J. 1997. "Supporting Working Women: YWCAs in the National Register." *Placing Women in the Past.* Special issue of *Cultural Resource Management* 20, no. 3: 16–17. Washington, D.C.: U.S. Department of the Interior.

Lehman, Jeffrey S. 1994. "Updating Urban Policy." Pp. 226–52 in *Confronting Poverty: Prescriptions for Change,* edited by Sheldon Danziger, Gary Sandefur, and Daniel Weinberg. New York: Russell Sage Foundation.

Lerner, Gerda. 1972. *Black Women in White America: A Documentary History.* New York: Random House.

———. 1974. "Early Community Work of Black Club Women." *Journal of Negro History* 59 (April): 158–67.

———. 1979. *The Majority Finds Its Past: Placing Women in History.* New York: Oxford University Press.

Lissak, Rivka S. 1989. *Pluralism and Progressives: Hull House and the New Immigrants,* 1890–1919. Chicago: University of Chicago Press.

Locust Point Social Settlement Association of Baltimore City. 1900. Annual Report. Baltimore.

———. 1904. Annual Report. Baltimore.

Lofland, Lyn. 1973. *A World of Strangers: Order and Action in Urban Public Space.* Prospect Heights, Ill.: Waveland Press.

———. 1975. "The 'Thereness' of Women: A Selective Review of Urban Sociology." Pp. 144–70 in *Another Voice: Feminist Perspectives on Social Life and Social Science,* edited by Marcia Millman and Rosabeth Moss Kanter. New York: Anchor Books.

———. 1998. *The Public Realm: Exploring the City's Quintessential Social Territory.* New York: Aldine De Gruyter.

Logan, Rayford. 1954. *The Negro in American Life and Thought: The Nadir,* 1877–1901. New York: Macmillan.

Loose, Cindy. 1999. "Acting on Their Convictions: Court-ordered 'Volunteers' Boost Work of Agencies." *Washington Post,* July 18, A1.

Luker, Ralph E. 1991. *The Social Gospel in Black and White: American Racial Reform,* 1885–1912. Chapel Hill: University of North Carolina Press.

Lupkin, Paula. 1997. "Manhood Factories: Architecture, Business, and the Evolving Urban Role of the YMCA, 1865–1925." Pp. 40–64 in *Men and Women Adrift,* ed. Mjagkij and Spratt.

Macdougall, Allan Ross, ed. 1952. *Letters of Edna St. Vincent Millay.* New York: Harper and Brothers.

MacLachlan, Lt. Col. Edith A., Women's Social Service Secretary. N.d. "History of the Women's and Children's Social Service Department."

Magnuson, Norris. 1977. *Salvation in the Slums: Evangelical Social Work,* 1865–1920. Metuchen, N.J.: Scarecrow Press and The American Theological Library Association.

Massey, Doreen, and John Allen. 1984. *Geography Matters!* Cambridge: Cambridge University Press.

Matthews, Glenna. 1992. *The Rise of Public Woman: Woman's Power and Woman's Place in the United States,* 1630–1970. New York: Oxford University Press.

Mayer, Harold M., and Richard C. Wade. 1969. *Chicago: Growth of a Metropolis.* Chicago: University of Chicago Press.

McCarthy, Kathleen D. 1982. *Noblesse Oblige: Charity and Cultural Philanthropy in Chicago,* 1849–1929. Chicago: University of Chicago Press.

———, ed. 1990a. *Lady Bountiful Revisited: Women, Philanthropy, and Power.* New Brunswick, N.J.: Rutgers University Press.

———. 1990b. "Parallel Power Structures: Women and the Voluntary Sphere." Pp. 1–31 in *Lady Bountiful Revisited,* ed. McCarthy.

McDonell, E. 1969. *The Beguines and Beghards in Medieval Culture.* New York: Octagon.

McKinley, Edward H. 1986. *Somebody's Brother: A History of the Salvation Army Men's Social Service Department* 1891–1985. Lewiston, N.Y.: Edwin Mellen.

———. 1995. *Marching to Glory: The History of the Salvation Army in the United States of America,* 1880–1992. 2d ed. Grand Rapids, Mich.: Eerdmans.

———. 1996. Personal communication with author. March 6.

McLaughlin, Charles C. 1983. *The Papers of Frederick Law Olmsted.* Baltimore: Johns Hopkins University Press.

Melosi, Martin V. 1980. *Pollution and Reform in American Cities,* 1870–1930. Austin: University of Texas Press.

Mero, Everett B. 1909. "How Public Gymnasiums and Baths Help to Make Good Citizens." *The American City* 1 (October): 69–76.

Meyerowitz, Joanne J. 1988. *Women Adrift: Independent Wage Earners in Chicago,* 1880–1930. Chicago: University of Chicago Press.

Mill, John Stuart. [1869] 1970. *The Subjection of Women.* Reprint, Cambridge: MIT Press.

Mills, C. Wright. [1959] 1967. "The Big City: Private Troubles and Public Issues." In *Power, Politics, and People,* edited by Irving Louis Horowitz. New York: Oxford University Press.

Miller, Page Putnam, ed. 1992. *Reclaiming the Past: Landmarks of Women's History.* Bloomington: Indiana University Press.

Milroy, Beth Moore, and Susan Wismer. 1994. "Community, Work, and Public/ Private Sphere Models." *Gender, Place, and Culture* 1:71–90.

Mizruchi, Ephraim. 1983. *Regulating Society: Marginality and Social Control in Historical Perspective.* New York: Free Press.

Mjagkij, Nina, and Margaret Spratt, eds. 1997. *Men and Women Adrift: The YMCA and the YWCA in the City.* New York: New York University Press.

Mohl, Raymond A. 1997. "Cultural Pluralism in Immigrant Education: The YWCA's International Institutes, 1910–1940." Pp. 111–37 in *Men and Women Adrift,* ed. Mjagkij and Spratt.

Monkkonen, Eric. 1988. *America Becomes Urban: The Development of U.S. Cities and Towns,* 1780–1980. Berkeley: University of California Press.

Moore, Charles. 1921. *Daniel H. Burnham: Architect, Planner of Cities.* Vol. 2. Boston: Houghton Mifflin.

Moore, Eva Perry (Mrs. Philip N.). 1909. "Woman's Interest in Civic Welfare." *The American City* 1 (September): 44.

Morgan, Morris Hicky. 1960. *Vitruvius: The Ten Books on Architecture.* New York: Dover Publications.

Moseley, Eva, Timothy Stroup, and Peter Webster. 1980. "North Bennet Street Industrial School, 1879– : Records 1880– ." Unpublished Finding Aid. Cambridge, Mass: Arthur and Elizabeth Schlesinger Library, Radcliffe College.

Mosell, Mrs. N. F. [1908] 1988. *The Work of the Afro-American Woman.* Reprint, New York: Oxford Press.

Mumford, Lewis. 1955. *The Brown Decades: A Study of the Arts in America, 1865– 1895.* New York: Dover.

Muncy, Robyn. 1991. *Creating a Female Dominion in American Reform, 1890–1935.* New York: Oxford University Press.

Murdoch, Norman H. 1994. *Origins of the Salvation Army.* Knoxville: University of Tennessee Press.

———. 1996. Personal communication with the author. April.

Murolo, Priscilla. 1997. *The Common Ground of Womanhood: Class, Gender, and Working Girls' Clubs, 1884–1928.* Urbana: University of Illinois Press.

Nasaw, David. 1993. *Going Out: The Rise and Fall of Public Amusements.* New York: Basic Books.

"National and Territorial Manual: Working Women's Home." c. 1940s. Alexandria, Va.: The Salvation Army National Archives and Research Center.

Neel, Carolyn. 1989. "The Origins of the Beguines." *Signs: Journal of Women in Culture and Society* 14:321–41.

Norris, Elizabeth. 1981. "Building of '600.'" Internal memo of the YWCA of the USA, National Board of the Young Women's Christian Association, New York. September 24.

———. 1996. Personal communication with the author. New York: National Archives, Young Women's Christian Association.

Nutter, Kathleen Banks. 1997. "Organizing Women during the Progressive Era: Mary Kenney O'Sullivan and the Labor Movement." *Labor's Heritage* 8:18–37.

Oakley, Mrs. Imogen B. 1912. "The More Civic Work, the Less Need of Philanthropy." *The American City* 6 (June): 805–13.

Odem, Mary E. 1995. *Delinquent Daughters: Protecting and Policing Adolescent Female Sexuality in the United States, 1885–1920.* Chapel Hill: University of North Carolina Press.

Osofsky, Gilbert. 1966. *Harlem: The Making of a Ghetto.* New York: Harper and Row.

Pattison, Mrs. Frank A. 1909. "The Relations of the Woman's Club to the American City." *The American City* 1 (November): 129–30.

Peiss, Kathy. 1986. *Cheap Amusements: Working Women and Leisure in Turn-of-the-Century New York.* Philadelphia: Temple University Press.

Peterson, Jon A. 1976. "The City Beautiful Movement: Forgotten Origins and Lost Meaning." *Journal of Urban History* 2 (August): 415–34.

———. 1985. "The Nation's First Comprehensive City Plan: A Political Analysis of the McMillan Plan for Washington, D.C. 1900–1902." *Journal of the American Planning Association* 51 (Spring): 134–50.

Phillips, Lily Todd. 1926. "The Branch Public Baths, Richmond, Virginia." *Journal of the American Association for Promoting Hygiene and Public Baths* 8:47–48.

Phillis Wheatley Association. 1912. Typed constitution of the Phillis Wheatley Association. Cleveland, Ohio: Western Reserve Historical Society.

———. 1913. Handwritten record of the Phillis Wheatley Association Amendment. Cleveland, Ohio: Western Reserve Historical Society.

———. 1917. Annual Report. Cleveland, Ohio: Western Reserve Historical Society.

——— 1921. Minutes of the Annual Meeting. Cleveland, Ohio: Western Reserve Historical Society.

Philpott, Thomas Lee. 1978. *The Slum and the Ghetto: Neighborhood Deterioration and Middle-Class Reform, Chicago, 1880–1930*. New York: Oxford University Press.

Pleck, Elizabeth Hafkin. 1979. *Black Migration and Poverty: Boston, 1865–1900*. New York: Academic Press.

Quincy, Josiah. 1898. "Playgrounds, Baths, and Gymnasia." *Journal of Social Science* 36:139–47.

Rabinovitz, Lauren. 1998. *For the Love of Pleasure: Women, Movies, and Culture in Turn-of-the-Century Chicago*. New Brunswick, N.J.: Rutgers University Press.

Rainwater, Clarence E. 1922. *The Play Movement in the United States: A Study of Community Recreation*. Chicago: University of Chicago Press.

Regnerus, Mark D., Christian Smith, and David Sikkink. 1998. "Who Gives to the Poor? The Influence of Religious Tradition and Political Location on the Personal Generosity of Americans Toward the Poor." *Journal for the Scientific Study of Religion* 37:481–94.

Reps, John W. 1965. *The Making of Urban America: A History of City Planning in the United States*. Princeton, N.J.: Princeton University Press.

Residents of Hull House. [1895] 1970. *Hull House Maps and Papers*. Reprint. New York: Arno Press.

Riis, Jacob A. [1890] 1957. *How the Other Half Lives: Studies among the Tenements of New York*. Reprint, New York: Hill and Wang.

Robbins, Mary Caroline. 1897. "Village Improvement Societies." *Atlantic Monthly* 79:212–22.

Robinson, Charles Mulford. [1901] 1913. *The Improvement of Towns and Cities; or, The Practical Basis of Civic Aesthetics*. 2d ed. New York: Putnam's Sons.

———. [1918] 1970. *Modern Civic Art; or, The City Made Beautiful*. Reprint, New York: Arno Press.

Rosenberg, Carroll Smith. 1971. *Religion and the Rise of the American City: The New York City Mission Movement, 1812–1870*. Ithaca, N.Y.: Cornell University Press.

Rosenzweig, Roy, and Elizabeth Blackmar. 1992. *The Park and the People: A History of Central Park*. Ithaca, N.Y.: Cornell University Press.

Rossi, Alice S., ed. 1973. *The Feminist Papers: From Adams to deBeauvoir*. New York: Bantam Books.

Rothman, David J. 1971. *The Discovery of the Asylum: Social Order and Disorder in the New Republic*. Boston: Little, Brown.

Rothman, Sheila M. 1978. *Woman's Proper Place: A History of Changing Ideals and Practices, 1870 to the Present*. New York: Basic Books.

Ruffins, Fath Davis. 1994. "Lifting As We Climb: Black Women and the Preservation of African American History and Culture." *Gender and History* 6:376–96.

Ryan, Mary P. 1979. *Womanhood in America: From Colonial Times to the Present.* New York: New Viewpoints.

———. 1981. *Cradle of the Middle Class: The Family in Oneida County, New York,* 1790–1865. Cambridge: Cambridge University Press.

———. 1990. *Women in Public: Between Banners and Ballots,* 1825–1880. Baltimore: Johns Hopkins University Press.

———. 1997. *Civic Wars: Democracy and Public Life in the American City during the Nineteenth Century.* Berkeley: University of California Press.

Salem, Dorothy. 1990. *To Better Our World: Black Women in Organized Reform,* 1890–1920. Brooklyn, N.Y.: Carlson.

Salvation Army, The. 1995a. *The Salvation Army 1994 National Annual Report.* Alexandria, Va.: The Salvation Army National Headquarters.

———. 1995b. *The Salvation Army Yearbook:* 1996. London: The International Headquarters of The Salvation Army.

Sandburg, Carl. 1992. *Chicago Poems.* Urbana: University of Illinois Press.

Sander, Kathleen Waters. 1998. *The Business of Charity: The Woman's Exchange Movement,* 1832–1900. Urbana: University of Illinois Press.

Sandercock, Leonie, ed. 1998. *Making the Invisible Visible.* Berkeley: University of California Press.

Sandercock, Leonie, and Ann Forsyth. 1992. "A Gender Agenda: New Directions for Planning Theory." *Journal of the American Planning Association* 58 (Winter): 49–59.

Schlesinger, Arthur Meier. 1961. *The Rise of the City:* 1878–1898. Chicago: Quadrangle Books.

Schneir, Miriam, ed. 1972. *Feminism: The Essential Historical Writings.* New York: Vintage Books.

Schultz, Stanley K. 1989. *Constructing Urban Culture: American Cities and City Planning,* 1800–1920. Philadelphia: Temple University Press.

Schuyler, David. 1986. *The New Urban Landscape: The Redefinition of City Form in Nineteenth-Century America.* Baltimore: Johns Hopkins University Press.

Scott, Anne Firor. 1990a. "Women's Voluntary Associations: From Charity to Reform." Pp. 35–54 in *Lady Bountiful Revisited,* ed. McCarthy.

———. 1990b. "Most Invisible of All: Black Women's Voluntary Associations." *Journal of Southern History* 56 (February): 3–22.

———. 1991. *Natural Allies: Women's Associations in American History.* Urbana: University of Illinois Press.

Scott, Mel. 1969. *American City Planning since* 1890. Berkeley: University of California Press.

Scudder, Vida D. 1890. "The Relation of College Women to Social Need." Scudder Papers. Sophia Smith Collection. Smith College, Northampton, Mass.

———. 1892. "The Place of College Settlements." *Andover Review* 18 (October): 339–50.

———. 1893. "A Glimpse into Life." *Wellesley Magazine* 1, no. 5 (February): 221–32.

———. 1896. Address to the 41st annual meeting of the Eastern Kindergarten Association. Scudder Papers. Sophia Smith Collection. Smith College, Northampton, Mass.

———. 1915. "The Challenge of College Settlements." *Radcliffe Magazine* (December): 32–34.

Scudder, Vida D., and Bertha Hazard. 1890. "The College Settlements Association." Scudder Papers. Sophia Smith Collection. Smith College, Northampton, Mass.

Scudder Papers. Sophia Smith Collection. Smith College, Northampton, Mass.

Settlement Cook Book Company. [1901] 1976. *The Settlement Cook Book: Treasured Recipes of Seven Decades.* 3d ed. New York: Simon and Schuster.

Settlements File. Various years. Sophia Smith Collection. Smith College, Northampton, Mass.

Shaughnessy, Erin, ed. 1997. "How Did African American Women Define Their Citizenship at the Chicago World's Fair in 1893?" http://womhist.binghamton.edu.

Shaw, George Bernard. [1907] 1957. *Major Barbara.* Reprint. New York: Penguin Books.

Shaw, Stephanie J. 1991. "Black Club Women and the Creation of the National Association of Colored Women." *Journal of Women's History* 3 (Fall): 10–25.

Sibley, David. 1995. "Gender, Science, Politics and Geographies of the City." *Gender, Place and Culture* 2 (March): 37–49.

Siegel, Arthur, ed. 1965. *Chicago's Famous Buildings.* Chicago: University of Chicago Press.

Simmons Bible College Records, 1869–1971. N.d. Louisville, Ky.: University of Louisville Archives and Records Center.

Sims, Mary S. 1936. *The Natural History of a Social Institution — The Young Women's Christian Association.* New York: The Woman's Press.

Sklar, Kathryn Kish. 1985. "Hull House in the 1890s: A Community of Women Reformers." *Signs: Journal of Women in Culture and Society* 10 (Summer): 658–77.

———. 1990. "Who Funded Hull House?" Pp. 94–115 in *Lady Bountiful Revisited,* ed. McCarthy.

———. 1993. "The Historical Foundations of Women's Power in the Creation of the American Welfare State, 1830–1930." Pp. 43–93 in *Mothers of a New World: Maternalist Politics and the Origins of Welfare States,* edited by Seth Koven and Sonya Michel. New York: Routledge.

———. 1995a. "Two Political Cultures in the Progressive Era: The National Consumers' League and the American Association for Labor Legislation." Pp. 36–62 in *U.S. History as Women's History: New Feminist Essays,* edited by Linda Kerber, Alice Kessler-Harris, and Kathryn Kish Sklar. Chapel Hill: University of North Carolina Press.

———. 1995b. *Florence Kelley and the Nation's Work: The Rise of Women's Political Culture, 1830–1900.* New Haven: Yale University Press.

Skocpol, Theda. 1992. *Protecting Soldiers and Mothers: The Political Origins of Social Policy in the United States.* Cambridge: Harvard University Press.

Smith, Carl. 1995. *Urban Disorder and the Shape of Belief: The Great Chicago Fire, the Haymarket Bomb, and the Model Town of Pullman.* Chicago: University of Chicago Press.

Smith, Norris Kelly. 1979. *Frank Lloyd Wright: A Study in Architectural Content.* Watkins Glen, N.Y.: The American Life Foundation.

"The Smoke Evil Must Go." 1909. *The American City* 1 (November): 47.

"Social Wing." 1898. *Disposition of Forces* (March): 4–7. Alexandria, Va.: The Salvation Army National Archives and Research Center.

———. 1900. *Disposition of Forces* (December): 4–13. Alexandria, Va.: The Salvation Army National Archives and Research Center.

Soja, Edward W. 1996. *Thirdspace: Journeys to Los Angeles and Other Real-and-Imagined Places.* Cambridge, Mass.: Blackwell.

Solomon, Barbara Miller. 1985. *In the Company of Educated Women.* New Haven: Yale University Press.

Spain, Daphne. 1992. *Gendered Spaces.* Chapel Hill: University of North Carolina Press.

———. 1995. "Public Housing and the Beguinage." Pp. 256–70 in *Gender in Urban Research,* edited by Judith A. Garber and Robyne S. Turner. Thousand Oaks, Calif.: Sage Publications.

Spear, Allan H. 1967. *Black Chicago: The Making of a Negro Ghetto, 1890–1920.* Chicago: University of Chicago Press.

Spencer-Wood, Suzanne M. 1987. "A Survey of Domestic Reform Movement Sites in Boston and Cambridge, ca. 1865–1905." *Historical Archaeology* 21:7–36.

———. 1994. "Turn of the Century Women's Organizations, Urban Design, and the Origin of the American Playground Movement." *Landscape Journal* 13, no. 2 (Fall): 125–37.

———. 1996. "Feminist Historical Archaeology and the Transformation of American Culture by Domestic Reform Movements, 1840–1925." Pp. 397–445 in *Historical Archaeology and the Study of American Culture,* ed. Lu Ann De Cunzo and Bernard Herman. Knoxville: University of Tennessee Press.

Stansell, Christine. 1982. *City of Women: Sex and Class in New York, 1789–1860.* New York: Knopf.

Stead, William T. [1894] 1978. *If Christ Came to Chicago! A Plea for the Union of All Who Love in the Service of All Who Suffer.* Reprint, Chicago: Laird and Lee.

Stebner, Eleanor J. 1997. *The Women of Hull House: A Study in Spirituality, Vocation, and Friendship.* Albany, N.Y.: State University of New York Press.

Steffens, Lincoln. 1904. *The Shame of the Cities.* New York: McClure Phillips.

Stern, Robert A., Gregory Gilmartin, and John Massengale. 1983. *New York, 1900: Metropolitan Architecture and Urbanism, 1890-1915.* New York: Rizzoli.

Stewart, Jane A. 1902. "Boston's Experience with Municipal Baths." *American Journal of Sociology* 7:416–22.

Still, Bayrd. 1974. *Urban America: A History with Documents.* Boston: Little, Brown.

Stimpson, Catharine R., Elsa Dixler, Martha J. Nelson, and Kathryn B. Yatrakis. 1980. *Women and the American City.* Chicago: University of Chicago Press.

Taylor, William R. 1992. *In Pursuit of Gotham: Culture and Commerce in New York.* New York: Oxford University Press.

Terrell, Mary Church. 1898. "The Progress of Colored Women." Address delivered before the National American Women's Suffrage Association, Washington, D.C., February 18. http://memory.loc.gov.

Thomas, June Manning, and Reynard Blake. 1996. "Faith-based Community Development and African American Neighborhoods." Pp. 50–62 in *Revitalizing Urban Neighborhoods,* edited by Dennis Keating, Norman Krumholz, and Philip Star. Lawrence: University of Kansas Press.

Tilly, Louise A. 1989. "Gender, Women's History, and Social History." *Social Science History* 13, no. 4 (Winter): 439–62.

Tilly, Louise A., and Patricia Gurin, eds. 1990. *Women, Politics, and Change.* New York: Russell Sage Foundation.

Trachtenberg, Alan. 1982. *The Incorporation of America: Culture and Society in the Gilded Age.* New York: Hill and Wang.

Trolander, Judith Ann. 1975. *Settlement Houses and the Great Depression.* Detroit: Wayne State University Press.

Tunnard, Christopher, and Henry Hope Reed. 1968. "The City Beautiful." Pp. 72–82 in *The Challenge of the City,* 1860–1910, edited by Lyle W. Dorsett. Lexington, Mass.: D. C. Heath.

Turner, Elizabeth Hayes. 1997. *Women, Culture, and Community: Religion and Reform in Galveston,* 1880–1920. New York: Oxford University Press.

Turner, Victor. 1977. "Variations on a Theme of Liminality." Pp. 36–70 in *Secular Ritual,* edited by Sally F. Moore and Barbara G. Myerhoff. Amsterdam: Van Gorcum, Assen.

Tyler, Helen E. 1949. *Where Prayer and Purpose Meet: The WCTU Story,* 1874–1949. Evanston, Ill.: Signal Press.

United Neighborhood Houses of New York, Inc. 1995. *1994 Annual Report.* New York, N.Y.

Upton, Dell, and Michael Vlach, eds. 1986. *Common Places: Readings in American Vernacular Architecture.* Athens: University of Georgia Press.

U.S. Bureau of the Census. 1975. *Historical Statistics of the United States, Colonial Times to* 1970. Bicentennial ed., Part 1. Washington, D.C.: U.S. Government Printing Office.

———. 1997. "The Foreign-Born Population: 1996." *Current Population Reports.* Pp. 20–494. Washington, D.C.: U.S. Government Printing Office.

U.S. Department of the Interior. 1923. Bureau of Education Bulletin, no. 26. "Educational Work of the Young Women's Christian Association." Washington, D.C.: U.S. Government Printing Office.

———. 1992. "National Register of Historic Places: Information." Washington, D.C.: U.S. Government Printing Office.

———. 1997. "Placing Women in the Past." *Cultural Resource Management* 20, no. 3. Special issue.

U.S. Department of Justice. 1997. *Statistical Yearbook of the Immigration and Naturalization Service,* 1996. Washington, D.C.: U.S. Government Printing Office.

Van Buren, Maud. 1915. "Women and Town Improvement." *The American City* 12:104–5.

Van Ness, Cynthia. 1996. Personal communication with author. Buffalo: Buffalo and Erie County Public Library, Special Collections Department.

Van Slyck, Abigail A. 1995. *Free to All: Carnegie Libraries and American Culture,* 1890–1920. Chicago: University of Chicago Press.

Verba, Sidney, Kay L. Schlozman, and Henry E. Brady. 1995. *Voice and Equality: Civic Voluntarism in American Politics.* Cambridge: Harvard University Press.

Wald, Lillian D. 1915. *The House on Henry Street.* New York: Henry Holt.

Walkowitz, Judith R. 1992. *City of Dreadful Delight: Narratives of Sexual Danger in Late-Victorian London.* Chicago: University of Chicago Press.

Ward, David. 1971. *Cities and Immigrants: A Geography of Change in Nineteenth-Century America.* New York: Oxford University Press.

Waring, George E., Jr. 1886. *Report on the Social Statistics of Cities.* Washington, D.C.: U.S. Bureau of the Census, Government Printing Office.

———. 1877. *Village Improvements and Farm Villages*. Boston: James R. Osgood and Company.

Warner, Sam Bass, Jr. 1968. *The Private City: Philadelphia in Three Periods of Growth*. Philadelphia: University of Pennsylvania Press.

Watt, David Harrington. 1991. "United States: Cultural Challenges to the Voluntary Sector." Pp. 243–87 in *Between States and Markets: The Voluntary Sector in Comparative Perspective*, edited by Robert Wuthnow. Princeton, N.J.: Princeton University Press.

Weimann, Jeanne Madeline. 1981. *The Fair Women: The Story of The Woman's Building, World's Columbian Exposition, Chicago 1893*. Chicago: Academy Chicago.

Weiner, Deborah E. B. 1994. *Architecture and Social Reform in Late-Victorian London*. Manchester: Manchester University Press.

Weisenfeld, Judith. 1996. "White Rose Mission and Industrial Association." Pp. 2827–28 in *Encyclopedia of African-American Culture and History*, edited by Jack Salzman, David Lionel Smith, and Cornel West. New York: Simon and Schuster.

Weisman, Leslie Kanes. 1992. *Discrimination by Design: A Feminist Critique of the Man-Made Environment*. Urbana: University of Illinois Press.

Weiss, Marc A. 1992. "Skyscraper Zoning: New York's Pioneering Role." *Journal of the American Planning Association* 58 (Spring): 201–12.

Wells, Camille. 1995. Summary Statement, Symposium on Women and Virginia Architecture, Virginia Historical Society, Richmond, Va., September 29.

———. 1996. Personal communication with author. March.

Wells, Ida B., ed. 1893. "The Reason Why the Colored American Is Not in the World's Columbian Exposition." Preface and chap. 1. http://womhist.binghamton.edu.

Welter, Barbara. 1966. "The Cult of True Womanhood, 1820–1860." *American Quarterly* 18:151–74.

Wesley, Charles Harris. 1984. *The History of the National Association of Colored Women's Clubs: A Legacy of Service*. Washington, D.C.: National Association of Colored Women's Clubs.

White, Deborah Gray. 1993. "The Cost of Club Work, the Price of Black Feminism." Pp. 247–69 in *Visible Women: New Essays on American Activism*, edited by Nancy A. Hewitt and Suzanne Lebsock. Urbana: University of Illinois Press.

White, Ronald C., and C. Howard Hopkins. 1976. *The Social Gospel: Religion and Reform in Changing America*. Philadelphia: Temple University Press.

Wick, Dorothy. 1999. Librarian/archivist of the YWCA of the USA. Personal communication with author. May 20.

Wiebe, Robert H. 1967. *The Search for Order, 1877–1920*. New York: Hill and Wang.

Willard, Frances E. 1893. "Woman's Department of the World's Fair." Pp. 448–70 in *The World's Fair, Being a Pictorial History of The Columbian Exposition*, edited by William E. Cameron. Syracuse, N.Y.: H. C. Leavenworth.

Williams, Marilyn Thornton. 1991. *Washing "The Great Unwashed": Public Baths in Urban America, 1840–1920*. Columbus: Ohio State University Press.

Williams, Lillian Serece, ed. 1995. "Records of the National Association of Colored Women's Clubs, 1895–1992." University Publications of America. http://uapubs.com.

Willis, Carol. 1992. "Form Follows Finance: The Empire State Building." Pp. 160–87 in *The Landscape of Modernity*, edited by David Ward and Olivier Zunz. New York: Russell Sage Foundation.

Wilson, Elizabeth. [1916] 1987. *Fifty Years of Association Work among Young Women,* 1866–1916. Reprint, New York: Garland.

Wilson, Elizabeth. 1991. *The Sphinx in the City: Urban Life, the Control of Disorder, and Women.* Berkeley: University of California Press.

Wilson, Grace H. 1933. *The Religious and Educational Philosophy of the Young Women's Christian Association.* New York: Teachers College, Columbia University.

Wilson, Margaret Gibbons. 1979. *The American Woman in Transition: The Urban Influence, 1870–1920.* Westport, Conn.: Greenwood Press.

Wilson, Richard Guy. 1979. "Architecture, Landscape, and City Planning." Pp. 75–95 in *The American Renaissance, 1876–1917,* edited by the Brooklyn Museum. New York: Pantheon Books.

Wilson, William H. 1964. *The City Beautiful Movement in Kansas City.* Columbia: University of Missouri Press.

———. 1989. *The City Beautiful Movement.* Baltimore: Johns Hopkins University Press.

Winston, Diane. 1999. *Red-Hot and Righteous: The Urban Religion of The Salvation Army.* Cambridge: Harvard University Press.

Wirka, Susan Marie. 1996. "The City Social Movement: Progressive Women Reformers and Early Social Planning." Pp. 55–75 in *Planning the Twentieth-Century American City,* edited by Mary Corbin Sies and Christopher Silver. Baltimore: Johns Hopkins University Press.

Wish, Harvey. 1968. "Urbanism and the Church." In *The Challenge of the City, 1860–1910,* edited by Lyle W. Dorsett. Lexington, Mass.: D. C. Heath.

"Women Approve Plan to Give Building to U. of B." 1915. *Buffalo Express.* January 24.

Women's Christian Association of Cleveland, Ohio. 1869. First Annual Report. Cleveland, Ohio: Western Reserve Historical Society.

———. 1870. Second Annual Report. Cleveland, Ohio: Western Reserve Historical Society.

———. 1879. Manual of the Women's Christian Association of Cleveland, Ohio. Cleveland, Ohio: Western Reserve Historical Society.

———. 1891. Twenty-third Annual Report. Cleveland, Ohio: Western Reserve Historical Society.

———. 1893. "After Twenty-Five Years: 1868–1893." Cleveland, Ohio: Western Reserve Historical Society.

Women's Educational and Industrial Union (Boston). 1907. "Bulletin of the Domestic Reform League," no. 2 (February).

Woods, Robert A., ed. 1898. *The City Wilderness: A Settlement Study by Residents and Associates of the South End House.* Boston: Houghton Mifflin.

Woods, Robert A., and Albert J. Kennedy, eds. [1911] 1970. *Handbook of Settlements.* Reprint. New York: Arno Press.

Woodward, C. Vann. 1955. *The Strange Career of Jim Crow.* New York: Oxford University Press.

Wortman, Marlene Stein. 1977. "Domesticating the Nineteenth-Century American City." Pp. 531–72 in *Prospects: An Annual of American Cultural Studies,* edited by Jack Salzman. New York: Burt Franklin.

Wuthnow, Robert. 1991a. "The Voluntary Sector: Legacy of the Past, Hope for the Future?" Pp. 3–29 in *Between States and Markets: The Voluntary Sector in Com-*

parative Perspective, edited by Robert Wuthnow. Princeton, N.J.: Princeton University Press.

———. 1991b. "Tocqueville's Question Reconsidered: Voluntarism and Public Discourse in Advanced Industrial Societies." Pp. 288–308 in *Between States and Markets: The Voluntary Sector in Comparative Perspective,* edited by Robert Wuthnow. Princeton, N.J.: Princeton University Press.

YWCA of Cleveland, Ohio. 1899. "After Thirty Years." Cleveland, Ohio: Western Reserve Historical Society.

———. 1911. Forty-third Annual Report. Cleveland, Ohio: Western Reserve Historical Society.

YWCA of the USA. National Board Archives. 1954. *The Residence and the YWCA.* New York: National Board of the Young Women's Christian Association.

———. 1982. "Photo Memories of '600.'" New York: National Board of the Young Women's Christian Association.

———. 1992a. "Some Readings on Early YWCA Residences." New York: National Headquarters.

———. 1992b. "The Story of the YWCA." New York: National Headquarters.

———. N.d. Inventory to the Records Files Collection. Sophia Smith Collection. Smith College, Northampton, Mass.

Zueblin, Charles. 1902. *American Municipal Progress: Chapters in Municipal Sociology.* New York: Macmillan.

Zunz, Olivier. 1990. *Making America Corporate, 1870–1920.* Chicago: University of Chicago Press.

Index

Daphne Spain is professor of urban and environmental planning in the School of Architecture at the University of Virginia. She received her Ph.D. in sociology from the University of Massachusetts. Her previous books include *Gendered Spaces, Balancing Act: Motherhood, Marriage, and Employment among American Women* (with Suzanne M. Bianchi), and *Back to the City: Issues in Neighborhood Renovation* (edited with Shirley Laska).

How Women Saved the City